the Jesus Machine

The Jesus Machine

How James Dobson,
Focus on the Family,
and Evangelical America
Are Winning the Culture War

Dan Gilgoff

St. Martin's Press ☙ New York

www.stmartins.com

Design by Nancy Singer Olaguera

Library of Congress Cataloging-in-Publication Data

Gilgoff, Dan.
    The Jesus machine : how James Dobson, Focus on the Family, and evangelical America are winning the culture war / Dan Gilgoff. — 1st ed.
        p. cm.
    Includes bibliographical references.
    ISBN-13: 978-0-312-35790-0
    ISBN-10: 0-312-35790-7
    1. United States—Church history—21st century. 2. Chrisitianity and culture—United States 3. Christian conservatism—United States. 4. Dobson, James C., 1936–5. Focus on the Family (Organization) 6. Evangelicalism—United States. I. Title.

BR526.G56 2007
277.3'083—dc22

                                                                        2006035648

10 9 8 7 6 5 4 3 2

For Rebecca,
who believed in me

Contents

Acknowledgments		ix
Introduction		xi
1	The Crossroads	1
2	Billy Graham's Heir	18
3	Vatican West	43
4	The Long War	71
5	The Beltway's Bible Belt	106
6	Dobson's D-Day	138
7	The Values Vote	173
8	The Bench Press	212
9	Looking for God in the Democratic Party	242
	Epilogue	268
	Notes	283
	Interviews	295
	Index	303

Acknowledgments

This book began as a *U.S. News & World Report* assignment in late 2004 from editor in chief Brian Duffy and then–managing editor Victoria Pope. I'm grateful to both for planting the seed. The assignment turned into a book proposal after a Saturday-morning phone call from Penny Nelson, at the time a stranger but now my trusted agent, who overcame my abundant doubts and provided guidance and cheerleading through all phases of the project. St. Martin's editor in chief, George Witte, kept faith in my ability to produce a readable manuscript, even when the evidence was to the contrary.

Sara Sklaroff had the patience and heart to review the manuscript in an early, raw form, and at a time when she had much more pressing concerns. My mom, Anna Gilgoff, read early versions of the manuscript and was always available for idea sessions—and gripe sessions. She was my first editor in life, for which I will always be grateful.

At *U.S. News*, Brian Duffy generously granted me the time off to turn this project around in short order. Gordon Witkin graciously endured my long absence from the office and, more important, facilitated my earlier conversion from cultural to political reporter. I am fortunate to work alongside a handful of authors, and Ken Walsh, Jay Tolson, and Marc Silver took time to share their experiences and wisdom and to entertain all my questions and concerns, no matter how inane. Fellow

*U.S. News*ers Silla Brush, Liz Halloran, Bret Schulte, and Anna Mulrine provided editorial and emotional support, along with sorely needed distraction.

I am deeply grateful to the people who took time from busy schedules to talk to me for this book, especially those who did so for many hours or on multiple occasions, including Randy Brinson, Phil Burress, Richard Cizik, Ken Connor, John Green, Russell Johnson, Richard Land, Connie Mackey, Tom McClusky, Manuel Miranda, Kelly Shackelford, and Paul Weyrich. Focus on the Family's Paul Hetrick and Gwen Stein were first-rate hosts during my trips to Colorado Springs and diligently worked to fill interview and informational requests. The Family Research Council's J. P. Duffy and the National Association of Evangelicals' Carolyn Haggard were also great help in arranging interviews.

My immediate and extended families lent much-needed support during this project, especially Ben, Josh, Dalia, Dad and Betsy, and Marilyn and Ira. My friends were more than understanding when I dropped off the planet for a year and a few months.

More than anyone, I owe thanks to my wife, Rebecca. It's impossible to list all she did to make this book happen, but it ranged from sketching out the earliest vision for the project to proofreading the manuscript to tending to the most mundane demands of our lives while I disappeared for vast stretches of time. I couldn't have done this without her, and can't wait to get to know her again.

Introduction

My first interview with James Dobson was pretty much a fluke.

It was just after Election Day 2004, and the Washington press corps was scrambling to report the story of how white evangelicals had handed President George W. Bush a second term. My editor at *U.S. News & World Report* called me into his office on the morning after the election with an assignment to write about these newly branded "values voters." I had forty-eight hours.

At the time, I was only marginally aware of Focus on the Family. I thought of it as a conservative Christian advocacy group, one of many such organizations. Still, it made sense for me to call and request an interview with its chief spokesman, James Dobson.

When the interview was granted, I wasn't in a place to truly appreciate my good fortune. Only later did I learn that Dobson hardly ever talks to the mainstream news media, apart from occasional interviews with *The New York Times*. In the week after Election Day, dozens of interview requests poured into Focus on the Family's Colorado Springs headquarters. Dobson would grant only three: to the *Times*, to George Stephanopoulos for the lead spot on ABC's *This Week*, and to me. My secret? Dumb luck. It turns out that Michael Gerson—who was then serving as President Bush's chief speechwriter—is a *U.S. News & World Report* alum and had penned a generous profile of Dobson for the magazine in 1998. Six years later, Dobson still had warm feelings toward *U.S. News*.

My telephone interview with Dobson lasted just over twenty minutes, during which time he made several bold proclamations. He told me that President Bush had made a mistake in his first postelection press conference when he brushed aside a question about the apparent religious divide between largely evangelical "red" America and more secular "blue" America. Dobson said that Bush should have taken the opportunity to thank evangelical voters for reelecting him. He also laid out an ultimatum for the president and his Republican allies in Congress: They had "four years to deliver" on issues like curbing abortion rights and passing an amendment to the U.S. Constitution to ban gay marriage. If they failed, Dobson said, millions of evangelicals would stay home in the next presidential election.

In my story for *U.S. News* that week, I wrote about what a scary prospect that was for the GOP, since evangelicals had just delivered two of every five Bush votes. But what I didn't know then was how potent that threat was, coming from Dobson. I thought that activists with household names, like Jerry Falwell and Pat Robertson, were still the most influential figures in the Christian Right. I had no idea that James Dobson had become the movement's new standard-bearer, or that he was more powerful than either of them ever were.

It didn't take long to find out. A couple of weeks later, a *U.S. News* editor called with an assignment for a follow-up to my postelection article. With the continued public interest in the growing role evangelicals were playing in the nation's political life, I was to identify the movement's top political power broker and profile him or her. I phoned a few of the country's most respected scholars on politics and religion, along with a few prominent Christian Right activists. All invoked the same name: Focus on the Family founder James Dobson. They told me that Dobson, having won his following by dispensing family advice on his daily radio show and through a string of bestselling books, was more powerful than any previous Christian Right leader because, unlike his predecessors, he was seen to be above the partisan political fray.

It was time to book a flight to Colorado Springs.

When I phoned Focus on the Family, however, Dobson's press aide had bad news: Dobson was upset that I had taken up so much of his time for our earlier interview—some twenty-odd minutes—considering that only one quote of his wound up in my story. This time, my interview request was declined. Having gained brief entry into Dobson's exclusive world, I was now locked out, along with virtually every other journalist in the country. On the phone with Dobson's aide, I explained that my postelection story had been only one page long and that I wanted to squeeze in as many evangelical voices as possible. The aide wouldn't budge. I pleaded my case in subsequent phone conversations, but got nowhere. Finally, I drafted a two-page letter that began "Dear Dr. Dobson," in which I resorted to flattery. I said that I was interested in speaking to Dobson because he had "unmatched" political influence in the evangelical world and was "uniquely able" to transcend evangelicalism's denominational lines. I apologized for taking up so much of his time in our postelection interview. It was all sincere. Still, nothing.

But Dobson's aide invited me to come to Colorado Springs anyway. He said I would get a tour of Focus's eighty-eight-acre campus and that I could interview some of its thirteen hundred employees, including top executives. He basically said that I could interview anyone *but* Dobson. When I asked if it was okay for a *U.S. News* photographer to accompany me, he said taking pictures of most Focus employees wouldn't be a problem, but that Dobson himself had a long-standing rule against being shot by press photographers. I had never written about a public figure who refused to be photographed. But those were the rules.

In mid-December 2004, I made my first trip to Focus on the Family headquarters. I interviewed about three dozen Focus staffers, from executives on down. I toured Focus's 75,000-square-foot warehouse, filled with Dobson's pamphlets, books, DVDS, and CDs. I listened to phone conversations between Focus on the Family therapists and Christian women across the country who said their husbands were abusive or that their kids were taking drugs. I watched Dobson tape a radio interview with two authors on how parents could use foods like carrots and tube-shaped pasta to teach adolescents about puberty. Focus was not merely a conservative Christian advocacy group after all. It was vastly more diverse and complex. That's what made it fascinating.

Still, no Dobson interview.

At the end of my second day in Colorado Springs, however, Dobson's aide told me that he might grant an interview the following morning, my last at Focus headquarters. Representatives from Focus's media relations department had been sitting in on all of my interviews with Focus staff, and thought my questions were well informed and, more important, unbiased. I had passed a crucial test. The next morning, hours before my plane was scheduled to take off from Denver, an hour and a half's drive north, the interview was confirmed. This time I went in with a full—or at least much fuller—appreciation of how much Dobson's views mattered to tens of millions of American evangelicals. Many of the conservative Christian activists I'd talked to before arriving in Colorado Springs said they considered Dobson to be the most influential evangelical figure since Billy Graham.

The interview was scheduled to last an hour, but it went about twenty minutes over. Dobson, seated in an armchair under a huge portrait of Winston Churchill, was expansive. He covered topics ranging from childhood memories to his daily exercise regimen to his plan, at sixty-eight years of age, to put off retirement for as long as possible.

But we mostly talked politics. Two broad themes emerged in the interview. The first was that, in Dobson's mind—and, he said, in the minds of millions of American evangelicals—the current historical moment marked a national crisis the likes of which had not been seen in a generation. Dobson said that secular liberals had spent decades gaining a stranglehold on America's most powerful institutions, including the Supreme Court, the news media, higher education, even professional groups like the American Medical Association, and had plunged the country into moral free fall. There was no clearer evidence than the legalization of gay marriage in Massachusetts the previous May, which Dobson feared would provoke a wave of similar actions by courts across the country. Dobson believed that legalized gay marriage was a plot engineered by godless liberals and gay activists and that it would set in motion the downfall of Western civilization.

The second theme to emerge in the interview was Dobson's belief that the 2004 election, which had occurred not two months earlier, had ushered in a historic season of hope for evangelicals. With the reelection of George W. Bush, Republicans firmly in control of Congress, and widespread recognition of the critical role evangelicals had played in the election, Dobson felt that the national political tide was finally turning to his advantage. "There's . . . greater hope now," he said, "than there has been in my lifetime."

That paradox, of despair mingled with a promise of speedy deliverance, has recurred over and over again throughout the thirty-year history of the Christian Right. But the story of Dobson's and Focus on the Family's place in that history, as the leading Christian Right figure and organization of the past decade, has gone almost entirely untold. Just as I had after the 2004 election, much of the mainstream news media still treat Jerry Falwell and Pat Robertson as the evangelical movement's political spokesmen, even though their political organizations—Moral Majority and Christian Coalition—crumbled a decade or more ago.

One reason Focus on the Family has been overlooked is that it is more complex than those organizations, which were straightforward political advocacy groups. Focus's political power, by contrast, stems from the very fact that it is primarily apolitical. Another reason is that Dobson and Focus have denied access to many journalists and authors. In his 1996 book *With God on Our Side: The Rise of the Religious Right in America*, the authoritative history of the movement, author William Martin writes that he failed to get access to Dobson or to Focus, even for his updated 2005 edition, which covered Dobson's political ascendancy in the late nineties. Billy Graham, Falwell, Robertson, and former Christian Coalition executive director Ralph Reed, by contrast, all cooperated.

So I was particularly fortunate when, after my 2004 interviews with Dobson, he continued to grant me access. Focus liked my early 2005

U.S. News profile of Dobson enough to have me mail a few dozen copies of the magazine to Colorado Springs to distribute to employees. Unlike the many journalists whom Dobson felt had betrayed him, I'd earned his trust. My story quoted critics of him and of Focus, including a prominent evangelical who said that Dobson's habit of making demands on politicians fed an image of evangelical leaders as "modern-day ayatollahs," but Dobson felt that it had been fair. In coming months, when I'd cover developments for *U.S. News* in which the Christian Right played a big part, like the March 2005 congressional intervention into the Terri Schiavo case, Dobson would answer my questions via e-mail. I was one of the only reporters in the country to be granted such a privilege.

When I started the research for this book in mid-2005, Focus continued to cooperate, hosting me on two additional trips to Colorado Springs headquarters for interviews with dozens more Focus employees. I also talked to many former top staffers, going back to Focus's founding in the late 1970s. But Dobson himself declined to be interviewed again. I never got an official explanation of why. I suspect that Dobson, an unyielding guardian of his public image, was more wary of how he would come off in a project that dug deeper than a magazine profile and that had a longer shelf life. His cooperation could make it appear as though the book, critical passages and all, had his imprimatur. So I relied on the couple of hours of interviews I'd already done with him, along with our e-mail exchanges. Of course, I also had access to hundreds of hours of Dobson's radio broadcasts.

But from the beginning, I wanted this book to do more than tell Dobson's personal story. I set out to explain how his sprawling organizational empire provides the national armature for the modern-day Christian Right, as Moral Majority and Christian Coalition had done in earlier decades, but to greater effect. The Family Research Council, for example, which Dobson took the lead in founding and which Focus calls its Washington embassy, has long replaced Christian Coalition's D.C. office as the capital's premiere Christian Right lobbying shop. At the same time, Focus on the Family's Family Policy Councils, state-level advocacy groups that act like Focus affiliates, have replaced state Christian Coalition chapters as the most powerful local Christian Right outfits in the country. And a new and highly secretive coalition of Christian Right activists called the Arlington Group, whose birth marks a new era in cooperation among the movement's elite, is more closely allied with Focus on the Family and the Family Research Council than with any other organizational network. At a moment when the Christian Right senses that there is more to be gained and lost than ever before—in presidential elections, Supreme Court appointments, and in an effort to amend the Constitution—this is the machinery through which the movement is waging its battle. I interviewed almost twenty top current and former Family Research Council personnel; traveled to Family Policy Councils in Ohio, Texas, and Alabama; and spoke with more than two dozen Arlington Group members for this book.

Dobson himself finally submitted to a list of written questions in late 2005, but he declined to answer most of them because he said they were too political—even though he is the most powerful political leader that the American evangelical movement has ever known.

When Focus caught wind of the title of this book in early 2006, Dobson's aide told me the organization was deeply offended. I was informed via e-mail that my access was shut down. Focus asked me not to cite the e-mail, though suffice to say that it was the nastiest I've received as a journalist. Now I'm locked out again. I don't believe, however, that Dobson or Focus will find this book offensive. What propelled me to write it in the first place was the blizzard of polemical literature that argued in favor of or in opposition to the Christian Right and its objectives, without offering a basic understanding of how the movement works. I hope this book plugs that hole.

—Dan Gilgoff
Washington, D.C.
August 2006

The Jesus Machine

1

The Crossroads

"He has the benefit of not being a partisan voice. He is the single most credible figure within the evangelical community."

—◆—

When James Dobson arrived in Montgomery in August 2003, the symbolism of the location was not lost on him. He had come to call for the return of a two-and-a-half-ton Ten Commandments monument to the Alabama Supreme Court. It had been wheeled away a day earlier in accordance with a federal judge's ruling that the statue represented an unconstitutional government endorsement of religion. More than a thousand Christian demonstrators had gathered in the plaza outside the courthouse to call for its return, and Dobson flew to Montgomery to address the crowd. He opened his remarks by noting that Rosa Parks had launched her bus boycott in the same city nearly half a century earlier. "She had no power," Dobson told the crowd, dotted with umbrellas opened against the 90-plus-degree midday sun. "She had no influence. She had no money. . . . But she saw something that she felt was evil. It was imposed on her and all black people by the rule of law."

Of course, white evangelical Americans, for whom Dobson had become the top political spokesperson, had helped form the backbone of opposition to the civil rights movement that Parks's 1955 boycott set in motion. Jerry Falwell condemned civil rights activists from his Virginia pulpit and opposed the Lyndon Johnson–era civil rights laws as "a terrible violation of human and private property rights."[1] Jim Crow proponents opened Christian schools to avoid subjecting their children to integration.

In Montgomery, though, Dobson drew a direct parallel between Parks's civil disobedience and that of Alabama Supreme Court Chief Justice Roy Moore. An evangelical Christian who'd been elected to his post by campaigning to "restore the moral foundation of law," Moore had been suspended from the bench by a state judicial ethics commission for flouting the federal order to remove the monument he'd installed two years earlier. But Dobson said Moore's suspension and the court-ordered removal of the Commandments were an attack on Christians, just as Jim Crow laws had attacked African Americans. "We as people of faith are also being sent to the back of the bus," he told the crowd in Montgomery.

Despite his passion for Moore's cause, Dobson was initially reluctant to journey to Montgomery. Not more than four months earlier, he'd stepped down from the presidency of Focus on the Family, the $130 million, thirteen-hundred-employee media ministry he'd founded in the late 1970s. And at sixty-seven he was war weary. "I can't fight every battle," Dobson remembered thinking, in a later interview in his Colorado Springs office. "This one is not mine." It was also true that many of the nation's most prominent evangelical leaders had publicly criticized Moore's intransigence. Richard Land, leader of the political wing of the Southern Baptist Convention, and Ted Haggard, then president of the National Association of Evangelicals—both usually in Dob-

son's corner on political matters—said that Moore was out of line in defying a federal order. The long evangelical tradition of deference to government authority, which included opposing the tactic of civil
disobedience, had partly explained evangelical objections to the civil
rights movement. Even the director of Alabama's Family Policy Council, a kind of state-level Focus on the Family affiliate, said that Moore
was wrong.

To Dobson, though, the removal of "Roy's Rock," as the granite Ten
Commandments monument had come to be known, and Roy Moore's
suspension were the last straws in a decades-long campaign by the
courts to expel religion from the public square. And the organizers calling from Montgomery needed him. A modest but growing assemblage
of mostly evangelical Christians was keeping vigil outside the Alabama
Judicial Building, praying for the return of Roy's Rock and planning a
climactic rally to focus the attention of the national news media. Moore
himself refused to appear, saying that the protest should focus on the
Commandments, not on him. Dobson was being asked to fill the keynote speaker's slot. No other Christian Right leader would have the same
impact or would attract as much attention within the huge evangelical
subculture. "It is not an exaggeration to say that he is to some people a
Martin Luther King, Jr., crusading for the liberation of people who
can't help themselves," said the National Association of Evangelicals'
Ted Haggard, whose organization includes thirty-five million Americans, before gay sex and drug-use allegations forced him to step down
in late 2006. "Martin Luther King helped African Americans unlike
anyone in a hundred years, and Jim Dobson is the leader for civil rights
of people who can't speak for themselves: unborn babies."

Reluctantly, Dobson boarded a plane.

His Montgomery speech walked the crowd through what Dobson
called a forty-year record of transgressions by the federal judiciary, beginning with the Supreme Court: its 1962 decision ending officially
sanctioned school prayer, its 1963 decision that ended devotional Bible
reading in public schools, and, of course, 1973's *Roe v. Wade*. Dobson

cited eighties- and nineties-era Supreme Court rulings that barred prayer at graduation ceremonies and ended the mandatory posting of the Ten Commandments in public schools. He pointed to a recent decision by a federal appeals court in California which found that the recitation of the pledge of allegiance in schools represented an unconstitutional government endorsement of religion because it included the words "under God."

And just a couple of months before, Dobson noted, a 6 to 3 vote by the Supreme Court in the case *Lawrence v. Texas* struck down the country's last state sodomy laws. In his dissent, Justice Antonin Scalia warned that the ruling threatened to undo the state-level bans on gay marriage that Dobson and his vast national activist network had helped pass in the 1990s. Particularly galling to Dobson was that Supreme Court Justice Anthony Kennedy, a Reagan appointee, had cited a European court's ruling in his majority opinion in *Lawrence*. "I just returned from Europe," Dobson told the crowd, "and I'm telling you, that is a very pagan place."

In fact, it is fair to say that in Montgomery, Dobson perceived that America had arrived at a historic crossroads, with nothing less than the survival of Western civilization hanging in the balance. Down one road lay a nation where a Christian God was acknowledged as the foundation of government, family, and morality—the kind of nation that Dobson believed America had been for two hundred years and had begun to drift from only in the 1960s. Down the other lay America as contemporary Europe, home to the planet's most secular society. The courts, Dobson believed, were gradually steering the country down this latter course, against the people's will, by scrubbing religion from public life, striking down abortion restrictions and anti–gay rights laws, and otherwise thumbing their noses at God's law.

But in Montgomery, Dobson also glimpsed the possibility of deliverance from the judicial oligarchy. For one thing, he was freer than ever to parlay his national influence into political clout, having just stepped down from the presidency of Focus on the Family, where IRS laws governing nonprofit organizations restricted his political activism. And, while the crowd in Montgomery hardly qualified as overwhelming—a couple of thousand, according to press reports, though some Focus staffers remembered more than five thousand activists showing up—Dobson interpreted its intensity as symbolic of a new level of disgust among the country's seventy million white evangelical Christians, and a new willingness to stand up and fight. Most importantly, Dobson knew the presidential election was just over a year away and that the outcome was likely to remake the federal judiciary from the very top by determining who would get to appoint the first Supreme Court nominees in more than a decade—George W. Bush or his Democratic opponent.

So even as he used the removal of Roy's Rock as a rallying cry for evangelicals to join the culture war, Dobson himself was probably more moved by his appearance in Montgomery than anyone else. "I saw that a segment of the American people needed a voice, needed a spokesperson," he said in the Colorado Springs interview. "I saw that the issues hung in the balance. . . . And I saw the crowds, saw what they were saying, saw the intensity of it, saw Roy Moore and what he was trying to do. And I came out of there and said, 'I can't sit this one out.' And it was that day that I said to my colleagues, 'For one thing, we got to do what we can to take Tom Daschle out.'"

It was, by historical standards, an audacious goal. South Dakota senator Tom Daschle had served for the last decade as the Democrats' Senate leader, and neither party's Senate leader had been defeated at the polls since the election of Barry Goldwater in Arizona in 1952. After knocking off a Republican incumbent in 1986, Daschle had twice cruised to reelection.

But Dobson was unfazed. He'd been incensed by Daschle's role in leading Senate Democrats to block ten of George W. Bush's nominees to U.S. Appeals Courts—though more than two hundred federal judicial appointees had been confirmed, a success rate in line with that of previous first-term presidents. Dobson saw defeating the Democratic leader as the surest way for Bush to be able to continue his rightward re-alignment of the courts, particularly on the eve of expected Supreme Court vacancies. Unseating the man the GOP had tagged the "obstruc-tionist in chief" would be the political equivalent of slipping a horse's head into the Democrats' bed.

So in 2004, Dobson endorsed John Thune, an evangelical Chris-tian and conservative Republican who'd served three terms in the House of Representatives. Thune had come within 525 votes of victory in his bid to unseat South Dakota senator Tim Johnson in 2002. In 2004, Thune played up his opposition to abortion and same-sex marriage, fo-cusing the race on hot-button social issues to an extent unprecedented in South Dakota history. His message found particular resonance among the one in four South Dakotans who is an evangelical Chris-tian. So would James Dobson's endorsement. "There is literally a gen-eration of Americans who have grown up with Dr. Dobson," Thune said in an interview in his Senate office after the election. "His voice is golden out there, particularly among Americans who had a conserva-tive value system or conservative worldview. He could speak to them like nobody else could, absent somebody like Billy Graham."

While Dobson had occasionally granted endorsements to conserva-tive Republican candidates in previous elections, he hit the campaign trail for Thune in 2004 with a zeal that he'd never shown any other can-didate. He stumped for Thune at a huge Christian music festival over Labor Day weekend and in a pair of October "Stand for Family" rallies sponsored by Focus on the Family Action, a new political organization that Dobson launched in 2004. Through his South Dakota appear-ances, Dobson reached roughly one tenth of the state's population. He also attacked Daschle in full-page newspaper ads paid for by evangelical activist Gary Bauer's political action committee. Appearing under the banner *An Important Message from Dr. James C. Dobson*, the ads ac-cused Daschle of "doing the two-step" on abortion and same-sex mar-riage, selling South Dakotans a conservative line while voting with the liberals back in Washington.[2] A high-profile culture warrior who'd run for president in 2000, Bauer knew that showcasing Dobson would be more effective than appearing in the ads himself. "If I go into South Dakota and say, 'Vote for Thune or against Daschle,' people say, 'Of course he's going to say that—Bauer's a political operative,'" Bauer said. "When Dobson says it, he has impact. . . . I can't think of anyone with more equity in a heartland state."

Unlike other Christian Right titans—Moral Majority founder Jerry Falwell, Christian Coalition founder Pat Robertson, or former Christian Coalition executive director Ralph Reed—Dobson has never run for public office or led a primarily political organization. A child psychologist, he won an enormous following by dispensing what many consider to be biblically based family advice, mostly about raising children and maintaining successful marriages, through a daily radio program also called *Focus on the Family*. "Dr. Dobson is almost like a father to me," said a forty-six-year-old mother of four from Cañon City, Colorado, who stopped by Focus's Colorado Springs bookstore in late 2004 to do some Christmas shopping. "I was having a difficult time raising my kids, and he helped rescue me."

Dobson's radio show is carried on upward of two thousand domestic radio stations, with six to ten million weekly listeners. He receives so much mail from fans that his organization requires its own zip code. His dozens of books, including *Dare to Discipline, Preparing for Adolescence,* and *What Wives Wish Their Husbands Knew about Women,* have sold in the tens of millions. His videos and DVDs have reached an even wider audience, via television broadcasts and church-sponsored screenings. In an interview, the Southern Baptist Convention's Richard Land, whose group claims sixteen million American members, called Dobson "the most influential evangelical leader in America. . . . The closest thing to his influence is what Billy Graham had in the sixties and seventies."

The politicians who have been influenced by Dobson say their admiration for him stems from his family advice, not his political advocacy. In Washington, Republican congressman Frank Wolf of Virginia was so moved by Dobson's 1981 child-rearing film *Where's Dad?*, particularly by a sequence in which Dobson recites the lyrics to Harry Chapin's seventies-era hit "Cat's in the Cradle," that he installed a separate phone line in his Capitol Hill office exclusively for his wife and kids to call on. Wolf stopped attending work-related events on Sunday to spend more time with his family. "If George Bush or Bill Clinton came to the end of my street on Sunday, I would not go," Wolf said in an interview in his House office, where a framed passage from one of Dobson's books hangs on the wall. "It's a firm, firm, firm, firm rule. . . . The message Dobson gives in [his books] is universal. It has no political overtones. Dobson has had an impact on my life to the point that my kids refer to me as B.D. and A.D., before Dobson and after Dobson. They saw the fruit of *Where's Dad?*"

When Dobson takes to the airwaves to urge listeners to call Congress in support of a Supreme Court nominee or to stop a piece of legislation from advancing, his admonitions are taken as those of a trusted family adviser, not a political shill. His influence among evangelicals outshines that of any previous Christian Right standard-bearer because he is not seen as the Christian Right's standard-bearer. "I have no political ambitions, and that puts me in a different category than somebody who does," Dobson said in an interview. ". . . I'm separate from [the political system]. I'm not owned by it. I don't want anything there. I wouldn't run for president if it was handed to me on a platter. I would be absolutely claustrophobic in the public eye every moment of the day."

Dobson prefers the role of a behind-the-scenes political fixer, publicly downplaying his level of political involvement to protect his credibility among his followers. He portrays himself, and is characterized by friends, as a reluctant warrior. He tends to frame each act of political advocacy as an unprecedented foray into politics born of a new crisis that demands he stop biting his tongue. In a newsletter to Focus constituents following President Clinton's inauguration, for example, Dobson wrote, "Nothing in my adult life has shaken me quite like the devastation we are seeing."[3] In short, Clinton's arrival, because of his support for abortion rights and gay rights and because of allegations that he'd been unfaithful to his wife, was treated as an unprecedented crisis. But twelve years later, in a 2004 letter to Focus on the Family constituents advocating a constitutional amendment banning same-sex marriage, Dobson's tone was remarkably similar in its urgency: "I do not recall a time since the beginnings of Focus on the Family, 27 years ago, when the institution of marriage faced such peril." And Dobson played the sky-is-falling card again in 2005, when a group of U.S. senators reached a deal to avert the so-called nuclear option—suspending the Senate's filibuster rule that requires 60-vote supermajorities to confirm President Bush's judicial nominees—telling his radio listeners, "This one hit me personally harder than anything ever has coming out of Washington."

In person he comes across as an antipolitico. Dobson's sandy, combed-over hair, blue eyes, gentle smile, and penchant for tan-colored suits give him the appearance of having just stepped out of a Hallmark card. His big, boxy eyeglasses, as seen in photographs going back to the early 1980s, announce that he is oblivious to fashion, and his six-foot-plus frame and lanky build tend to make the chair he's occupying look too small, giving him an air of paternalistic authority. Even when worked up in a lather, as he frequently is, Dobson's speech is unhurried, and the slight western drawl and note of hesitancy in his voice give it an almost exaggerated folksiness. On the radio dial, amid the racket of overly caffeinated DJs and fast-talking automobile salesmen, Dobson's daily *Focus on the Family* broadcast is an island of placidity. Even when speaking in baleful terms, as in 2006 when he said *The Da Vinci Code* "has all the evidences of something cooked up in hell" and was a "satanic plot," Dobson sounds a lot more like a quaint grandfather than a fiery Baptist preacher. When he devotes an episode of his program to political issues, such as Supreme Court nominees or an upcoming election, he apologizes to his listeners for preempting a previously scheduled program, creating the impression that even he would rather be focusing on the family.

And yet Dobson is hardly a political neophyte. The biggest portrait in his Colorado Springs office isn't of Jesus Christ; it's of Winston Churchill. Dobson fell in love with the painting when he saw it at a Tampa art gallery in the mid-1990s, but his wife refused to let him buy it, fearing he'd hang it in their bedroom. So Dobson told one of Focus's board members about the portrait, and the board promptly took up a collection and bought it for him. "Churchill knew in forty-one he could never beat Germany," Dobson said in a late 2004 interview, rising to fetch a biography of the statesman from his bookshelf. "So his hope was to help the British people hang on until the Americans came. For the last twenty years, all the centers of power have been influenced by a different world-view than what we share as evangelical Christians," he continued, citing Congress, the judiciary, higher education, and Hollywood as examples. "Our strategy has been to let people who see things the way we do know what's at stake and to encourage them to hang on until change occurs."

But when asked about his political activities—as opposed to his political *opinions*—Dobson can be remarkably coy, as if he senses that discussing such matters on the record would tarnish his image as an above-the-fray family counselor. His political résumé includes having cofounded the Washington-based Family Research Council, which would eventually replace Christian Coalition as the Christian Right's top beltway advocacy group in 1983; joining President Ronald Reagan's federal task forces on gambling and pornography; successfully promoting a Colorado ballot initiative barring the state from passing antidiscrimination laws for homosexuals in 1992; meeting with all the major Republican presidential candidates in 1996; and endorsing conservative Republican candidates beginning in the 1990s, including Randall Terry, founder of the militant antiabortion group Operation Rescue, in his unsuccessful 1998 bid for the House of Representatives.

And yet Dobson declined to answer a list of questions for this book about his political advocacy on the basis that the questions were too political. "[R]esponding to the majority of your questions . . . would drag Dr. Dobson further into the public policy arena than he is willing to go," his spokesman said via e-mail in late 2005. "Furthermore, Dr. Dobson has dealt with most of these issues from a <u>personal</u> perspective and not as President/CEO/Founder/Chairman of Focus on the Family or [sister organization] Focus on the Family Action." In the late 2004 interview in his Colorado Springs office, Dobson went so far as to dismiss his own political clout. "You can't even tell someone else's dog what to do," he said. "If they don't want to do what you're suggesting, they don't do it. You can't manipulate people like that. . . . So that's a phony argument that somehow I have used these child-rearing and marriage principles to warp and twist people into doing things they wouldn't want to do. That is off the wall, man. That is crazy."

Before 2004, Dobson had always been tightfisted with Republican endorsements. But 2004 was different, and not just because the Supreme Court was at stake. Dobson's top legislative priority was passing an amendment to the U.S. Constitution to ban same-sex marriage. In May 2004, Massachusetts became the first state to legalize gay marriage. Even before that, Dobson had singled out gay marriage as the biggest threat facing the American family—bigger than the soaring divorce rate, the rise in the number of unmarried cohabiting couples raising children, or the increase in absentee dads and working moms. "My greatest concern is for the relentless attack by homosexual activists who are determined to destroy the institution of marriage," Dobson told his official biographer, Dale Buss, in the 2005 book *Family Man: The Biography of Dr. James Dobson*. "[T]here are very few conservative leaders who are willing to stand up against this most powerful lobby, which has the passionate support of every branch of the media."[4]

In summer 2003 a powerful new coalition of Christian Right leaders called the Arlington Group began convening in Washington to plot strategy for passing a constitutional amendment that would ban gay marriage. According to sources at one of the first Arlington Group meetings, which were and continue to be strictly off-the-record, Dobson was struck by an observation offered by a legendary Washington

strategist named Paul Weyrich. Weyrich was an early and influential architect of the Christian Right, cofounding Moral Majority in the late
1970s. At the 2003 meeting, which included more than a dozen top
Christian Right figures, Weyrich estimated aloud that conservative Republicans would need to gain seven to ten Senate seats if they hoped to
pass a constitutional amendment, which requires two-thirds support in
the House and Senate. At the time, the GOP held a one-seat majority in
Congress's upper chamber. There was no Arlington Group member, no
Christian activist anywhere, with the public following to influence Senate races like Dobson could. And there was no shortage of Republican
candidates who wanted him. "Unlike any campaign surrogate we could
send out there, he would get a massive crowd," said Gary Marx, national
conservative coalition director for the Bush-Cheney 2004 campaign.
"He has the benefit of not being a partisan voice. He is the single most
credible figure within the evangelical community."

In South Dakota, Dobson's appearances, along with a patchwork of
efforts on the part of Christian Right groups and evangelical pastors,
helped nudge John Thune to a 51 percent to 49 percent victory over
Senator Tom Daschle. Dobson campaigned for four other conservative
Republican Senate candidates, including former Republican congressman Tom Coburn, who was running in an open seat race in Oklahoma. Oklahoma was one of a dwindling handful of red states where
Democrats still held out hope for winning a Senate seat. And if anyone
could pull it off, it was Brad Carson, a moderate Democratic congressman with a compelling political profile: he is part Cherokee, a Southern Baptist, and a Rhodes scholar. All through his Senate campaign,
Carson took pains to distance himself from the national Democratic
Party and from Democratic presidential nominee John Kerry by bran-
dishing his vote for the partial-birth abortion ban and reaffirming his
support for gun rights.

In fact, one of the Coburn campaign's greatest concerns was that
Oklahoma's culturally conservative voters were having trouble distin-
guishing the two candidates' stances on abortion. Coburn had left the
House in 2000 and returned to Muskogee to continue his previous

work as an obstetrician and had frequently boasted of delivering upward of four thousand babies, so his campaign was indignant that the news media weren't portraying him as the clearly more pro-life candidate. The Coburn campaign also worried about an internal poll taken two months before Election Day that showed Coburn with a relatively thin lead among white born-again Christians, who account for almost half the state's population. Alarmed by the poll, Coburn's campaign manager, Mike Schwartz, encouraged his pollster to craft and test messages tailor-made for evangelicals. But the pollster shrugged him off. "You'd think that pollsters do what they're told, but this one didn't want to," Schwartz said. "I wasn't about to change the team in late September, so I just figured a way around it."

The solution to Coburn's problems, establishing him as more pro-life than Carson and making an explicit appeal to evangelicals, was to bring in James Dobson. "If we get Dobson into the state on our behalf, we don't have to do anything else special," said Schwartz. "It sends the message to everybody that's listening, and consolidates us among a core constituency." Coburn, a conservative evangelical Christian, had known Dobson from his days in the House of Representatives in the 1990s. After leaving the House in 2000, Coburn joined the board of directors at the Family Research Council, the Washington advocacy group that Dobson helped found and is closely aligned with.

"There's no question [Dobson] has a great following in Oklahoma," Coburn said in an interview after the election. "And it cuts across party lines."

Less than a month before Election Day, Dobson campaigned for Coburn in four Oklahoma cities. "Jim Dobson coming to town is the biggest thing that ever happened in Durant, Oklahoma," said Schwartz. Added John Hart, Coburn's communications director during the campaign: "It's his moral authority. . . . Millions of parents in America have read his books. He comes in and is covered by the *Tulsa World* and by local TV stations, and he can describe the difference between candidates in ways that traditional media can't." Coburn won decisively, 53 to 41 percent, though earlier polls put Carson in front.

Carson blamed his loss squarely on the Democrats' alienation of evangelical voters with its stances on abortion and other cultural issues. "The culture war is real," he wrote in the *The New Republic* shortly after Election Day. ". . . For the vast majority of Oklahomans—and, I would suspect, voters in other red states . . . transcendent cultural concerns are more important than universal health care or raising the minimum wage or preserving farm subsidies."[5]

Even as he doled out more candidate endorsements than ever before, Dobson was nonetheless selective. He rebuffed overtures from beer magnate and GOP Senate candidate Peter Coors in his home state of Colorado. Dobson was disturbed by Coors's beer commercials, which targeted young people, and by some of the company's cheeky endorsement deals. He also frowned on the company's domestic partner benefits program for gay employees and its refusal to exempt evangelical Christians who object to homosexuality from participating in diversity training.[6]

But in 2004, Dobson was able to make a real difference in the election by creating Focus on the Family Action, a fund-raising outfit free from the IRS rules imposed on the nonprofit Focus on the Family. He sent a fund-raising letter for the new organization promising that "All the funds . . . go straight to the battle for righteousness." Focus on the Family Action allowed Dobson to draft letters to hundreds of thousands of Focus constituents supportive of Republican Senate candidates in Louisiana, North Carolina, South Carolina, and Florida, in addition to South Dakota and Oklahoma. Those candidates all won their races. Dobson also headlined six "Stand for Family" rallies that promoted the constitutional ban on same-sex marriage and were sponsored by Focus on the Family Action. They were all held in states with competitive Senate races and attracted from six thousand to more than thirteen thousand people each, along with local media attention. He keynoted a separate series of megachurch rallies, beamed to hundreds of churches nationwide and carried live by Christian radio and cable channels, where he promoted the constitutional amendment and implored evangelicals to vote for conservative candidates. In its first six months of existence, Focus on the Family Action, whose employees all work at Focus on the Family as well, raised nearly nine million dollars.

In 2000, as word spread that then presumptive Republican presidential nominee George W. Bush might select a pro-choice running mate, such as former New Jersey governor Christine Todd Whitman, Dobson warned Bush that he would lose evangelical votes, and with them, the White House. In 2004, Bush received Dobson's first presidential endorsement. Why the change of heart? The president had signed the ban on the procedure opponents call partial birth abortion, endorsed a constitutional amendment to ban gay marriage, and appointed conservative judges to the federal bench. He'd appointed well-known evangelical John Ashcroft to be attorney general. Perhaps most importantly, Bush spoke openly about his faith in an evangelical lexicon, telling senators during the Ashcroft confirmation battle to consider "Ashcroft's heart and his record" and talking frequently about the role Jesus played in his decision to give up drinking, including his oceanside walk with Billy Graham during which Graham had asked him "Are you right with God?" "This president is more actively pro-life and pro-family and pro-moral than any previous president, especially with his willingness to speak openly about his faith," Dobson said in an interview. "During the first campaign, he referenced Jesus Christ. I don't know any other presidential candidate in history, maybe going back to Jimmy Carter . . . talking about Jesus Christ. So in that sense, we have a certain affinity with George W. Bush.

"But the specter of John Kerry was probably a bigger concern . . . ," Dobson continued. "The possibility of John Kerry appointing, in eight years if that's the way it worked out, maybe three to five Supreme Court justices, which would have allowed them to reinterpret the Constitution, that was terrifying to many people, us included."

After the 2004 election, Republicans were in firm control of the Senate—thanks largely to the net gain of four conservative members whom Dobson had supported—along with the White House and the House of Representatives. Dobson and other graying Christian Right leaders saw Washington realign in a way it hadn't since the Eisenhower era. Overnight, agenda items for which the Christian Right had been clamoring for decades seemed within reach. The Supreme Court could be reconstituted. Congress could impose the first real curbs on abortion rights since *Roe*. And if there weren't yet enough votes to amend the Constitution to ban gay marriage, the numbers in Congress were at least moving in that direction.

But it all needed to happen quickly. "There's a window which may only remain open a short time to make some critical changes in the government of this country," Dobson said in the 2004 interview. ". . . . I believe what happened is something of a reprieve, not a final victory. And if the Republicans who have been handed power in the White House and Senate squander this opportunity, I believe they will pay a price for it in four years, and maybe two."

After all Dobson and his followers had done during the campaign, conservative Republicans were eager to start 2005 in his good graces. So it was little surprise that a black tie dinner sponsored by the Family Research Council and Focus on the Family during the week of President Bush's January 2005 inauguration festivities drew Senate majority leader and White House hopeful Bill Frist, House majority whip Roy Blunt, and newly elected Louisiana congressman Bobby Jindal, president of the Republican freshman class. The White House was represented by a top Karl Rove lieutenant and by President Bush's just-named domestic policy adviser, former Health and Human Services deputy secretary Claude Allen. (The following year, Allen would resign from the White House and be sentenced to two years probation after pleading guilty to bilking Washington-area department stores in a bogus refund scheme.)[7] Speaking to an audience of a few hundred inside the plush Willard Hotel, two blocks from 1600 Pennsylvania Avenue, Allen announced that the first call he took after being offered the White House job was from James Dobson. Outgoing Republican National Committee chairman Ed Gillespie showed up later, wife in tow. On an evening when Washington's Republicans had a full menu of lavish preinauguration soirées to choose from, the most powerful were at a banquet where the most potent drink on hand was sweet lemonade.

Still, Dobson looked uneasy that night. Keynoting the event, he laid out the battle ahead by describing the enemy pro-family forces were up against—liberal Democrats—through an allegory. "A missionary in Africa came home one day and walked into the house and there in the living room was a large python," Dobson told the audience. "And it scared him, obviously, and he went back to the truck and he got his pistol and he realized he had only one bullet. He aimed carefully and shot the snake in the head, but the snake was not mortally wounded, but it was severely, badly wounded. And he closed the door and the snake just went crazy, just writhing in that house and he tore up everything on the inside as he was responding to the attack. . . .

"Those who are coming from the left side of the spectrum are wounded," he concluded. "They got wounded on November 2, and they are angry and they are not going to just limp away. They are going to fight, and we're going to need all the help we can get."

2

Billy Graham's Heir

"His folksy style made listeners believe that
he was their friend. And they wanted to
help him because of it."

—◊—

It is not uncommon for the news media to refer to him as the Reverend James Dobson. And though his great-grandfather received a prophesy that all members of the next four generations would belong to the Lord, and though his father made his living as an itinerant minister, James Dobson, Jr., never heard the call to preach. Which isn't to say his great-grandfather's premonition rang false. Dobson has often spoken of an exchange between his dad and the Lord in which Dobson's own future was foretold. It happened the day before his father, James Dobson, Sr., suffered a heart attack at the age of sixty-six. In declining health, the elder Dobson had been praying for more time to win souls for the Lord when, according to Dobson Jr.'s telling, he received a message from

God. "My father didn't say that often; he didn't throw those words around," Dobson said, according to his biographer. "When he said the Lord talked to him that morning, you could be sure he'd had a conversation with the Lord."[1]

According to James Dobson, Jr., the message from God to his father was simple, unequivocal, and came as something of a shock: "I have heard your prayer. I know your love for my people and your passion for the gospel of Jesus Christ, and I know you asked to have more time to reach others for me. And I'm going to grant that request. You're going to reach thousands of people, perhaps millions of people, coast to coast and around the world. But it . . . [is] going to be through your son."[2]

Two and a half months later, after a second heart attack, James Dobson, Sr., was dead.

It was 1977, the year after James Dobson, Jr., had left his positions as a medical school professor and a medical researcher to spend more time writing and lecturing in public, and to launch a weekly radio program. From the start, he called the radio show *Focus on the Family*. Dobson wouldn't learn of his father's revelation until the mid-1980s, in a letter from a relative. By that time, Focus on the Family was a booming organization, doubling or tripling the size of its staff, budget, and mailing list nearly every year. When Dobson got the letter, it all became clear. "I saw for the first time that Focus on the Family isn't a product of my creativity or my words or my thoughts or my writings; this is God's answer to my father's prayer," Dobson told his biographer, "and it explained why every door has sprung open for the ministry from the early days. . . . It came out of my father's prayer life, his intense relationship with the Lord, and his desire to serve him. . . . And the Lord has just transferred that one generation down [to me], as he did with Solomon when he allowed him to build the Temple instead of David."[3]

An outspoken proponent of involved dads and stay-at-home moms, Dobson had neither as a young child. Born in Shreveport, Louisiana, in 1936, to James Sr. and Myrtle Dobson, Dobson Jr. was left in the care of relatives as his parents toured the revival circuit of the Deep South and the Southwest.[4] But his mother quit the road when Dobson was seven, and the family moved into a house outside Oklahoma City. Myrtle Dobson's doting on her only child would help ensure that Dobson Jr. would grow up to be as confident, talkative, and emotionally transparent as his father was taciturn and self-doubting.[5] Describing Dobson's relationship with his mother to *Christianity Today* in 1988, Dobson's wife, Shirley Deere Dobson, recalled, "No matter what Jim said to her, even if she didn't agree with it, she would never put it down. She would always let him say whatever he wanted to say. . . . She would never give an opinion."[6]

Dobson's ancestors had been charter members of the Church of the Nazarene, a small Christian denomination established in the United States in the first decade of the twentieth century.[7] In 2004 it counted just under 1.5 million members worldwide.[8] Nazarene theology stresses the free will and responsibility of each individual in choosing to accept the grace of Jesus Christ.[9] It calls on adherents to lead holy lives by following a strict code of behavior that proscribes smoking, drinking, and other worldly pleasures.[10] Dobson has said he shies away from discussing his Nazarene faith because outsiders have misconstrued its holiness doctrine—the command to continually renounce sin after being saved in order to emulate Christ—as a claim to perfection or sinlessness.[11] Dobson has also said, however, that sin is an intentional act, "a *willful* disobedience or defiance to *known* law," suggesting that he believes it impossible to sin without knowing one is doing it.[12]

By the time Dobson launched his *Focus on the Family* radio show in 1977, he'd already had a successful seventeen-year career in medicine. In 1958, he graduated from Pasadena College outside Los Angeles, a small Nazarene school where he'd majored in psychology, made tennis captain, and met his future wife, Shirley, who was homecoming queen there. Dobson took her to Sunday-evening services on their first date.[13] He was drawn to Christian psychology by a professor named Paul Culbertson, who was forced to heavily supplement secular textbooks with his own teachings because the field was so new. "Culbertson was not teaching spirituality as opposed to psychology, but about the whole person as physical, mental, and spiritual," recalled Wil Spaite, a friend of Dobson's at Pasadena and a fellow psychology major. "Psychology was a means to bring about healing in a person, and God was the ultimate source of the healing. It was God who desired the person to be whole."

Dobson pursued a Ph.D. in psychology at the University of Southern California. While completing his doctorate, he took a position with Childrens Hospital Los Angeles, where he supervised a five-million-dollar study of a treatment for phenylketonuria (PKU), a rare disease that can cause severe mental retardation.[14] Within a few years, he'd also become professor of pediatrics at the University of Southern California School of Medicine.

Lacking an ultimate career aspiration, Dobson's ambition was nonetheless unmistakable. "He had a real sense of destiny," remembered Spaite.

Even before leaving Pasadena College, Dobson gave a glimpse of his future during a ride in Wil Spaite's '56 Chevy. Spaite's wife, Polly, and their newborn son were in the car, and Polly was grousing about the permissive parenting techniques of Dr. Benjamin Spock. "I'm going to do something about the family," Dobson, a college junior, declared, surprising the Spaites.

Dobson said it was his exposure to the swelling ranks of troubled youth during the 1960s that really shaped his child development theories. "[M]y involvement in the field of child psychology is precisely what convinced me, beyond a shadow of a doubt, that the family was in serious trouble," he said via e-mail in 2005. "My years at the USC School of Medicine and Childrens Hospital, which came right on the heels of the sexual revolution, only served to confirm my belief that the institution of the family was disintegrating. I worked with children on a daily basis, and saw firsthand how divorce, abuse, and other forms of familial strife were tearing their lives apart. . . . I became convinced that the only hope for these broken and disillusioned kids—as

well as for future generations of children — lay in the strengthening of
the family unit and returning to the Judeo-Christian concepts of
morality and fidelity."

Many American evangelicals saw the turbulent 1960s as a case
study in the perils of moral relativism, even as the civil rights and anti-
war movements had clear moral imperatives — and, in many instances,
religious underpinnings. The modern American evangelical movement
emerged in the early twentieth century largely as a reaction to the birth
of modern scientific and cultural ideas, such as Darwinian evolution,
and their application to biblical interpretation. In the face of such developments, evangelicals clung intently to biblical authority and literal-
ism, while mainline Protestants updated their beliefs and traditions.[15]
In the 1960s, Dobson and other evangelicals continued to subscribe to
what they considered to be a biblically based system of right and wrong,
with bright-line absolutes that jarred with the era's ethic of tolerance
and experimentation. The decade's civil unrest, giving birth to the militant black power movement and the sexual revolution, gave the evangelical movement a culture to define itself against. Surveying the
sixties-era college scene in a later book, Dobson asserted that "drug
abuse was not only prevalent, but became almost universal for students
and teachers alike. The Viet Nam War [sic] soon heated campus pas-
sions to an incendiary level, generating anger and disdain for the government, the President, the military, both political parties, and indeed,
the American way of life. . . . Accompanying this social upheaval was a
sudden disintegration of moral and ethical principles, such as has never
occurred in the history of mankind. All at once, there were no definite
values. There were no standards. No absolutes. No rules. No traditional
beliefs on which to lean. . . . And as will be recalled, some bright-eyed
theologians chose that moment of confusion to announce the death of
God. It was a distressing time to be so young — to be groping aimlessly
in search of a personal identity and a place in the sun."[16]

Dobson's response to the 1960s was *Dare to Discipline*, his first
book for a general readership (he'd previously coauthored a medical

text on mental retardation in children). Published in 1970, it railed against the child-rearing techniques popularized by Benjamin Spock, which eschewed a disciplinarian posture and encouraged parents to get in touch with their kids' feelings. Dobson actually admired Spock, but felt many parents misinterpreted him. While Dobson's book was a parenting manual first, it doubled as an anti-1960s manifesto whose response to the "if it feels good, do it" culture was to channel Jonathan Edwards, the eighteenth-century New England theologian who penned the famous sermon "Sinners in the Hands of an Angry God." "Permissiveness has not just been a failure; it's been a disaster!" Dobson wrote in *Dare to Discipline*'s introduction, pointing to what he said were the increased proclivities of the current generation of young adults toward violence, drugs, and general immorality.[17]

The book offered suggestions for inflicting minor, temporary pain on children to instill respect for authority, including spanking with a belt or a switch. It recommended keeping such items on a child's dresser as a reminder that bucking authority has consequences. Dobson offered specific instructions for administering corporal punishment, like spanking *"immediately* after the offense or not at all" and following the act with a clear reaffirmation of parental love for the child. *Dare to Discipline* quickly sold two million copies to a largely evangelical readership. But it failed to cause much of a stir in post-sixties pacifist parenting circles; few moms and dads outside the evangelical subculture took notice.[18]

Even before *Dare to Discipline*, Dobson had begun giving presentations on his old-fashioned parenting techniques to church and PTA groups in Southern California, perhaps partly to escape the cloistered world of medical research and to recapture something of the revival atmosphere of his youth.[19] By 1976, his presentations were enough in demand for him to take a sabbatical from USC and Childrens Hospital to concentrate on public speaking.[20] By then, he'd published two more books, including his first foray into marital relations, *What Wives Wish*

Their Husbands Knew about Women, and would release two more titles, including *Preparing for Adolescence,* before the decade's end. As his books continued to sell in the millions, the crowds turning out for his "Focus on the Family" seminars swelled into the thousands. Crisscrossing the country to speak at ticketed events, Dobson's schedule soon had him feeling that he was repeating the mistakes of his own peripatetic father; the Dobson household now included a young daughter and an adopted son.

So Dobson made his mind up to retire from the road, just as his mother had done after years of touring the revival circuit with her husband. Before he did, though, a Christian publishing house approached him with a novel proposal: taping one of his final presentations to sell to churches as a film series. Dobson was skeptical of the scheme, and worried about squandering the publisher's money, so he actively discouraged the company from following through. But the publisher wound up making a seven-part Focus on the Family series that featured Dobson holding forth on child-rearing and husband-wife relationships, which was distributed to evangelical churches on 16-millimeter film and in Betamax format compatible with the first VCRs. The publisher also packaged one segment of the series, about the importance of interested and active fathers, as a separate one-hour TV special called *Where's Dad?* Dobson sent a representative around the country to raise money from evangelical businessmen to air *Where's Dad?* in local markets during prime time. By the early 1980s, an estimated one hundred million plus people had seen it worldwide.[21]

In 1977, while on sabbatical from USC and Childrens Hospital— which turned out to be his retirement from the academic and medical worlds—Dobson had launched his first radio show. It was a fifteen-minute weekend program underwritten by a Christian publisher that had distributed some of his early books. In 1981, Dobson expanded it to a thirty-minute daily format, and by the following year it was on nearly two hundred stations. Five years later the daily broadcast had been picked up by nearly eight hundred stations nationwide.[22] "The majority of Christian radio programming at that time was pastors who would edit their preaching from a Sunday service and put it on the radio," remembered Peb Jackson, who did promotion for Dobson's early seminars and joined the Focus on the Family board of directors in 1977. "There weren't many talk shows. There were shows with missionaries and about church people doing things, but this was different."

Dobson's avuncular manner and his capacity for letting grown men break down with the tape rolling were a sharp break with Christian radio's customary fire-and-brimstone sermons.

To a no-frills evangelical radio culture inhabited by graying, out-of-touch preachers, Dobson brought all the professionalism of his medical CV to bear, interviewing contemporary Christian authors about the challenges of bringing up kids and creating happy marriages. But Dobson was no softy. Defying the affirmation-heavy tactics of the psychologists who were cropping up on television and radio in response to a generation of therapy-hungry baby boomers, he applied the same rules-based approach as *Dare to Discipline*. "During those years, psychologists were not prone to give answers—they were more prone to draw you out," recalled Jackson. "Jim was never shy about giving answers. He did not hem and haw around with folks and say, 'Tell me how you're feeling.' He'd say, 'Let me tell you what I think.'"

The subject matter, and Dobson's practical approach, won him an overwhelmingly female listenership. He encouraged parents to talk to their kids about sex and sexuality before the onset of puberty. He opined that masturbation, a controversial subject among many religious Americans, "is not much of an issue with God." And even as he was uncompromising on premarital abstinence, asserting that the harshest consequence of premarital sex is the "judgment of God in the life to come," he stressed that it's never too late to reverse course and become a "secondary virgin." "His folksy style made listeners believe that he was their friend," recalled former Focus on the Family chief operating officer Paul Nelson. "And they wanted to help him because of it."

Dobson was intensely aware of that fact. Early on, he perceived that his broadcast, by connecting him to listeners every day, presented him with the opportunity to win their trust and to help instill in them an orthodox Christian worldview that rejected the reigning postmodernism. "He was skeptical as to the lasting impact of just speaking once to any group," said Peb Jackson, who would become Focus's first public affairs director. "He was more interested in long-term relationships. That was why the daily radio show was a perfect medium. He is in your face every day, talking about the issues and values and he felt that happened over a period of time. . . . You could get people whipped up with music or by a great speaker, but he felt radio was transformational in helping people define their thinking on issues."

Dobson had incorporated his speaking and media ventures as Focus on the Family in 1977, but his most important innovation came in 1979, when he hired five women to answer the letters that had been pouring in at a rate of more than a hundred a day in response to his radio show. Dobson's fans were writing to him for two reasons. One was to order something from Focus's growing repertoire of books, pamphlets, videos, and taped broadcasts that they'd heard or heard about on *Focus on the Family*. The other was to ask for Dobson's advice on a wide array of topics. Coming mostly from women, the letters asked about proper potty-training techniques, how to confront a cheating husband, where to seek help for depression, and countless other matters. By the early eighties, Dobson was receiving thousands of letters a month. He'd hired more than sixty staffers to answer the mail, who came to be known at Focus as "correspondents." The organization also hired a team of part-time Christian therapists to call troubled "constituents," as Dobson called the people who wrote and called him and Focus.

The volume of letters was so great that Focus waited a few years before beginning to advertise a toll-free number for placing orders and seeking help. "Dobson's background was as a psychologist, so he didn't want to send out brief or incomplete answers to questions," said Mike Trout, who joined Focus in 1981 and was Dobson's on-air cohost from 1986 until 2000. "He wanted a professionally trained staff to respond to people in a complete and thorough way, so you didn't want to overwhelm the phone lines. There were times we went on air and apologized for the backlog. We knew a lot of folks out there were in dire circumstances, desperately asking for help."

Though Focus on the Family never required payment for its advice and advertised "suggested donations" for its products rather than firm prices, financial support was quick in coming. By 1987 the ministry had a roughly thirty-four-million-dollar budget, more than Christian Coalition's at its high point a decade later, and almost all from individual donors. By 1995, Focus's budget topped one hundred million. In contrast to donors who support charities like the Salvation Army or ministries like Campus Crusade for Christ, donors to Focus benefited personally from their donations, by listening to Dobson's show, having access to a warehouse of reasonably priced Christian resources, and knowing someone was out there if they ever needed some free guidance. "People didn't feel like they had to give a dime, and with that credibility, people would get on the mailing list and we developed this sense of communication," said Jackson. "The idea was not just to be a resource for people to tap into when they listened to the radio show. We wanted to design a superstructure of assistance to people that went deep."

By 1988, Focus on the Family was receiving 150,000 pieces of mail a month, almost all addressed to Dobson and mostly from fretful mothers and wives.[23] Correspondents culled their reply letters from Dobson's books and broadcasts, flipping through thick, two-foot-by-two-foot catalogs of handwritten broadcast transcriptions to find Dobson's advice on a given topic.

To Dobson, the survival and growth of his organization, which he called a "ministry," depended on each individual who called or wrote to Focus getting speedy, customized help. Phone calls were to be answered in three rings. Answering services or automated phone attendants were out of the question. Letters were to be turned around in three days. Dobson reviewed constituent mail and built broadcasts around what was on his listeners' minds. "It shocked people at times to realize [Dobson's] need to satisfy the customer," recalled Jackson. "He would find out if phone calls were not answered or mail wasn't answered or if something was not promised or did not get to a person. He always had a way of sniffing out failure. With his own massive personality and effort, he kept everyone's nose to the grindstone. It would shock people who came in and pictured this very sensitive, understanding guy they had heard on the radio, and you found out this guy wielded a heavy hammer." Jackson, who'd come to Focus from the corporate world, could appreciate Dobson's heavy-handed management style. Many of the Christian women who staffed the organization's correspondence department had a more difficult time getting comfortable.

With a line of bestselling books, a popular film series, a widely distributed radio show, and a rapid-response call and letter-writing operation, Focus on the Family had developed into a full-blown evangelical media empire by the mid-1980s. The organization sent monthly letters and occasional fund-raising pitches to each person who called, further cementing its relationship with constituents. By 1985, Focus had collected seven hundred thousand names and addresses.[24] A decade later, Focus cleared two million names.[25] "The marketing was just incredible," said Paul Nelson, the former Focus chief operating officer. "I was always putting the brakes on, saying we have to be careful because we can sell a dog on [Dobson's radio show]. I told Jim, 'For crying out loud, you can go to the mountain with some heresy and a hundred thousand people will follow you there, because the marketing was there.'"

As letters and phone calls mounted through the 1980s, Focus compiled Dobson's advice on hundreds of different topics into computer databanks that were accessible to its phone and letter correspondents. There was Dobson's guidance on how to stop bed-wetting, how to confront a teenager about drug use, how to communicate with a remote husband, how to talk to a suicidal person. "The people who would call or write really did not care what the [Focus correspondents] who they were talking to felt about the issue," said Nelson. "They cared what Dr. Dobson thought." Letter-writing correspondents would simply mine the database for Dobson's advice, then spend a few minutes customizing each response to fit an individual constituent's specific situation.

But the mission as defined by Dobson remained that no constituent should feel as though he or she was receiving a form letter. As the nineties approached, Focus's correspondence department wanted to study other big letter-writing operations. The only similarly sized effort was managed by the White House, so Focus flew the White House's letter-writing supervisor to its Southern California headquarters. "The woman was amazed at our system, that we were every bit as efficient as the White House," remembered then correspondence department supervisor Diane Passno. "I felt good about that, because we were flying by the seat of our pants. We just knew we had to answer the mail. We didn't know what we were doing."

But Dobson knew. Unlike leaders of other Christian ministries, Dobson was so confident in pursuing his vision for Focus on the Family that he wasn't afraid to hire business world executives into the top tiers of Focus management to see that it was carried out. "He has a confidence, sometimes even arrogance . . . he had such a belief in what he felt God had given him in both his purpose and his expertise," Jackson said. "Jim had the uncanny ability that even when his fellow professionals were going in one direction and he had a belief in something that was counter, it didn't make any difference. . . . If everybody was on the same train in one direction, it almost made it more delicious for him to go in the opposite direction."

—m—

Dobson launched Focus on the Family just a year or so before the modern Christian Right was born in the late 1970s, but he initially took pains to insulate himself and his ministry from partisan politics. "Extremely anxious not to over-politicize his message, Dobson keeps the fo-

cus on helping and encouraging families," *Christianity Today* wrote in
1988. ". . . Yet he is clearly fascinated with Washington, and has been
spending increasing amounts of his personal time there."[26] Washington
first noticed Dobson with the 1981 release of the film and TV special
Where's Dad? Republican congressman Frank Wolf and Republican
senator Dan Coats, an evangelical Christian, sponsored screenings of
the film for their fellow elected officials, whose ranks included plenty of
workaholic fathers. *Where's Dad?* impressed Democratic House majority leader Jim Wright and a hard-drinking Republican freshman from
Texas named Tom DeLay, the future House majority leader. DeLay
was so moved by the film—"I started crying because I had missed my
daughter's whole childhood," he told the *Washington Post* later—that
he credited it with sparking his transformation into a born-again
Christian.[27]

Throughout the 1980s, Dobson led delegations of top Focus on the
Family donors to the capital for meetings with congressmen, senators,
and White House officials, who saw him as a parenting guru and as a
broadcasting star. On one trip, Reagan chief of staff James Baker—
whose wife would later become a Focus board member—hosted a dinner in Dobson's honor.

But even as his Washington friendships tended toward the Republican side of the aisle, Dobson's early advocacy in Washington was largely
nonpartisan. It included pushing for time off for military personnel to
be structured around weekends and evenings, when their children were
most likely to be home, and for placement of Focus resources like
Where's Dad? in military bases worldwide. Christian Right architect
Paul Weyrich spent much of the decade urging Dobson to capitalize on
his celebrity by taking up conservative political causes, but to no avail.
Dobson worried that his activism would taint him in the eyes of his followers. "I've spent all this time gaining credibility with these people
who are hurting," Dobson would say, according to Weyrich. "They
come to me because they're having problems with their families, they're
having problems with discipline, they're having problems with divorce,

any kind of problem you can think of. . . . I can't afford to get politically involved."

As a product of the same network of evangelical radio and TV stations that was dubbed the "electronic church" in the 1970s and that had launched Jerry Falwell onto the national stage, Dobson drew frequent questions about whether he was the heir to Falwell and his political organization, Moral Majority. Dobson insisted that he was not. "When headlines say I'm the new leader of the New Right, that implies a whole lot that I wouldn't touch with a 10-foot pole," Dobson told a newspaper reporter in 1989. ". . . The Moral Majority talked about South Africa and Central America, the INS treaty, and Jerry endorsed George Bush two years ago. We never talk about anything but the family. We never endorse a political candidate. And we do very little with legislation."[28]

Still, Dobson began taking an active role in Washington's public policy debates as far back as 1980, the year Jimmy Carter convened the White House Conference on the American Family. Campaigning for president in 1976, Carter promised to stage such a conference, though the fact that it wasn't held until a few months before he was up for re-election led to charges that he was merely trying to shore up sagging Catholic and evangelical support.[29] After witnessing 1977's congressionally funded National Women's Conference in Houston, chaired by liberal New York congresswoman Bella Abzug and featuring the leading lights of the National Organization for Women, Dobson was skeptical about the Conference on the Family even before it opened.[30] So he asked his radio audience to write to the White House with requests that Dobson be invited. The effort unleashed eighty thousand letters on conference organizer Jim Guy Tucker.[31]

"Tucker was scared of me," Dobson recalled. "He didn't know who I was, and he tried to keep me at arm's length because he didn't want anyone with a constituency." But Tucker had nonetheless invited Dobson to address a preconference event on child development. "After I spoke that night . . . he came up to me and said, 'It's really interesting what you have to say,'" Dobson recalled. "He said, 'I don't agree with you, but I want to tell you it's the first time I heard those things.' He asked to have a Coke together, and he said, 'People like you are not in this town. . . . I didn't know that people like you from a credible university existed [and] have the kind of views that you have.' We had a long talk that night."

The encounter prompted Dobson to help found the Family Research Council. FRC would be a Washington-based clearinghouse for conservative professors and researchers who could testify before Congress or provide policy briefings on "pro-family" policy. The FRC was intended to shield Dobson and Focus from Washington's political fights while giving them an inside-the-beltway proxy. But Dobson's 1985 appointment to Ronald Reagan's Commission on Pornography brought him even closer to Washington. Speaking about the allure of weighing in on political issues to *Christianity Today* in 1988, Dobson said, "You talk about tension, there's a constant tension for me. I could turn Focus into a full-time issues program. The need is there. But it would change the whole ministry."[32]

Focus on the Family *was* changing in the late eighties, becoming more politically active. In 1988, around the time that Jerry Falwell's Moral Majority closed its doors, Focus started planting state-level groups called Family Policy Councils across the country to lobby state legislatures for "pro-family" legislation.[33] A year later, it launched a public policy magazine called *Citizen*. It began distributing a radio feature called *Family News in Focus*, which carried reports on political developments and was distributed separately from Dobson's daily broadcast. That same year, 1989, the struggling Family Research Council was folded into Focus on the Family, and Dobson hired Gary Bauer, a top domestic policy adviser to Ronald Reagan, to revive it. By the time Bauer left a decade later, FRC had become the most powerful Christian Right group in Washington.

In the late 1980s, Dobson also became more prone to broach controversial issues on his daily broadcast, calling on listeners in 1988 to boycott the Martin Scorsese movie *The Last Temptation of Christ* and urging them to call Congress to protest the Civil Rights Restoration Act, which Dobson said could require religious organizations that receive government funds to hire alcoholics, homosexuals, and AIDS patients.[34] "[Politics] grew from almost nothing to a sizable chunk of what we did," said Bobbie Valentine, who was Dobson's on-air producer for seventeen years, ending in 2000. "There were people who were very vocal to [Dobson] about this, and listeners who would write and complain that they wanted to hear about their marriage or raising their children. The programming staff had concerns that we weren't doing much on the good old raising-your-family things. Occasionally, we'd chat with Dr. Dobson about it, but he was very, very firm in his conviction that part of his responsibility was to represent families in the political world. . . . He said, 'This is what I believe God is calling me to do, and I'm going to do it.'"

Of course, most Americans continued to be completely unaware of Dobson. The national news media didn't have occasion to fixate on him until 1989, when serial killer Ted Bundy granted Dobson the one interview he was permitted on the eve of his execution by electrocution. Bundy requested the Dobson interview after reading the two-thousand-page report issued by Reagan's Commission on Pornography, on which Dobson had served. In their twenty-nine-minute sit-down interview, conducted at Florida State Prison near Starke, Florida, Dobson homed in on the role Bundy said his obsession with hard-core pornography had played in precipitating his violent sex killings.[35] Bundy had admitted to slaying more than thirty women and was suspected of killing even more. In his interview with Dobson, Bundy claimed that porn acted like "fuel for his fantasies" and said, "There are loose in the towns and their communities people like me today whose dangerous impulses are being fueled day in, day out, by violence in the media . . . particularly sexual violence."[36] Dobson was roundly criticized in the mainstream press for overemphasizing the role of pornography in Bundy's crimes and for downplaying other factors, like Bundy's upbringing in a broken home and his mental health problems. Focus on the Family drew fire for selling a videotape of the interview for twenty-five dollars, prompting it to donate the proceeds to Christian antipornography groups.

Committed to protecting the reputation of Focus in the public eye, Dobson was even more careful about protecting its reputation, and his own, among his evangelical constituents as he stepped up his political activism. When Ronald Reagan asked him to consider serving as commissioner of the Federal Administration for Children, Youth, and Families, managing a four-hundred-million-dollar budget, Dobson not only demurred, he insisted that news of the offer be kept from the media. "I didn't want my name to come up with it," Dobson said. "Because people know that they trust me in a way that they wouldn't if they thought I was trying to manipulate them."

To this day, Focus on the Family employees wince at the news media's portrayal of the ministry as a political organization. "The press makes such a big deal out of the public policy involvement, and it's such a small part of what the ministry does," said Diane Passno, the one-time Focus correspondence supervisor, who rose to be a senior vice president at Focus. "I don't think the press understands why people love Dr. Dobson and Focus on the Family. It's like this one man who was there right at a time when they were facing a crisis, and we didn't ask for anything in return. We were there, and that's why people love him."

But it was precisely that loyalty that allowed Focus, beginning in the early 1990s, to build what became possibly the most effective grassroots strike force in the nation. In 1992, a year after Focus relocated from Pomona, California, to Colorado Springs, Dobson joined an effort to promote an amendment to the Colorado state constitution that would prohibit the passage of gay rights laws, including those that barred employers and landlords from discriminating on the basis of sexual orientation (which were already on the books in Aspen, Boulder, and Denver).[37] Until Dobson backed the measure, known as Amendment 2, the signature drive to place it on the ballot looked like a long shot. But after Dobson promoted Amendment 2 on his radio show, "Our phones began ringing off the wall," according to the campaign's chief organizer. "We had volunteers suddenly begging to carry petitions."[38] With Focus producing the campaign's public service announcements, Amendment 2 passed with 53.4 percent of the vote.[39] (The law was later struck down by the Supreme Court.)

With results like that, Dobson's radio show won a reputation as an unrivaled platform for mobilizing evangelicals. There was no better proof than in 1994, when a Democratic congressman from California introduced an amendment to an education bill in Congress that would require all home-school teachers—parents, for the most part—to receive state certification in every subject they taught.[40] Worried that the amendment would effectively vanquish the home-schooling movement, Virginia-based home-school advocate Michael Farris launched a campaign against it in which Dobson would prove critical.[41] The home-schooling movement was growing rapidly at the time, with estimates of anywhere from 250,000 to a million children being home-schooled, including a huge contingent of evangelical Christians. Farris, an evangelical, had become the movement's chief spokesman by founding the Home School Legal Defense Association, which by the early 1990s included thirty-seven thousand families.[42] Farris mobilized that membership against the 1994 education amendment and pushed the cause on a nationally syndicated Christian radio program, generating two hundred thousand angry calls to Congress.

But Farris knew he could unleash an even greater tsunami of phone calls by landing on Dobson's daily show. "It was the biggest game in town," Farris said. After his debut *Focus on the Family* appearance, calls to Congress surged to a million in a week's time. The home-school amendment was not only quashed, but the House overwhelmingly passed an alternative amendment granting new autonomy to home schools by rewriting the federal definition of schools to exclude them.[43]

According to Farris, the victory marked a turning point in the home-schooling movement. After 1994, home-schooling parents were no longer dismissed by official Washington as a fringe movement. At the same time, Focus's machinery remained invisible to blue state America, which didn't tune in to Dobson's show. "The average person in the establishment is not aware of what Dobson is saying to five or ten million people every week," said Richard Viguerie, the conservative activist who pioneered the use of direct mail for the Republican Party in the sixties and seventies. "That has served us beautifully."

As the political victories kept coming, some Focus executives and other employees began to worry that Dobson was narrowing the organization's appeal and steering it away from its original mission. Jerry Falwell's Moral Majority, the Christian Right's leading organization in the 1980s, and Pat Robertson's Christian Coalition, the movement's standard-bearer in the early and mid-1990s, were both envisioned as political machines from the start. But Focus on the Family grew out of Dobson's parenting seminars and family-oriented radio show, with a membership born of the organization's commitment to help troubled people. "Certain leaders within the organization were expressing concern that the organization was becoming too political," remembered Rolf Zettersten, one of Dobson's top lieutenants in the eighties and early nineties. "Jim's defense was that when he'd go out to see the public, people would hug him and tell him how much they'd appreciate his stand on abortion, but that he was not getting hugs or thanks for potty-training people's children."

But even if a segment of Focus's vast constituency could be prodded to phone Congress, there were signs that the majority had little interest in becoming citizen activists. They simply wanted to hear Dobson's parenting advice.

When Focus began selling subscriptions to *Citizen* magazine in the late eighties, according to one former Focus staffer, only 10 percent of its mailing list signed up. Even after Focus waived the subscription price, there was virtually no jump in subscriptions. "The average American mom is concerned with *How do I raise my children?*, and debates over public policy issues are not absorbed in her thought life," said the former staffer. "That's why we couldn't get the typical Focus constituent to buy *Citizen*. . . . The original purpose was to get moms and dads to be better moms and dads, and husbands and wives to be better husbands and wives."

But Dobson, with the support of many Focus staffers, insisted his forays into national public policy debates were moral, not political, in nature. They argued that it was not the ministry that was changing, but the culture—growing coarser and more tolerant of behavior once considered taboo, like homosexuality and the idea of same-sex marriage. "The idea of being in politics is a negative for much of our evangelical community, and [Dobson] didn't want to be identified as a political person but as someone who supported family values and biblical scriptures," said Ted Engstrom, a former president of the international relief organization World Vision International and a Focus on the Family board member since 1979, before his death in 2006. "He is very sensitive about that."

In a 2004 interview, for example, Dobson rejected the characterization of his call to eliminate the federal tax code's so-called marriage penalty (which was reduced by President Bush's 2001 tax cut) as a political issue. "That's not a political issue, that's a family issue," he snapped. "And if you look at the things that I have cared about and fought for from the beginning, it has been morality and family and life, and that's not disguising anything. It's not all that different from teaching parents how to raise their kids. So it's not like *Dare to Discipline* and *The Strong-Willed Child* were a subterfuge for a hidden agenda. . . . The people out there who know about us understand that. I'm not trying to get Republicans elected, and it's been that way from the beginning."

In order to retain its tax-free, nonprofit status in the eyes of the IRS, Focus needed to show that, even with its increased political involvement, less than $250,000 annually was being spent on broadcasts and mailings intended to rally constituents to lobby elected officials. "We were constantly going through and self-monitoring, and we'd get into

debates about 'Is this direct mail dealing with legislation or morality?'"
recalled Zettersten, the former Dobson lieutenant. "And I can remember [Dobson] getting very defensive with the team, explaining that this
was not a public policy–related letter, and others saying, 'I really think
it is.'"

While Dobson has insisted that Focus on the Family's political advocacy is limited to taking public policy positions on moral issues, and
that it avoids partisan politics, some former Focus insiders report otherwise. For instance, one former highly placed Focus employee said that
the Clinton administration's invitation to Dobson's wife, Shirley, to attend the White House's National Day of Prayer event in the mid-1990s
ignited a heated internal debate about how to respond. Shirley Dobson
had chaired the National Day of Prayer Task Force since 1991. But "Jim
refused to let her go because he felt Clinton would use her for political
purposes, to attract evangelicals and conservatives," said the source.
"And we [staffers] said we should use the White House to push our
causes. Jim saw it as a political issue, and I think Shirley wanted to
go. . . . He would cite Chuck Colson"—the convicted Watergate felon
turned evangelical intellectual—"who said that in the Nixon White
House, they would use the trappings of the White House to get evangelicals on board, but it was just a political strategy, a photo opportunity. . . . That was a politicization of the organization, where it began to
look at decisions based on politics rather than on pure agenda.

"Those are Jim's decisions to make," the source continued, "but I
don't think you can make them and then say that it's the media's fault
[that Focus is seen as a political organization]. He was making decisions
based on politics, and once you become a power in Washington, it's
hard not to do that. . . . When you think of what Dobson is today, you
think of him as a leader of the conservative political movement, and
that perception is not a fabrication of the liberal media."

The former Focus source also said Dobson was infuriated to learn
that Focus on the Family board member Bill Hybels, pastor of the gi-
gantic Willow Creek Community Church outside Chicago, had ac-

cepted President Clinton's invitation to serve as a religious adviser in the early 1990s. Hybels left Focus's board shortly after. He declined requests to be interviewed for this book.

While Dobson was stage-managing Focus's political reorientation from the inside, external forces were also conspiring to make him the new leader of the Christian Right. The collapse of Pat Robertson's Christian Coalition after Executive Director Ralph Reed's 1997 departure created a power vacuum within the movement. And with the exponential growth of the closely allied Family Research Council under Gary Bauer, Focus's huge mailing list—which crossed the 2.5-million-name mark in the late nineties—and Dobson's own transformation into values advocate, he seemed like the Christian Right's natural heir. "I don't know at that point if [Dobson] would have been thinking in terms of competing with Jerry [Falwell] or Pat [Robertson], but he would have been cognizant of the vacuum, that they had reached their zenith and were on the decline," said Don Hodel, who served as Focus on the Family president for two years after Dobson stepped down in 2003. "He would have said, 'Somebody has got to say something.' I don't think he'd be thinking in terms of 'Well, it's time for me to be the leader,' but in terms of 'I've got this broadcast, and I've got this mailing list, and I'm going to say what I think.' In other words, he's in a leadership position not because he wanted to be the leader, but because he wanted to deal with problems and he has a big megaphone."

Other Dobson confidantes agreed, saying that Dobson knew he was becoming the next Pat Robertson although it wasn't a role he aspired to. Another former top Focus employee, however, said that Dobson relished his growing political power. "He told me that closing down the congressional switchboard was more interesting than talking about changing diapers and potty training," said the source, who requested anonymity. "He talked to me about getting bored with the same old parenting issues . . . but to get a meeting with the president or to consult with a senator on the telephone proved more interesting."

Of course, Dobson's political influence among the evangelical masses stems from having created precisely the opposite impression. And by avoiding the bizarre and incendiary remarks that Jerry Falwell and Pat Robertson became well known for—as recently as 2006, Robertson suggested that a stroke suffered by Israeli prime minister Ariel Sharon was God's retribution for Israel pulling out of Gaza— Dobson put a kinder, gentler face on the Christian Right. Focus sources said that Dobson actually studied Falwell's and Robertson's gaffes in order to avoid similar ones himself. "He would say, 'I don't want to come off as half-cocked and have to take three steps back and everyone around us looks foolish,'" said Mike Trout, Dobson's longtime radio co-host. "He was always being very careful and making sure that he wasn't offending someone. In other ministries, that level of detail was not carried through, and there would be a lot of comments that were said wrong, or off the cuff, and [Dobson] got more sensitive."

In a further attempt to minimize missteps, Dobson frequently seeks advice on political matters from Washington insiders like Gary Bauer and Chuck Colson before making public statements.

Dobson's vigilant stewardship of his public image has paid off. According to a 2004 poll conducted for the PBS *Religion & Ethics Newsweekly* and *U.S. News & World Report*, American evangelicals give Dobson an average favorability rating of more than 76 on a 100-point scale. The same poll found that evangelicals give Robertson a 55 and Falwell a 46. Dobson also scored a higher favorability rating than Robertson and Falwell among nonevangelicals, but less than 30 percent were able to identify him, far fewer than those familiar with Robertson and Falwell.[44] Many in the evangelical world chafe at the public perception of Falwell and Robertson as the political spokesmen for their movement, preferring Dobson in that role. But with Dobson making himself unavailable to the news media—the television interviews he grants are almost exclusively to select shows on FOX News Channel—they continue to lavish attention on Robertson, whose stranger proclamations still lead the evening news, and Falwell, whose invitation to Senator John McCain to speak at Liberty University's commencement in spring 2006 generated hundreds of headlines across the country.

Adding to Dobson's popularity among evangelicals is his success in maintaining a spotless personal reputation in the scandal-plagued world of media evangelists. In 1987, televangelist Jim Bakker was revealed to have had a sexual encounter with former church secretary and future *Playboy* model Jessica Hahn, who was paid $250,000 to keep quiet. Bakker was later sent to jail for four years for swindling supporters out of $158 million. It was also reported that Bakker's wife, Tammy Faye, had checked into the Betty Ford Clinic with a prescription drug problem.[45] Around the same time, photographs surfaced of Jimmy Swaggart, perhaps the most popular TV preacher of his time, leading a prostitute into a motel outside New Orleans.[46] The scandals helped hasten the decline of Moral Majority, the first Christian Right group of its size and power.

Dobson, for his part, has been married to his wife, Shirley, for more than forty-five years. Their daughter, Danae, has published more than twenty Christian-themed books for children and young adults.[47] Their son, Ryan, has coauthored books for Christian young adults, including *Be Intolerant,* an argument against moral relativism, and founded a youth skateboarding ministry. Ryan is married and the father of James Dobson's only grandchild, born in October 2006. Danae is single. "[S]he acknowledges the difficulty of any potential husband measuring up to the standards she sees in her father—or passing his muster," writes Dobson's official biographer.[48] James Dobson keeps a reportedly modest town house in Colorado Springs and has never collected a salary from Focus, living off his astronomical book sales. "Everybody has a bad secret, but he has no secret," said the National Association of Evangelicals' Ted Haggard, who is also based in Colorado Springs. "He sleeps with his own wife, spends his own money." Late last year, when a former gay prostitute went public with allegations that Haggard had paid him for drug-fueled trysts, Haggard denied the specific charges but admitted to "sexual immorality" and called himself "a deceiver and a liar."

Focus on the Family, meanwhile, has moved quickly into crisis management mode upon discovering indiscretions among high-profile employees. When Dobson's on-air cohost Gil Moegerle revealed in 1985 that he and his wife were experiencing serious relationship problems, Moegerle left the show while staying on at Focus. But after Moegerle divorced his wife in 1986 and announced that he planned to marry his secretary, Focus pressured both to resign, triggering a lawsuit that was later thrown out.[49]

Then, in 2000, Moegerle's on-air replacement, longtime Dobson cohost Mike Trout, revealed that he was having an affair and left Focus of his own volition.

Recently, though, Dobson's more brazen public statements and behavior have attracted some bad press. He made headlines in early 2005 for accusing the cartoon character SpongeBob SquarePants of having participated in a "pro-homosexual video" promoting tolerance, prompting Focus to quickly assemble an in-house crisis management team. Later that year, he compared Republican Senate Majority Leader Bill Frist's call for federal funds for expanded embryonic stem cell research to Nazi experiments in World War II. Dobson has also attracted public scrutiny for calling attention to his impressive political connections. In 2005 he attracted threats of a subpoena from the U.S. Senate after disclosing on his radio show that he'd had private conversations with Karl Rove about Harriet Miers's nomination to the Supreme Court. His 2006 on-air announcement that he'd received a thank-you note from recently confirmed Supreme Court Justice Samuel Alito also caused a stir. Sources close to Dobson say such moves are indications that he has become much more accustomed to criticism in the mainstream media and more dismissive of it. "My purpose in living is not to take a good reputation to the grave with me," he said in an interview. ". . . I did not attempt to build an empire here and I'm not inclined to try to preserve it. I want to do what I think God wants me to do and I want to do it as wisely and judiciously as possible and let the chips fall where they may."

3

Vatican West

"People come in here, they spend three days, they crawl all over the place, and then go away and say we're a right-wing hit squad. And that's really a small percentage of what we do."

—⁂—

Colorado Springs feels like a holy place.

The city—population 360,000 and climbing—is spread like a spilled drink against the eastern base of the colossal and permanently snowcapped Rocky Mountains. When the sun descends behind 14,000-foot-high Pike's Peak, a fountain of rays shoots over the range, framing even the rush-hour trudge down Interstate 25 in grandeur. The Springs sits more than 6,000 feet above sea level, in an alpine desert whose landscape is blasted on late summer afternoons by torrents of rain that clear out as abruptly as they arrived, leaving behind the same stark lucidity as an hour before. The names of exits along the highway, like Briargate and Garden of the Gods, sound like they were plucked from the Book of Revelation. Looking down on the spot from the Rockies in 1893, a Wellesley College professor named Katharine Lee Bates was moved to write the lyrics to "America the Beautiful."

The Springs has witnessed a massive influx of evangelical Christian organizations in recent decades, with a particularly sharp spike following Focus on the Family's arrival from Southern California in 1992, and some evangelicals wryly refer to it as Vatican West. The global missionary group Compassion International, the International Bible Society, and the Association of Christian Schools International are all headquartered there. The population of surrounding El Paso County has nearly doubled since 1980, to more than half a million, and if you start asking transplants what led them there, it won't take long to find someone who says he or she was called by God. (The city's booming high-tech economy, with major Oracle and LexisNexis offices, and its handful of military installations, including the U.S. Air Force Academy, also deserve much of the credit.) In 1984, a pastor named Ted Haggard, who said he'd been called by God from Baton Rouge, launched a church in his Colorado Springs basement, using a stack of upturned buckets for a pulpit and rows of lawn chairs for pews. Today, his eleven-thousand-member New Life Church, just up the road from Focus on the Family, is the biggest in the state. Sunday services are held in a 55,000-square-foot sanctuary that features enough jumbotron video screens, special effects lighting, and costumed dancers to rival a Madonna concert, though its ten-piece house band is bigger than hers.

Largely because Colorado Springs is home both to Haggard—who was elected president of the thirty-five-million-member National Association of Evangelicals in 2003 and who participated in the weekly White House conference call to evangelical leaders before stepping down in late 2006—and to James Dobson, countless journalists venture there each year in search of the crossroads of evangelical Christianity and American politics. With a game-show host's smile and Ken-doll hair, Haggard had a policy of granting every interview request, time permitting. In a single week in fall 2005, he was shadowed by the filmmaker Alexandra Pelosi for HBO, drove to Denver for a photo shoot for the cover of *Christianity Today,* and was waiting to hear from NBC about the schedule for airing an hour-long special about New Life that Tom Brokaw traveled to the Springs to tape.

When members of the press ask to speak with Dobson, on the other hand—he received several thousand requests in 2005 alone, according to Focus on the Family—he almost always declines. "What you're doing here today has brought great frustration in the past, which is why we were so reluctant to talk to you," Dobson said in a late 2004 interview in his Colorado Springs office. "People come in here, they spend three days, they crawl all over the place, and then go away and say we're a right-wing hit squad. And that's really a small percentage of what we do."

It's *because* political advocacy is a relatively small percentage of what Focus on the Family does, in terms of dollars and staff, that the organization is so effective at rallying the evangelical grassroots, at being a "right-wing hit squad." Dobson hired the first Focus on the Family staff in the late 1970s to answer mail from radio listeners and from those who'd seen his *Focus on the Family* film series and who needed help or wanted more information, and what Focus calls "meeting needs" is still the engine of the organization. Even as Dobson and Focus grew much more politically active in the 1990s, it is still their work helping families and individuals that gives them political capital.

Housed in an 81-acre brick office park at the suburban northern end of Colorado Springs, Focus has a public policy team that accounts for around seventy of its roughly thirteen hundred employees. Almost a third of Focus's employees, meanwhile, are directly involved in communicating with the ministry's constituents. In a typical month in 2005, Focus received more than 10,000 e-mails, nearly 50,000 phone calls, and about 173,000 pieces of mail, enough to justify having its own zip code. (With a visitor's center and a 10,000-square-foot bookstore, daily tours, and a sprawling indoor playground for kids, Focus also gets about a quarter of a million visitors annually.) People usually contact Focus to order one of the roughly forty-seven hundred pamphlets, books, DVDs, CDs, and other resources the organization offers, on topics ranging from coping with postpartum depression to handling children who reject Jesus as their savior to bringing sexual passion back to a marriage. Orders ship within twenty-four hours from a 75,000-square-foot warehouse. "It's not a customer ordering a book," said one warehouse employee, explaining the speedy turnaround. "It's a woman whose daughter is considering abortion."

As of 2005, Focus's mailing list of constituents who'd contacted the ministry in the last eighteen months comprised nearly 2.5 million names. Add the names of those who haven't been in touch that recently but whose name and address information Focus maintains, and the list swells to around six million. According to a consultant hired by Focus in 2005, seventeen million Americans have contacted the organization since its founding in 1977, the equivalent of the combined populations of New York, Los Angeles, Chicago, and Houston, the nation's four biggest cities.

Every call to Focus's 800-number is answered by a person, not a machine, within three rings. A team of roughly 120 phone attendants handle telephone orders, while other teams process requests placed by mail and online, the most popular method. About one in ten callers has a question or problem but is unsure about which resource to order. Those callers are transferred to one of about seventy-five specialists in Focus's correspondence department, who recommend specific materials. On an afternoon in late 2004, one caller worried that her husband was being too strict with their college-aged daughter; she was sent one of Dobson's parenting books, at a cost of roughly twenty dollars. Another felt depressed and wanted information on herbal remedies; a correspondent prayed with her over the phone and sent a book on alternative medicine by a Christian doctor at a more than 75 percent discount, because the caller was short on money. Still another was hoping a hundred dollars could get her an autographed copy of Dobson's *The New Strong-Willed Child*; she was told that Dobson doesn't do autographs.

Phone correspondents receive a month of training and typically work in eight-hour shifts, half spent on the phone and half spent placing orders from callers and entering summaries of each call into a computer database. On a typical day, each correspondent takes twenty-five calls. Much of the phone traffic is driven by the daily thirty-minute *Focus on the Family* broadcast, which typically features James Dobson and which is piped in each morning to the warren of cubicles where the correspondents sit. Many correspondents hang their cubicles with lavish holiday decorations—artificial trees and garlands for Christmas, wood branch cornucopias and silk leaves for Thanksgiving—Thomas Kinkade calendars, and bumper stickers from the Bush-Cheney campaigns. Twenty-five-year-old Lindy Morgan's cubicle is comparatively plain, though biblical and inspirational quotations, like "REMEMBER WHOSE YOU ARE AND WHY YOU ARE HERE," are Scotch-taped to the borders of her computer screens. Each correspondent has two screens, one for pulling up a caller's file and another for searching the Focus database for resources.

On an afternoon shortly after Hurricane Katrina struck in September 2005, many of the callers routed to Morgan, who had worked as a Focus correspondent for three years after getting her art degree from Indiana Wesleyan University, were seeking reputable Christian charities. Dressed in a tight paisley top, denim skirt, and sandals, Morgan was armed with a list of Focus-recommended charities, which included the Salvation Army and, curiously, the Family Research Council, the conservative Washington-based lobbying shop that's closely connected to Focus. The FRC had convened a Pastor's Resource Council to help coordinate church relief efforts in the Gulf Coast. A few minutes after a hurricane-related call, Morgan's phone lit up again. She hit a button on her keypad to connect with Focus's constituent services department, which acts as central receiving for all incoming calls. "I have a woman with a daughter who was in an abusive relationship," said the grandmotherly voice of the Focus phone attendant on the other line.

"What's her number?" Morgan asked, then punched the caller's ID code into her computer keyboard. The caller's file quickly appeared on the monitor, showing that she last called around nine months earlier and ordered a book called *Healing for Damaged Emotions*. The phone attendant transferred the call to Morgan.

"I understand you have some concern about your daughter," Morgan said into her headset.

"She dated this boy for a year and a half. She's almost nineteen," said the caller, a middle-aged Texan who sounded surprisingly at ease given that she was talking intimately with a stranger. "She's really angry. She's angry at me, angry at everything."

"Was he verbally abusive?"

"He *was* verbally abusive—and there are some bruises on her arm," the caller explained. "He bit her, too. She needs something to deal with its aftermath. She went to sort of a counselor at a battered moms' shelter, but she'd stopped going a while back and appears to be harboring a growing bitterness."

Morgan listened for a few more minutes before encouraging the caller to check out a Focus on the Family Web site—the organization operates nearly twenty, including its main site, family.org—called troubledwith.com. The site is a trove of advice on dealing with everything from gambling and drug addictions to eating disorders to overcoming intimacy problems. It also offers guidance that is more controversial, though widely accepted within evangelical Christian circles, on topics like homosexuality, which is called a "relational problem of satisfying emotional needs in an unhealthy way" and the use of pornography, which is treated as a five-stage addiction that culminates in the addict transitioning "from the paper and plastic images of porn to the real world." The caller said that she had visited the site, but that all the information about abusive relationships focused on how to get out of them; there was nothing about dealing with the fallout from past relationships. So Morgan suggested the caller give her daughter the toll-free number for Focus's counseling department, which offers a free phone session with a licensed therapist and a referral to a Focus-approved Christian counselor in the caller's area. "It might be a good starting place because there's more anonymity—it's not face-to-face," Morgan said, cautioning the caller not to pressure her daughter into calling Focus because it could be counterproductive.

"I didn't know that that was even available," the caller replied.

A moment later, Morgan put the caller on hold and typed the word *abuse* into a keyword search of Focus's database. After speed-scanning descriptions of a few books and pamphlets, she found a book about recovering from abusive relationships by a Christian author, then clicked over to the caller to tell her that the suggested donation for the book was eleven dollars.

"Is it all right to send a check?"

Morgan said sure, then asked the caller for her daughter's name, so they could pray for her together over the phone. "Lord Jesus, I pray for [caller's name], who has to be going through a lot of questions and a lot of hurt. Give her the courage to address what has happened, and I pray for [name of caller's daughter] to have the courage to seek the help she needs. You are enough for these times, Lord."[1]

After hanging up, Morgan looked like she might cry. "I grew up in an abusive home, so those calls will pull some heartstrings for me," she said, eyes cast downward. Asked how she kept her spirits up through hours of depressing phone calls, Morgan looked up. "I believe in Jesus Christ, and I know that I'm not ultimately responsible," she said. "I'm able to trust that the Lord will walk them through the next chapter." When correspondents occasionally field a call about politics or public policy, like a complaint about Focus's opposition to gay marriage or a question about Dr. Dobson's opinion on a Supreme Court nominee, they read from a statement Dobson has prepared on the issue. But the vast majority of calls are of a personal nature.

*   *   *

Callers who require more help than a Focus correspondent can provide—more than a thousand a week—are transferred from correspondents like Morgan to a licensed Focus counselor, who will conduct a brief phone session before referring the caller to one of the two thousand therapists in Focus's national network. Like calls to correspondents, phone traffic to the counseling department is steered largely by Dobson's daily broadcast. When a popular Dobson radio series called *Love Must Be Tough*, about dealing with unfaithful partners, was rebroadcast in the late 1990s, the counseling department was flooded by three thousand calls in a single day. A good number of calls also come from people in financial trouble, facing eviction notices, or having difficulty finding work. The department grants small onetime monetary gifts, typically no more than a hundred dollars each, from an annual pot of around sixty-five thousand dollars.

Many of the Focus counseling department's phone sessions are aimed at helping people confront widely acknowledged problems, like alcoholism and child abuse. But, as in the correspondence department, some callers' predicaments—like learning that a friend is gay or that a husband uses pornography—concern behavior that is considered acceptable or even normal outside conservative religious circles. When a pastor's wife called in 2004 to say her husband was verbally abusing her, a counselor zeroed in on the husband's use of pornography. "If you continue to enable him to walk in sin," the counselor warned, "you are allowing him to walk into hell."

The overwhelming majority of those calling and writing Focus have always been female. And though evangelical Christians have sparked controversy by calling for wives to submit to their husbands, and though Dobson has decried what he considers the deleterious effects of the feminist movement, Focus counselors frequently sound like female empowerment coaches during their phone sessions.[2] In fall 2005 a counselor named Joann Condie took a call from a homemaker in her late twenties or early thirties who had been married to a recovering alco-

---

holic for a decade. The couple had two children together, but the caller said her husband had had multiple affairs. After listening to her describe their relationship for around ten minutes, Condie gave her diagnosis, firm and direct: "You don't really have much of a marriage. There's deceit at every turn. Who is your support system? Friends? Family? Do you have a pastor you can get guidance from—or do you feel like you're out here on your own?"

The caller explained that she and her husband had gone to see a marriage counselor but that she neglected to tell the counselor about her husband's infidelity. Instead of confronting her husband about his use of online and magazine porn, she unplugged his computer and canceled his magazine subscriptions.

"When it's an addictive relationship, we do things behind the scenes to make it better," responded Condie, whose office shelves—unlike correspondents, the much smaller team of about sixteen state-licensed Focus counselors get their own individual offices—displayed a brass candlestick formed into the word JOY and a menagerie of wooden Easter bunnies. "You're in the role of traffic cop. You're trying to catch him, and he's trying to hide everything. Those power struggles don't work in a relationship. You need to sit down and say, 'What is not going to be acceptable anymore?' You're a stay-at-home mom and need to get food on the table and gas in the car and have to pay the mortgage, but at what price are you getting that security? You're making a decision based on fear.

"What your husband is saying is life isn't going the way he wants it to go, so he's getting his fix," Condie continued. "Whether it's drugs or porn, he needs more and more to get the same high." By now, Condie explained, the woman's husband's disrespect for her had likely metastasized into contempt, and she needed to confront him, preferably with the help of a pastor. "You don't need to be his mom," Condie said. "But Dr. Dobson talked about this in *Love Must Be Tough*. You chose to marry him and he you. You have kids who are dependent on you to stand in the gap." Condie told the caller that she was sending her the book version of *Love Must Be Tough* free of charge. The book, like Dobson's radio series of the same name, advises spouses to step back and demand respect from unfaithful partners rather than act needy or desperate. Since the caller was not at home, Condie gave her a toll-free Focus number to call to find a Christian counselor in her area. By the time Condie hung up the phone, forty-five minutes had elapsed.

To outsiders, the work of Focus's correspondence and counseling teams can seem to have little to do with either the organization's or Dobson's political advocacy. But most Focus staff members see a direct connection. Willie Wooten, the former military chaplain who directs Focus's counseling department, construes all the phone calls born of divorce, unwanted pregnancies, and porn-obsessed husbands as symptoms of a culture run amok. "What we do is more triage for people who are already hurt," he said. "We're the emergency room of the ministry." To Wooten and his colleagues, reducing Focus's emergency room clientele requires reforming the culture, which requires help from Washington. In fact, the attention Focus has placed on political advocacy—on what it calls "defending family" as opposed to its original mission of "nurturing family" through providing resources on marriage and parenting—has grown so much in recent years that the organization changed its motto after the 2004 election, from "for the preservation of the home" to "nurturing and defending families worldwide." Focus casts the shift as a reaction to the corroding culture rather than the mark of a changing organization. "That's where the culture has taken the values that we hold dear," said John Fuller, Dobson's cohost on the daily broadcast. "Who would have thought twenty-five years ago that marriage would be politicized or that speaking publicly about our faith would be politicized?"

—m—

At Focus on the Family's Colorado Springs headquarters, faith is nothing if not public. Those applying to work at Focus must sign a "Statement of Applicant's Christian Faith." According to a Focus spokesperson, the statement "turns on the crucial matter of whether a person is a committed Christian, asks about current church attendance and involvement, as well as about the applicant's Christian testimony and experience."

Each workday at Focus begins at 8:15 A.M. with morning devotions, when the entire Focus workforce, from top executives to warehouse stock boys, breaks into groups of ten to fifteen for half an hour of communal prayer. Attendance is mandatory. Gathered on swivel chairs amid the administrative building's vast stretches of cubicles, Focus employees pray together for relatives undergoing surgery, for friends struggling with marital strife, for their old jalopy cars to hold out for a couple thousand more miles, for their teenage children to resist worldly temptations: sex, drugs, and (secular) rock and roll. Every meal inside Focus's "chapelteria," a full-service cafeteria that spills into a huge cathedral-windowed hall, begins with someone at the table saying grace.

As in much of the broader evangelical universe, Focus's atmosphere of public faith mingles easily with conservative politics. Passages from the New Testament and from Ronald Reagan's speeches hang on cubicle walls. The monthly speaker series at the chapelteria hosts nationally known preachers and Christian authors as well as right-wing political figures such as television and radio host Sean Hannity and Oliver North, the Iran-Contra figure turned broadcaster and author. The first-floor concourse of Focus's main administrative building is lined with pictures of James Dobson posing with Republican icons like Reagan, Reagan attorney general Ed Meese, and former House Speaker Newt Gingrich.

But amid the patchwork of oak-framed photographs, there's also a more sinister item on display: a bullet hole in the north wall from a 1994 standoff in which four Focus employees were taken hostage. A construction worker who'd been critically injured while at work on a new building on the Focus campus had taken the hostages with a handgun and demanded more workers' compensation. While no one was injured in the nearly six-hour ordeal, the gunman was sentenced to more than thirty years in prison.[3] The preserved bullet hole, from a shot fired by the construction worker, serves as a constant reminder to Focus staff that they are on the front line in the battle against a culture gone mad.

If Focus employees sense real danger in pursuing their mission— gay rights activists shattered some headquarters windows after Dobson championed a 1992 amendment to Colorado's constitution that pre- vented the passage of antidiscrimination laws for homosexuals—they say it also requires sacrifice. Many of the organization's executives took salary cuts of up to 80 percent to come to Colorado Springs. As of 2005, the highest-paid executive earned well under two hundred thousand dollars. Jim Daly, who became president of Focus on the Family in early 2005, was racing up the corporate ladder at the International Pa- per Corporation when he passed up a big promotion to join Focus as a twenty-seven-year-old in the late 1980s. Daly now says that he's living his Christian faith at work rather than just on Sundays. "I have a very pure motivation," he said. "I don't have an agenda, I just want to help people be a good dad. . . . I grew up in the sixties, and you'll hear the *Leave It to Beaver* analogies and Ward Cleaver and all that, but you know, I can *remember* that: dads and moms and the roles they played and the stability of the home and coming home and your mom's there and there's warm cookies. That was me growing up. That was kind of traditional America."

Actually, Daly's upbringing was not nearly so idyllic. His mother died of colon cancer when he was ten years old, and his father, an alco- holic, died of exposure two years later, after spending the night in an abandoned building. The future Focus on the Family president was left to fend for himself during his teen years. Still, his and Focus's mission boils down to the restoration of a bygone "traditional" America, and it has political implications far beyond the political advocacy done by Fo- cus's public policy division and its new sister political organization, Fo- cus on the Family Action. The mission adds a political dimension to many of the organization's ostensibly apolitical pamphlets and Web sites, *Focus on the Family* broadcasts, and even conversations between Focus correspondents and constituents. The phenomenon can hardly be described as outright political advocacy, but speaks to a wholly distinct worldview—a sense of what it means to do good in the world that clashes with that of many elites and of the mainstream media. It is a reminder of why the battle between red and blue America is called the *culture* war.

The best example may be "Love Won Out," a ministry Focus launched in the late 1990s with the goal of training pastors and churchgoers to build biblically based relationships with gays and lesbians within their congregations and families. The program is vintage Focus because it puts a gentler face on a controversial social issue without compromising the orthodox position. Love Won Out's message is to love homosexuals and to treat them humanely while rejecting their sexual behavior, bearing in mind "the power of God's love and His desire to transform the life of a struggling homosexual to find freedom in Jesus Christ," according to Focus materials. It sounds like a "love the sinner hate the sin" approach, though Love Won Out director Mike Haley rejects that formulation because he says most homosexuals hear only the words *hate* and *sin*. Haley lived as a gay man for twelve years but, after years of therapy and prayer, was married in 1994 and now has two sons. As of 2006, he was also serving as chairman of the board of Exodus International, the main organization working to convert homosexuals to straight lifestyles, boasting 125 local ministries in North America. "The church in the past would either ignore, condemn, or condone homosexuality," Haley said, explaining Love Won Out's mission. "But you can be accepting of a person without condoning their homosexual behavior. You love them unconditionally. If your son is going to come home with his partner and you beat on him with a sermon, they're going to stop coming home."

Love Won Out sponsors five conferences around the country each year, which had reached more than twenty-five thousand people by the end of 2005. (The events sometimes feature Nancy Heche, mother of well-known actress and former Ellen DeGeneres girlfriend Anne Heche, who has also been in straight relationships and was married in 2001.) While finding churches willing to host the events was difficult at first, there is now a two-year waiting list. Haley said the fact that pastors know Dobson "isn't squishy on homosexuality" has been a huge help in convincing them of the program's legitimacy.

While Dobson prides himself on his secular medical credentials, particularly his former positions with Childrens Hospital Los Angeles and at the University of Southern California School of Medicine, Focus on the Family's views on homosexuality depart sharply from those of the mainstream medical establishment. The American Psychiatric Association removed homosexuality from its list of mental and emotional disorders in 1973. The American Psychological Association has issued more recent statements asserting that homosexuality "does not require treatment and is not changeable" and has dismissed the claims of conversion therapists, going so far as to state that it is "concerned about such therapies and their potential harm to patients." Focus has said that both organizations are frequently motivated more by politics than science and that their position statements are often devised by liberal activist members. "Research and science is more and more validating scripture," said Bill Maier, Focus on the Family's psychologist-in-residence, citing statistics that gay men have shorter life spans and higher suicide rates than their straight counterparts. Of course, many mainstream public health officials explain those statistics as the result of cultural and public health phenomena rather than as evidence that homosexuality is unnatural or undesirable. "Homosexuality is not inborn, and there is evidence that homosexuals come from abusive, dysfunctional backgrounds," Maier said. "Homosexual orientation is not a sin. It's acting it out—the behavior—that is."

Focus generated headlines in September 2000 when Love Won Out founder John Paulk, a self-described former gay man who had appeared on the cover of *Newsweek* with his wife, a self-described former lesbian, was photographed in a gay bar in Washington, D.C. While acknowledging the incident was embarrassing, Focus maintained that Paulk hadn't engaged in a gay sex act, and he continued at the organization for a few more years. Haley, the current Love Won Out director, said his battle against homosexual urges is ongoing. "Will I ever go back to homosexuality? I pray not, but I know what my temptations are," he said. "It used to be 365 days twenty-four/seven. It enveloped me. Now it's 180 degrees different. All things are centered around, number one, I'm a Christian, and around my identity as a worshiper of Jesus Christ. The opposite of homosexuality is not heterosexuality, it's holiness. I'd still rather go shopping for fine china and still hate sports. Now would I be stupid enough to go into a gay bar? No—I couldn't handle it. It's my Achilles' heel."

An even starker illustration of how political ideology permeates Focus's work outside of its official political advocacy, and of the blurry line between the religious beliefs and political views of many committed evangelical Christians, is the Focus on the Family Institute. Launched in 1995, the institute is a semester-long program for college students and recent college graduates housed on Focus's Colorado Springs campus. It was a pioneer in what has become the full-blown industry of training young evangelicals to fight the culture war. Washington, D.C., is now home to a handful of similar programs, and Patrick Henry College, the first institution of higher education designed specifically to train home-schooled evangelicals for careers in politics and public policy, opened in Virginia in 2000. Each year, more than two hundred students attend the Focus on the Family Institute to take classes in two general subject areas: "nurturing family," which includes courses such as Marriage Studies and Family Life Studies, and "defending family," with classes such as Christian Worldview and Family, Church, and Society.

About half the institute's students attend Christian colleges and half attend other public and private schools. Nearly 80 percent are female. "A lot of men think the institute is all about family issues, so

they're less interested," said Sheryl DeWitt, the institute's faculty director. "A lot of moms hear about the program, and they want their daugh-
ters to come because they think it's all about family, too." While
virtually all the women in the program are planning to be stay-at-home
moms, according to DeWitt, most want to launch careers before settling down, with some planning to return to the workplace after their
kids are grown.

Representatives from the media are barred from speaking to institute students directly, but some are permitted to sit in on classes. A fall
2005 session of the Family Life Studies course opened with a discussion
on the dangers of sexual "hookups" among adolescents and teenagers.
"When I was in school, if you had oral sex, well, you were one of *those*
people," DeWitt, who is in her forties, told her class. "Now it's as common as kissing. What these kids are seeking is a connection and intimacy, and they don't know how to get it, and it leaves them empty." A
licensed psychologist who ran her own practice before joining the institute full-time, DeWitt said that many of these emotionally bruised kids
used to wind up in her office.

Halfway through the ninety-minute class, a pair of female students
delivered a presentation about a survey that showed teens are much
less comfortable with a wide range of sexual activities, from "petting
above the waist" to sexual intercourse, than is popularly perceived.
Later, DeWitt returned to the front of the classroom to deliver a lecture
on the differences in what men and women are seeking from relationships. Standing beside a big projector screen, she clicked to a slide that
read, "Men fall in love through their eyes, women fall in love through
their ears." The next slide was split into two columns, one with the title
heading "men," with the words *needs respect, logical, steady, desire to
lead* listed underneath. The "women" column featured the words *nurture, intuitive, personal, subjective, needs security.* "What you men
don't realize," DeWitt told the smattering of male students in her class,
"is that if you go out on one date, the girl is already thinking about
your children."

The next morning, Focus students convened for Christian World-view, one of the courses that fall under the "defending family" rubric. It was taught by Del Tackett, president of the Focus on the Family Institute and a former official in the National Security Council under George H. W. Bush. The class opened with Tackett queuing up a slide titled "The Battle Over History" onto the same projector screen that DeWitt had used. One side of the screen featured a circle around the words *truth/reality*. In a circle on the other side of the screen were the words *lies/illusion*. Tackett held up a copy of *I, Rigoberta Menchú*, the memoir of a woman who claimed to have witnessed widespread torture at the hands of the U.S.-backed Guatemalan military regime, published in 1982. The author went on to win the Nobel Peace Prize, and the book was widely assigned in colleges across the country, but it was later alleged to be partially fabricated. "This book is pro-feminist, anti-capitalist, anti-American," Tackett told his class. "That's why it became the darling of academia, which said, 'Whether or not the book is true, I don't care. We should teach about the brutality of the Guatemalan military, financed by America, and about the horrors of capitalism.'" Tackett used the book to segue into a lecture on what he called the current scourge of revisionist history. "What is the target of historical revisionism in this country today?" Tackett wondered aloud. "Christianity."

Tackett proceeded to recount a revelation he'd had during his tenure in Washington, while attending a two hundredth anniversary celebration of George Washington's farewell address to the nation. Contrary to what he'd learned in high school history and civics classes about the long tradition of the separation of church and state in America, Tackett was astounded to hear that Washington's speech was brimming with religious references. "Of all the responsibilities and habits which lead to a national prosperity," Washington had said, "religion and morality are indispensable supports."

"My jaw dropped," Tackett told his class. "My stomach went out. I had the unmistakable feeling that I'd been lied to." The experience inspired Tackett to reread the Founding Fathers, among whose writings he was shocked to find reference after glowing reference to Christianity. Tackett squeezed his clicker to queue a slide featuring a bust of John Adams next to these words of his: "It is religion and morality alone that can establish the principles among which freedom can stand." The next slide featured a portrait of Declaration of Independence signer Benjamin Rush, alongside Rush's words: "The ultimate education of our youth is the principles of Christianity by means of the Bible." For the next ten minutes, pictures of other Founders flashed across the screen. "It was like no matter what I read," Tackett said, "they were all saying the same thing: You could not have a government without morality and you could not have morality without a Christian worldview.

"I used to think if you went to the basement of this country, what would be there is the U.S. Constitution," Tackett continued. "But no— not from the Founding Fathers' perspective." He approached the markerboard and sketched out a two-story house, labeling the second floor "Constitution," the first "Morality," and the basement "Christianity." The slide show made no mention of James Madison or Thomas Jefferson, the Founders who most shaped the relationship between church and state during the formation of the Republic, and who advocated for strict separation of the two.

Tackett concluded by fast-forwarding to the present. Invoking a battle described in the Book of Judges in which the Jews were defeated because they'd abandoned God, Tackett said America's advanced state of moral decay had the same underpinnings. "If you ever could rip out the Christians' passion for their country, what would happen?" Tackett asked the class. "Well, look at what *has* happened." He ticked off a litany of social ills wracking the country, from the high rate of sexually transmitted diseases among teenagers to the high divorce rate to the millions of Americans swimming in debt. Then Tackett issued a call to arms, telling his evangelical students that it was up to them to reclaim their country. "It's very easy to say it's all the liberals' fault, it's the Democrats' fault," he said. "But light overtakes darkness. So if there's a darkness spreading across the land, it's not because a person opened a box of darkness somewhere. It's because someone hid the light." Tackett suddenly broke into prayer, and his students quickly bowed their heads. "Father, help us resist the notion that it's all about me," he said. "Let us have the strength to stand, in Jesus' name we pray." With that, class was dismissed.

—m—

By way of illustrating his modesty, James Dobson's admirers frequently note that he resisted naming the organization he founded after himself—à la the Billy Graham Evangelistic Association—and that his name graces none of the buildings on Focus on the Family's Colorado Springs campus. But Focus headquarters is nonetheless a temple to its founder, or at least a museum of his life, work, and family. The first thing visitors notice upon entering the main headquarters building is a large oil painting of Dobson and his wife hanging just inside the front door. The lobby features dozens of framed photographs of James and Shirley Dobson, from Pasadena College yearbook head shots circa 1959 to a montage of James Dobson's surprise sixtieth birthday party in 1995. The walls are bedecked with Dobson's awards, from a 1979 Who's Who of the West commendation to a 1986 certificate for serving on Reagan's Commission on Pornography. There are framed notes to Dobson from Reagan, and Dobson's 1982 invitation to a White House lunch, mounted with Dobson's place card from the occasion and the menu: tenderloin of beef, rice pilaf, and coconut cake.

A room where visitors gather for Focus tours is hung with poster-size panels detailing Dobson's genealogy back four generations, to the mid-nineteenth century. "Dr. Dobson's maternal great-grandfather prayed daily from 11 A.M. until noon for the spiritual welfare of his family," reads one panel, "including generations yet unborn." The welcome video at the Focus visitor's center includes taped messages to Dobson from Presidents Reagan, George H.W. Bush, and George W. Bush, along with a gallery dedicated to the paintings of Dobson's father, who had planned to enroll in art school but joined the ministry instead. The high point of the Focus tour is the viewing gallery outside Dobson's radio studio, where visitors wait in auditorium-style chairs to catch a glimpse of him taping a show. It's not hard to leave Colorado Springs with the impression that Focus on the Family *is* James Dobson.

To be sure, Focus on the Family has grown exponentially since Dobson launched the organization with his radio show and video series in the late 1970s. It now comprises two dozen separate "ministries," and Dobson has little direct involvement with most of them. The projects encompass a huge range of activity, from a million-dollar-a-year effort to place ultrasound equipment in crisis pregnancy centers nationwide, to a pastors' support network that includes a mailing list of more than one hundred thousand names, to housing the offices of the National Day of Prayer Task Force.

But Focus has long called itself a "media ministry," and most of its staff and resources are directed toward turning out a vast and still-growing repertoire of print, radio, online, and video/DVD products. Its nine monthly magazines include *Clubhouse Jr.*, for kids age four to eight; *Brio*, for girls age twelve to sixteen; *Brio & Beyond*, for girls sixteen and older; *Breakaway*, for boys twelve and older; *Citizen*, which covers politics and public policy from a conservative Christian perspective; and *Plugged In*, which features movie, music, and television reviews that rate specific titles for spiritual, sexual, and violent content. *Plugged In*'s 2005 review of *Harry Potter and the Goblet of Fire* said "the film's wall-to-wall sorcery is birthed from a faulty worldview that taps into the occult and never recognizes any divine authority."

Focus's radio stable, in addition to the daily *Focus on the Family* broadcast, includes a widely distributed children's drama called *Adventures in Odyssey* and *Weekend Magazine*. Focus also distributes shorter radio features, including daily news updates called *Family News in Focus*, which "shed light on pressing moral and social issues." The organization is continually launching new Web sites, including focuson-yourchild.com, for parents, and thetruthproject.org, a resource aimed at helping the small groups that make up many evangelical churches to teach what evangelicals call Christian worldview.

Focus translates Dobson's *Focus on the Family* commentaries and a short segment called *Family Minute* into twenty-six languages for broadcast around the world, including an estimated audience of hundreds of millions of listeners via state-run radio in China, where Dobson is called "Dr. Du." In the 1990s, Focus on the Family began establishing independent international affiliates, with organizations in eighteen countries by 2006, including Australia, Belgium, Costa Rica, Egypt, Ireland, Japan, and South Africa. In response to South Africa's AIDS epidemic, Focus has promoted an abstinence-only curriculum called *No Apologies . . . the Truth About Life, Love, and Sex.* In Latin America, Focus says its affiliates have collected hundreds of thousands of "sexual purity pacts," whose signers pledge to forgo sex until marriage.

These myriad Focus on the Family ventures may have little to do with Dobson personally, but they owe their success largely to their affiliation with him. Even as he had a relatively small hand in launching programs like Love Won Out or Focus's state-level Family Policy Councils, for instance, Dobson's visibility and credibility were crucial to the evangelical subculture embracing them early on.

The clearest indication that Focus's identity may be inextricably bound to Dobson's comes from its constituents, the lifeblood of the ministry. When they call, write, or e-mail Focus on the Family with a question or problem, they almost invariably ask specifically for Dobson's advice. Its huge mailing list notwithstanding, Dobson's fans tend to identify with him personally, through his books, radio show, and parenting seminars, more than they do with Focus on the Family. Dobson's role as Focus's founder and public face and the centrality of his radio broadcast to the whole enterprise raise serious questions about the sustainability of the organization and its political influence in the post-Dobson era, even as it is at the height of its political power. The organization's political clout rests on its ability to mobilize millions of evangelicals; if its audience and mailing list begin to shrink, so does its influence. "I don't foresee any dramatic downturn in our audience anytime soon," said John Fuller, cohost of the daily *Focus on the Family* broadcast. "The only thing that can affect that is if Dr. Dobson steps away from the microphone. . . . The day he steps away, voluntarily or involuntarily, we have an issue. What the audience response will be, I don't know."

Dobson marked his seventieth birthday in April 2006, and speculation surrounding what happens when he leaves has been a major preoccupation at Focus for at least a decade. As of early 2006, he was in good health. "Yesterday was my four thousand and second day of exercise since December 14, 1993, and I've missed fourteen days of exercise in eleven years," he said without prompting in a December 2004 interview. But since 1990, Dobson has suffered a heart attack, a major stroke, and has been treated for prostate cancer. "Focus has developed a plan for the day Jim is no longer active," said Gary Bauer, the former Family Research Council president. "I think all Focus's friends worry about whether that plan will work out or not. . . . These organizations can become very personality centered, so that Christian Coalition really was Ralph Reed. Once he went on to something else, it almost became impossible to keep that thing going."

Will Focus meet the same fate? Dobson, for his part, said the organization's future is in God's hands. "I will probably, as years go on, phase out and other voices will begin to be heard more on the radio and I think it will be a smooth transition, but I don't know," he said. "Only God knows that. . . . Everything has a shelf life."

On the administrative end, Focus on the Family's transition to life after Dobson is already complete. Dobson stepped down from the presidency in 2003, transferring control of day-to-day operations first to former Reagan cabinet member and former Christian Coalition president Don Hodel and then to Focus veteran Jim Daly, who was forty-three years old when he took the position. While there is still a good deal of uncertainty about who will replace Dobson as Focus's primary spokesman, the organization has been grooming a handful of personalities to divide radio duties rather than attempt to find a single Dobson heir. Focus psychologist-in-residence Bill Maier, a longtime FM disk jockey on the West Coast and the current host of Focus on the Family's *Weekend Magazine*, is Dobson's most obvious understudy. Dobson's co-host on the daily program, the molasses-voiced John Fuller, has also grown familiar to Focus listeners.

At the same time, the organization is working to codify Dobson's written, on-air, and videotaped work in order to mine it for decades to come, planning to prolong Dobson's close public affiliation with Focus until long after his death. "Focus on the Family needs to become the repository of the wit and wisdom of James Dobson and the communicator of it," former Focus president Don Hodel told Dobson's official biographer before stepping down in 2005. "We have his views and his speeches and his writing based on his commitment to scriptures that covers almost everything that the family could encounter. . . . They may need to be packaged a little differently. . . . But fundamentally, there is no reason for that to change any more than scripture changes."[4]

Indeed, the canon of Dobson broadcasts, writings, and videos has come to be treated almost as holy text within Focus, where every corner of the organization is viewed by staff as a manifestation of Dobson's ideals. As Dobson was preparing to step down from the Focus presidency in 2003, he became worried about the sprawling organization's ability to consistently adhere to and express his positions on every conceivable topic. So he appointed a top executive to work full-time enforcing the Dobson orthodoxy across the organization, supervising everything from public policy pronouncements to bed-wetting pamphlets. "Over the last twenty-five or thirty years, Dr. Dobson has written or talked, publicly or privately, about almost every issue," said Diane Passno, who joined Focus in the early 1980s and is now its orthodoxy czar. "You can't have the founder-president with an opinion and the ministry coming out with a different opinion. Ninety-nine times out of a hundred you're on target, but you have to be aware that the one percent that you're not on target is going to cause the ministry embarrassment." Passno reviews every Focus product before it becomes available to constituents and trains what she calls "orthodoxy experts" within various departments to do self-policing.

Aside from the challenge of preparing for Dobson's departure while remaining true to his every principle, Focus also has more immediate troubles. While the daily *Focus on the Family* radio program continues to be Dobson's and Focus's main pipeline to the evangelical masses, its audience numbers have remained flat since around 2000. As of late 2005, the age of the typical listener had risen to thirty-eight, and the average age of constituents on Focus's mailing list was fifty-two. For an organization whose primary mission is helping parents raise their children, the numbers are unsettling. "The people that have connected with [Dobson], they've aged right along with him," said Focus president Jim Daly. "We've got to reach a very different twenty-something parent, and to the degree we need to communicate with them differently, that will be the stretch for us."

Complicating the task is the decision of more and more Christian radio stations, one of the few formats seeing growth in the radio industry, to abandon talk-centric formats in favor of Contemporary Christian Music. Those stations are much less likely to carry half-hour talk programs like *Focus on the Family.* So-called teach-and-preach stations, meanwhile, are migrating from FM to AM, where reaching young listeners is much harder.

In order to strengthen its FM presence, Focus has begun packaging much shorter segments, like *James Dobson Family Minute* and sixty-second *Plugged In* movie reviews. But those formats make it virtually impossible to develop the level of loyalty and influence that Dobson won with his daily half-hour show. "You can't get real emotional in sixty seconds," said John Fuller, Dobson's cohost on the daily program. "It's not the kitchen table conversation that we enjoy now."

In spring 2005, Focus launched a new FM-friendly program called *Sharing Life Together*, hosted by a longtime Seattle-based Christian radio personality named Martha Hadley. Targeting female listeners, the weekday evening show blends five hours' worth of Contemporary Christian Music with Hadley's advice to live callers, who ask about taming rebellious teenagers, operating in blended "stepfamilies," and repairing marriages after separation. The show was being carried by more than fifty affiliates as of early 2006, and Focus sees it as a likely model for future programs. That's because it has connected with a younger demographic—it has been the most popular radio show among women age twenty-five to fifty-four in the Seattle and Columbus, Ohio, markets—and because it does not feature James Dobson.

But even within Focus on the Family, there is debate over whether, in the age of the Internet, mp3s, and cable on demand, Focus can attract a new generation of constituents through radio, a rigid format that peaked half a century ago. To be sure, the daily *Focus on the Family* broadcast is now carried on satellite radio, on the XM and Sirius networks. But once Dobson goes, can anyone within Focus, or within the evangelical universe, match his track record of drawing millions of listeners a day?

Many in Focus's broadcasting department think so. New Focus president Jim Daly thinks otherwise. After assuming the presidency in 2005, Daly led a one-man revolution within Focus with a novel idea: In order to attract new constituents, Focus should reach beyond the traditionalist evangelical subculture into the broader evangelical and even nonevangelical Christian demographic. Watching TV one night, Daly stumbled across the perfect test vehicle for his new strategy: an ABC reality show called *Supernanny*. Debuting in winter 2005, the program dispatches a stern British nanny to help American parents reform their out-of-control children. As Daly observed the *Supernanny's* tactics, which include sending children to a "naughty corner" and demanding apologies for willfully defiant behavior, he thought of *Dare to Discipline*, the book that had launched Dobson's career thirty-five years earlier by advising parents to spank unruly children.

At first, Daly's idea of buying TV commercials to air during *Super-nanny* met with skepticism from Focus executives. Up to that time, a big media buy for the organization had been a full-page ad in *Working Mother* magazine, and old Focus hands thought spending a few hundred thousand dollars on TV was a careless use of limited resources. But Daly prevailed. The *Supernanny* ads wound up driving 150,000 new users to focusonyourchild.com, Focus's main Web site for parenting advice. About 17,000 new subscribers signed up to receive *Focus on Your Child* newsletters.

Emboldened, Focus created a first-of-its-kind department, devoted exclusively to attracting new constituents. One of its first initiatives was orchestrating what it called "image campaigns" in a dozen different media markets, concentrated in the evangelical-heavy South and Midwest. The campaigns featured TV, radio, and print ads and, like the *Supernanny* commercial, played up Focus's "nurturing" side as an outlet for child-rearing and relationship advice. "Focus is very good at talking to people who know Focus, but we have not been able to penetrate the general market," said Steve Maegdlin, a former marketing executive at PeopleSoft who arrived at Focus in 2004 and was soon appointed head of the new department, called constituent acquisitions. "Eighty-three percent of Americans consider themselves Christian. The question is, where do they live and how do we reach them in a way that isn't necessarily Christian radio or through a Christian bookstore? Because a good percentage of them don't listen to Christian radio or shop at a Christian bookstore. This is not your father's Focus on the Family."

With this aggressive new posture, Focus has begun hunting for new constituents in unlikely places. From Thanksgiving to Christmas 2005, for example, the group leased a billboard in New York City's Times Square to promote its troubledwith.com site.

While the new outreach model is still in its infancy, Focus president Daly believes that by reaching beyond the traditionalist evangelical base, he can grow Focus's active mailing list to twenty million names—up from around 2.5 million in 2006—just in the next decade or so. "I see greater influence ahead for Focus," Daly said. "The culture needs help, and we want to be out there. . . . The question is how do we deliver our content in a way that's listened to and not tuned out?"

Focus thinks it found part of the answer with the launch of focusonyourchild.com in 2003. Rather than reacting to constituent mail, phone calls, or e-mail, the site asks parents to sign up for a free membership, which includes eight newsletters and four CD journals annually, plus access to premium Web content, all focused on child-rearing advice. There are separate newsletters and CD journals for four different age levels, and subscriptions change automatically as the child ages. As of early 2006, a quarter of a million users had signed up. Now Focus is looking to institute the interactive model on its other Web sites. "If you come to Focus and you're single and want advice on helping to find a spouse, Focus wants to be in a relationship with you and secure healthy boundaries to find that person," said Focus chief Internet officer Rob Flanegin. "And then when you're engaged, we want to transition you into the early married segment, because the first five years of that are foundational to long-term success for the marriage. Then, when you're expecting that first child, we want to transition to that and follow that child through until the kids are out of the house and you're an empty nester."

It is a cradle-to-grave model for serving Focus constituents, taking Dobson's longtime fixation on customer service to new heights. Of course, Focus also believes that the more people it can help and form intimate, lasting relationships with, the more soldiers it can enlist in the culture war. "Eventually, we can get them to mobilize on our behalf," said Maegdlin, the director of constituent acquisitions. "They essentially become an extension of who we are."

And yet, as James Dobson becomes ever more public about his political activism under the auspices of Focus on the Family Action, branding Focus as a political organization in the public eye, he complicates the organization's strategy of reaching new constituents through spotlighting its "nurturing" side. In 2005, for example, Focus attracted the most media attention for Dobson's criticism of SpongeBob SquarePants's participation in a "pro-homosexual" film and for Dobson's on-air discussions of confidential conversations with Karl Rove over the nomination of Harriet Miers to the Supreme Court. These were not effective strategies for winning over young parents. "Even in Colorado Springs, there's such a caricature of the organization," Daly said. "If I'm at a restaurant, or if I'm at the store, it feels like what it must have felt like being African American in the fifties or sixties. Someone says, 'Where do you work?' and I'm not sure how the person's going to respond, because sometimes it's positive but sometimes it's cold. It's the closest that I've come to experiencing bigotry."

While only about 5 percent of Focus's budget goes toward public policy advocacy, Daly continued, "I'd say that the brand is all about that 5 percent as opposed to the 95 percent. We deserve some of the criticism ourselves. Whenever we talk to the press, we tend to speak toward public policy issues. . . . For the future this is the piece I really want to drive on: we've got the public policy area well addressed, and we're pressing it. I think we have to continue to reach into households and help parents and help marriages stay together. I compare it to lifting dumbbells. We have this great bicep called public policy and we have this rather anemic muscle here on the nurture side that's doing a lot of work. But it's not known."

4

The Long War

"Christian conservatives of the evangelical
and fundamentalist type had been told for
years—ever since the Scopes Trial—that
they should not be involved in politics.
That it was a sin to be involved in politics.
That you would lose your soul if you were
involved in politics."

—m—

In its capacity as a political machine, Focus on the Family is the
culmination of a dream nearly half a century in the making. The dream
was to somehow persuade millions of evangelical and fundamentalist

Christians, who'd withdrawn from American public life for decades, to rise above their separatist impulses and join the political fray, and in such large numbers that they could tip local, state, and even national elections or flood Congress with enough phone calls to stop a bill in its tracks. To inject old-fashioned biblical morality into a Republican Party whose bourgeois base was mostly interested in keeping Uncle Sam off their backs and out of their pocketbooks. To groom Christian leaders with such political clout among the evangelical and fundamentalist masses that the White House would call them with the name of the next Supreme Court nominee before announcing it to the public. Today, Focus on the Family has achieved all those goals, and in greater measure than any previous Christian Right organization. But as late as the 1970s, none it seemed remotely possible. The very thought of creating a Christian Right had occurred to almost no one.

Certainly not to James Dobson. When he launched Focus on the Family in 1977, Dobson never imagined he'd have the power to influence a Senate race in South Dakota, as he did in 2004, or to scuttle a landmark pro–big business bill simply by distributing the phone number of Congress to his radio listeners, as he did in 2002, or that he'd receive calls from the White House to help sell a Supreme Court nominee, as he did in 2005. Dobson was simply trying to build a Southern California audience for his radio show. For someone who'd spent a career in medicine and academia, just making it as an on-air personality would be hard enough.

The vision for launching the Christian Right, and for constructing a nationwide evangelical political machine as sophisticated and effective as Focus, originally belonged to Paul Weyrich. Little known outside Washington, D.C., Weyrich played a leading role in organizing the post–Barry Goldwater New Right. In 1973 he cofounded the Heritage Foundation, which soon became Washington's premier conservative think tank, with seed money from beer mogul Joseph Coors and Pittsburgh multimillionare Richard Scaife. In 1979, Weyrich recruited Jerry Falwell to launch the evangelical right's most important early organization and came up with its name: Moral Majority. To this day, Weyrich's weekly Capitol Hill powwows draw Washington's top conservative activists and the most powerful conservative Republicans from the Senate and House, along with top White House officials. The incessantly glowering Weyrich, in round spectacles and with a thinning silver pate, presides over the sessions from a dais in the front of a windowless basement room, while fifty to a hundred activists pick over soggy fried chicken and steamed-till-limp vegetables on paper plates. To the rare reporter allowed to attend, the scene is a time capsule of in-the-trenches political organizing, with guest speakers like the chairman of the Republican National Committee and the director of the White House Office of Public Liaison taking questions—and fielding grievances—from county-level GOP chairmen, right-wing bloggers, and representatives of evangelical groups such as the Family Research Council.

Weyrich is a proud curmudgeon. After concluding that the Roman Catholic Church had grown too liberal and modern, he left for the Melkite Greek Catholic Church. He was ordained a deacon in the church in 1990, then became a protodeacon. A 1996 fall on ice caused severe spinal injuries that frequently relegated Weyrich to crutches or a wheelchair, and necessitated the amputation of both his legs at the knee in 2005. Still, Weyrich has managed to keep his sharp, sardonic wit. In an interview in early 2006, he recounted a 1988 meeting with Pat Robertson's presidential campaign staff at a time when the candidate's fortunes were clearly sinking. Robertson nevertheless announced that God had told him he would still win the White House. "I said, 'Did he tell you when, because it's certainly not gonna be this year,'" Weyrich recalled. "I never got invited back."

Weyrich is roughly seven years Dobson's junior—the two have been close since the late 1970s—but he dreamed up the idea of creating the Christian Right even before Dobson had completed his Ph.D. at the University of California. It was 1962, and the Supreme Court had just ruled that state-sponsored school prayer violated the Constitution's establishment clause. Decided on a 6 to 1 vote, the case would later be singled out by Christian conservatives as the opening shot in what they see as the federal judiciary's decades-long campaign to rip religion out of the public square. It would be followed by rulings that banished Bible reading from public school classrooms, struck down laws mandating that the Ten Commandments be posted in schools, and outlawed organized prayer at graduation ceremonies.

In 1962, though, when the landmark school prayer ruling came down, the conservative political and religious establishments responded with a shrug. At the time, Weyrich was a nineteen-year-old budding Republican activist and a program director for a Kenosha, Wisconsin, radio station. Hailing from an extended family of immigrant Roman Catholics and evangelical Protestants, Weyrich saw the Supreme Court's decision as a golden opportunity to convince evangelical and fundamentalist Christians to finally cast off decades-old political inhibitions—and for the GOP to reap a windfall of new voters. The marriage of old-line country club Republicans and blue-collar church folk stood to wholly transform the American political landscape. The merger of the two constituencies would eventually deliver the historic Republican victories of the late twentieth and early twenty-first centuries, including the election of Ronald Reagan, 1994's Republican Revolution, and the Republican gains of 2004.

But at the time of the 1962 Supreme Court decision, the Republican establishment wasn't interested in middle-American church folk. "I called the chairman of the Wisconsin Republican Party, and I said, 'If you come out swinging against that Supreme Court decision, there are a lot of people who will be very upset about it and you'll get them into the party,'" Weyrich recalled. "And he said, 'Oh, we can't get involved in something like that, you know, separation of church and state. . . .' And I said, 'That's got nothing to do with it. You have a right to disagree with the Supreme Court.' He said, 'Well, our businesspeople would think it was strange that we are getting involved in a religious issue.'

"That was the moment that I said to myself, 'By golly, this is just off the track,'" Weyrich continued. "'I'm going to see to it that one day the party will listen to these kinds of issues.' And that really became my mission in life."

But before he could get the GOP to listen, Weyrich needed to convince evangelicals and fundamentalists to speak up. "Christian conservatives of the evangelical and fundamentalist type had been told for years — ever since the Scopes Trial — that they should not be involved in politics," Weyrich said. "That it was a sin to be involved in politics. That you would lose your soul if you were involved in politics."

It hadn't always been so. Prior to the 1925 Scopes Monkey Trial, evangelicals had been growing more politically outspoken with each passing year. The birth of the contemporary American evangelical movement in the early twentieth century was conceived in a fierce battle over the future of Protestantism in light of modernism's new scientific and cultural ideas. The coalition of churches that would coalesce into the evangelical movement constituted one side in the battle, and it was vociferous and determined. It was also outnumbered. The largest block of Protestant churches was embracing modernism, gradually adapting beliefs and traditions, and would come to comprise mainline Protestantism. But the other, smaller block tenaciously held to its traditional worldview, leading to the rise of fundamentalism and the emergence of the Pentecostal and charismatic movements. Ethnic Protestant churches, like the Lutheran Church–Missouri Synod, and southern churches like the Southern Baptist Convention, also rejected the mainliners' new direction, rounding out the patchwork of denominations that constitute modern evangelicalism.[1]

The fault lines between evangelical and mainline Protestants would come to broadly define the two sides in the culture wars. Religion and politics scholar John Green has written that "The fundamentalists argued for an 'individual gospel' of personal transformation and government moral regulation, while the modernists advocated a new 'Social Gospel' of public welfare programs and reform of private economic institutions."[2] It still holds up as a good characterization of the contemporary red state/blue state divide.

The fundamentalists took their name from a series of booklets titled *The Fundamentals: A Testimony to the Truth*. Published in 1909, the booklets reasserted biblical infallibility on matters such as Christ's virgin birth, physical resurrection, and the promise of his second coming, in the face of less literal interpretations that were fed partly by the application of new scientific thinking.[3] In fact, one of the fundamentalists' primary targets was the theory of biological evolution, which was gaining traction—Darwin's *The Origin of Species* had been published half a century earlier—and which challenged fundamentalist notions of biblical authority and creationism. A handful of new Christian organizations cropped up to mobilize against the teaching of evolution in public schools, including the Anti-Evolution League of America and the World's Christian Fundamentals Association. The movement was given greater legitimacy by William Jennings Bryan, a former secretary of state under President Woodrow Wilson and a onetime Democratic presidential candidate. Bryan joined fundamentalist leaders in successfully lobbying for the passage of laws barring the teaching of evolution in five southern states by 1928.[4]

When schoolteacher John Scopes challenged one such law in Tennessee in 1925, he precipitated one of the most famous trials in U.S. history, pitting Bryan against star trial lawyer Clarence Darrow and the American Civil Liberties Union. While Bryan secured Scopes's conviction, "the trial was a public relations disaster for the movement," according to John Green. "Bryan, fundamentalists, and by implication all who agreed with them were portrayed as ignorant and backward. . . . The [evangelical political] movement quickly dissipated."[5]

The experience left evangelicals and fundamentalists feeling not only spurned by the mainstream but skeptical as to how much could be accomplished through politics and engagement with the broader society. They didn't just disappear into their homes, though. Evangelicals and fundamentalists began constructing a vast and vibrant subculture of new denominations, missionary groups, Bible schools, publishing houses, and broadcasting networks.[6] In the 1940s they waded back into national politics by founding organizations like the International Council of Christian Churches, which acted as a conservative alternative to mainline Protestantism's Federal Council of Churches, later the National Council of Churches. This fundamentalist new guard was particularly active in the anti-Communist movement of the 1950s, partnering with secular allies like Senator Joseph McCarthy and the John Birch Society.[7]

Around the same time, a growing breed of more moderate "neo-evangelicals" founded the National Association of Evangelicals, staking out a middle ground between fundamentalism and mainline Protestantism. Billy Graham was an early proponent.[8]

Even with the arrival of these new organizations, however, political engagement among in-the-pews evangelicals remained low. The 1973 *Roe v. Wade* decision provoked conservative Roman Catholics to organize pro-life lobbies. Catholic lawyer Phyllis Schlafly embarked on a decade-long and ultimately successful campaign to stop the Equal Rights Amendment around the time Congress passed it in 1972. And Paul Weyrich had embarked on a remarkably successful career in Washington by laying the groundwork for the New Right in the sixties and seventies, cofounding the Heritage Foundation as a conservative counterweight to the Brookings Institution, and opening the Committee for the Survival of a Free Congress, which would later become the Free Congress Foundation, a training institute for conservative activists. All the while, among evangelicals and fundamentalists, "I simply couldn't get traction," Weyrich said. "Their attitude was 'If there are abortions and if there's no prayer in the public school and there are all these problems, we're living in our own little communities, and there's not going to be any abortions among our kids, and we have opened Christian schools and prayer will be recited there, and we simply don't need to be involved. That changed, not with *Roe v. Wade*, not with the Equal Rights Amendment, not

with school prayer. That changed when Jimmy Carter tried to go after Christian schools."

While the Religious Right has been allied with the Republican Party
since the election of Ronald Reagan in 1980, fundamentalist and evangelical Christians actually returned to political prominence with the
election of Jimmy Carter four years earlier. After the tumultuous 1960s
and the divisiveness and disillusionment wrought by the Vietnam War
and Watergate, America embraced the honesty and humility that
Carter, a born-again Sunday school teacher, seemed to embody. At the
same time, Carter's rise triggered an avalanche of questions from the
news media and from nonevangelical Americans over what it actually
meant to be "born again."[9] The 1976 Democratic National Convention,
which drew frequent comparisons to a revival meeting in press accounts,
provided part of the answer, with Martin Luther King, Sr., closing the
final night by telling the audience: "Surely the Lord sent Jimmy Carter
to come on out and bring America back where she belongs."[10]

As evangelicals relished the attention and legitimacy Carter
brought them—Newsweek ran a cover story designating 1976 "The Year
of the Evangelical"—they also spoke up for him, with particularly
strong support from leaders of the huge Southern Baptist Convention.[11]
Carter also won an endorsement from future Christian Coalition
founder Pat Robertson, then a registered Democrat. On Election Day,
evangelical turnout jumped to 55 percent, 10 points higher than in
1972, and Carter took about half of it. In the South, Carter won the
white evangelical vote.

Carter's support among evangelicals and fundamentalists slipped in
his first term, largely for the same reasons it slipped among the electorate at large: the energy crisis, spiraling inflation, and the U.S.
hostages in Iran. But his tumble within the Christian conservative community was exacerbated by his support for abortion rights and for the
Equal Rights Amendment, which conservatives warned would lead to
unisex bathrooms and women in combat. Paul Weyrich goes so far as to
credit the Carter administration with launching the Christian Right in

1978, when the Internal Revenue Service announced it would revoke the tax-exempt status of private schools that it determined to be insufficiently integrated.[12] At the time, Christian day schools were reportedly proliferating at a rate of one a day, and they would no doubt be among the IRS's primary targets.

The IRS announcement had roots predating Carter's arrival in the White House. A 1972 federal court decision had found that racially segregated schools no longer qualified as charitable institutions. But evangelicals took the IRS plan as "nothing less than a declaration of war on their schools, their churches, and their children," in the later words of Christian Right activist Ralph Reed.[13] The plan also threatened to raise tuition costs. Either way, the move was taken by evangelicals as a betrayal by Jimmy Carter, who'd claimed to be a devout Baptist—claimed to be one of them. "That was the junction of the conservative movement's mantra that big government is dangerous to the interests of these [religious] groups, which understood for the first time that they could not insulate themselves in any kind of ghetto," said Weyrich. "Big government was coming after them as well. There was an overnight conversion. It was electrifying."

Sensing that his moment had finally arrived, Weyrich pleaded with an Indiana-based Baptist minister and failed congressional candidate named Robert Billings, a well-known leader of the Christian School movement, to relocate to Washington and lead the charge against the IRS. Billings eventually acquiesced, launching Christian School Action and traveling to different churches each Sunday to enlist pastors and Christian school parents. He'd have preachers take up a second collection to fund the cause. Billings was also aided by a handful of evangelical television and radio broadcasters who were then almost unknown outside evangelical circles, including Jerry Falwell, Pat Robertson, and James Dobson. The combined effort generated half a million pieces of mail to the White House, Congress, and the IRS, and triggered hearings on Capitol Hill. The IRS wound up scrapping its private school desegregation campaign before it began.[14]

Within a year or so after arriving in Washington, Billings was serving as executive director for an organization that would turn the efforts of a modest-sized pastors network into a full-blown movement. It was called Moral Majority.

If Focus on the Family is the fulfillment of Weyrich's forty-year-old dream of creating a Christian Right, Moral Majority was its first incarnation. Like the birth of Christian School Action, Moral Majority formed as a reaction to a clash between the evangelical subculture and the broader secular society. In February 1979, Dallas–Fort Worth television affiliate WFAA kicked a nationally syndicated preacher named James Robison off the air after Robison accused some gays of luring children into sex.[15] To show the station, an ABC affiliate, how much support was behind him, Robison quickly organized a rally in the Dallas Convention Center. It drew a reported crowd of more than ten thousand. Robison invited Weyrich, who'd already converted to the orthodox Eastern Catholic Church, and asked him to muster a few Catholics to round out the mostly evangelical audience.

The rally succeeded in getting Robison back on the air, but it also had a much more lasting impact. After the event, the most powerful pastors present, including Robison, Southern Baptist Convention president Adrian Rogers, W. A. Criswell—who led the Southern Baptist Convention's largest congregation—and the Virginia-based televangelist Jerry Falwell, repaired to a small room inside the convention center to talk strategy. To his surprise, Paul Weyrich was drafted on the spot to brief the group on how to parlay the evening's tremendous turnout into a permanent movement. "I literally didn't have time to think about it," recalled Weyrich, who nonetheless knew almost every face in the room from his frequent organizing trips across the country. "I said, 'As I've talked to you all, the big thing you keep telling me is that you'd like to be involved in public policy and politics, but that your first mission is Jesus Christ, and you don't think your congregations will tolerate your involvement in public policy.' And they all said, 'Amen—that's right.'"

Accompanying Weyrich that evening was a friend named Lance

Tarrance, a well-known pollster. Using Tarrance as a prop, Weyrich told the pastors that the only way to determine whether or not their fears were well founded was to commission a poll of religious Americans. The poll would need to ask two questions. The first was whether churchgoers approved of their pastors becoming politically active and outspoken. The second question, Weyrich said, was more important: Would they financially support a religiously based political organization on top of their contributions to traditional church activities? Tarrance estimated the project would cost around thirty thousand dollars, and Weyrich circled the room taking pledges. One of the most generous came from Bob Perry, a Houston home builder who would eventually become one of the country's top Republican donors, bankrolling the anti–John Kerry group Swift Boat Veterans for Truth in 2004.

When the pastors who'd met in Dallas reconvened in Washington later that year under the auspices of a group called the Religious Roundtable, Weyrich had good news. The results of the poll had come back. "The upshot of my presentation was that, among evangelicals and fundamentalists, not only did they want their leaders involved in public policy, they were clamoring to have their leaders involved in public policy," Weyrich said. "And moreover, they said, 'Yes, we will financially support both organizations. We won't stop giving to your church.' That was a life-changing experience, because all these guys who had been saying, 'We can't get involved,' all of a sudden saw their people wanted them involved. By the end of the meeting, I had people tripping over themselves to come to me and say, 'What do we do? Tell us what to do.'"

One of those in attendance was Jerry Falwell, who'd founded the Thomas Road Baptist Church in Lynchburg, Virginia, and who was nationally known through the *Old Time Gospel Hour,* one of a growing legion of religious TV shows that constituted what had come to be known as the "electronic church." In between the Dallas and Washington confabs, Weyrich had traveled to Lynchburg with a team of Washington-based conservative activists, including Nixon administration alumnus and Conservative Caucus founder Howard Phillips and

Richard Viguerie, who'd spent the previous two decades pioneering direct mail as a fund-raising and organizing tool for Republican and conservative causes. Up until that point, Weyrich, Phillips, Viguerie, and others in the Washington delegation had worked together to launch a wave of pioneering right-wing organizations in the capital. But they knew that until they could tap into a grassroots movement out in the country, they'd remain beltway lieutenants without armies. They also knew that mobilizing the dormant battalions of evangelical and fundamentalist Christians would be impossible unless they could recruit a popular and respected preacher. "I was a political novice," Jerry Falwell said in an interview, recalling the circumstances of the 1979 Lynchburg meeting. "I was seeking practical advice on how a religious leader could legally and loudly get involved in returning America to the Judeo-Christian ethic."

In the preceding years, the well-known evangelical theologian Francis Schaeffer had been lobbying Falwell to use his mounting influence to combat the rising tide of secular humanism. Besides hosting a TV show, Falwell had founded Lynchburg Baptist College, later renamed Liberty University, in 1971. "Evangelicals were slow arising to the battle over the abortion issue because of a lack of evangelical leadership," Falwell said. "Dr. Schaeffer challenged me to . . . provide leadership in what he called a 'salt ministry' of confronting the culture on life, family, and faith issues." At the Lynchburg meeting, Weyrich told Falwell that there were tens of millions of conservative evangelicals, fundamentalists, Catholics, Mormons, even mainline Protestants, who could form one mighty voting bloc by working past theological differences in the pursuit of common political goals. "I said, 'Out there is what you might call the moral majority. . . ,'" Weyrich said. "And Falwell turned to his guy and said, 'If we get involved, that's the name of the organization.'"

After hearing the results of Weyrich's 1979 poll, Falwell was sold. Launched in June 1979, Moral Majority would have been hard-pressed to find a more committed or energetic leader. By 1981, it boasted a six-million-dollar annual budget, its *Moral Majority Report* reached

840,000 homes, and its daily commentary was carried by upwards of three hundred radio stations. The organization reported a membership list of four million early on, though that number might have been wildly inflated.[16] From the beginning, Moral Majority laid out three broad goals: registering, educating, and mobilizing conservative religious voters. Crisscrossing the country in a chartered plane, his Lynchburg-based Liberty Singers in tow, Falwell hosted "I Love America" rallies in state capitals, drawing thousands of people and attracting local news coverage.[17]

Direct-mail companies had long been denied access to the evangelical and fundamentalist universe by pastors who zealously guarded their church directories, but Falwell opened the floodgates. He used mail pieces to say things that were too incendiary for the mainstream media, that "we are losing the war against homosexuals," and for railing against legalized abortion, feminism, flag burning, and threats to school prayer.[18]

Falwell focused his efforts on pastors, knowing they shaped the views of churchgoers not only with regard to issues and candidates but also on the very propriety of voting and political activism. "I was deeply concerned about convincing thousands of evangelical pastors and leaders that it was not wrong to get involved in politics," he said. ". . . This was not easy. I began conducting breakfast, lunch, and dinner meetings with hundreds of pastors each week. One by one, I was able to mobilize [them]. . . . For several years, I virtually left my church and Liberty University in the hands of my associates and began traveling over two hundred thousand miles annually and speaking on an average of twenty-five times weekly." Falwell urged pastors to overcome their separatist ways and link arms with like-minded Catholics, Protestants, Mormons, and even Jews, an ecumenical warfare technique that Francis Schaeffer called "co-belligerency."

On paper, the 1980 Republican nominee for president did not appear to be someone whom Moral Majority and the broader new evangelical right would unite behind. Ronald Reagan was a veteran of Hollywood, had divorced and remarried, and did not attend church regularly. As governor of California in the 1960s and 1970s, he had signed relatively liberal abortion rights laws and had opposed legislation that would bar gay teachers from public schools.[19] But Reagan's fierce anticommunism and outspoken support for a stronger national defense appealed to conservative Christians' sense of patriotism and American exceptionalism, and he was surely more conservative than Jimmy Carter on the social issues they cared about most. The GOP also stepped up its appeals to the evangelical demographic that Carter's campaign had shone a light on four years earlier. At the 1980 Republican National Convention, the party's platform withdrew its support for the Equal Rights Amendment, inserted support for a constitutional amendment banning abortion, and recommended that only pro-lifers be appointed to the federal judiciary.[20]

Even more essential to Reagan's successful courtship of the Christian Right was his conscious attempt to learn their language. He sounded authentic in talking about his own faith and made a special attempt to couch such discussions in evangelical theology, saying he'd ask to be admitted to heaven not as a reward for his deeds but "because of what Jesus Christ did for me at Calvary."[21] At a seventeen-thousand-person rally in Dallas in 1980 hosted by James Robison—the televangelist who'd convened a huge rally there the previous year after being forced off the air—Reagan brought down the house with his opening line: "I know you can't endorse me, but I want you to know that I endorse you."[22] "When Reagan stepped onto that stage, the crowd's roar was so high, it was a roar that overtakes you," recalled Arizona congressman Trent Franks, who was then a Texas-based businessman. "Apart from that meeting, I don't think I'd be in Congress today."

By the time Election Day 1980 arrived, Moral Majority claimed to have registered four million new voters, though a more reliable figure may have been around half that.[23] Whatever the exact number, Moral Majority's courtship of conservative pastors and its promotion of hot-button social issues as top priorities for evangelical and fundamentalist voters, coupled with Ronald Reagan's own determination in targeting conservative Christians, seemed to have paid off for the GOP. The white born-again Christians who'd split their votes about evenly between Carter and Gerald Ford four years earlier broke two to one for Reagan in 1980.[24] Christian Right forces were also key in defeating liberal senators like South Dakota's George McGovern and in electing new movement conservatives, like Indiana senator Dan Quayle. The 1980 election put the Senate in Republican hands for the first time in twenty-six years.[25]

In the weeks following Reagan's inauguration and the onset of the new congressional session, however, it became clear that the Christian Right would reap few rewards for its efforts. Reagan appointed almost no evangelicals to top administration posts. The White House also lost little time in announcing, with the new Senate majority leader, that action on a conservative social agenda would be delayed for at least a year as Washington struggled to revive an anemic economy.[26] Incredulous, Paul Weyrich convened a conference call with Falwell, Robison, televangelist Pat Robertson, and other evangelical leaders. He opened the call by reminding his colleagues that the people they represented were essential to Reagan's landslide victory. "I said, 'Look—this is an outrageous statement,'" Weyrich recalled. "'Supposing that a Democratic president got elected and the chief of staff to the Democratic president along with the Democratic majority leader would issue a statement saying, "Civil rights is on the back burner, we've just got more important things to do." . . . There would be people marching in the streets.' And I said, 'If we sit down and take this, it will be a very bad omen as to where we're going to go with this movement.'

"Well, I got pummeled," Weyrich continued. "There was nobody that spoke up for me. Falwell said, 'Weyrich, you're just too hotheaded. He's our president, and we elected him, and if he says economic issues are important, that's just the way it is. . . . And I said, 'Gentlemen, you will regret this. Remember this conference call, because you will look back and say, "Oh my gosh, we haven't accomplished anything."' And of course, that was the case."

*   *   *

Reagan shunned the Christian Right over and over again through his first term, and each time was forgiven. When the president named Sandra Day O'Connor as his first Supreme Court appointment in 1981, Weyrich convened another conference call to mobilize opposition to her nomination. As an Arizona state senator, O'Connor had fought for legalized abortion and for the Equal Rights Amendment.[27] Once again, Weyrich got nowhere. Part of the reason was that, before announcing O'Connor's nomination, Reagan had called Falwell to assure him that she held the "views and values that I campaigned on."[28] Reagan secured a pledge from Falwell to withhold criticism of the nominee until her confirmation hearings began and Falwell had the opportunity to learn more about her. "I told President Reagan I would honor his request and not oppose Sandra Day O'Connor," Falwell said. "I kept my word. To this day, I sincerely believe that President Reagan truly felt Justice O'Connor would honor his policies on the Court. She generally did not. Hindsight is always twenty/twenty."

O'Connor wound up delivering the crucial swing vote on the 5 to 4 Supreme Court decisions that most incensed the Christian Right, including those that banned prayer at high school graduation, reaffirmed a woman's right to have an abortion, and struck down a state ban on the procedure critics call partial birth abortion.[29]

Even before the O'Connor nomination, though, the Reagan administration had declined an opportunity to help deliver a major victory for the Christian Right by keeping mum on the so-called human life statute. The bill attempted to subvert *Roe v. Wade* by defining human life as existing from conception, and its passage would have opened the door for state legislatures to pass antiabortion laws. But the Reagan administration's silence helped ensure the bill's defeat.[30] No doubt sensing the Christian Right's disappointment, Reagan appeared with Jerry Falwell in the Rose Garden in 1982 to propose an amendment to the Constitution enshrining a right to voluntary prayer in public school. But the administration did nothing to build the congressional supermajorities required by constitutional amendments, and it too failed.[31]

Another big disappointment was the work done by Reagan's surgeon general C. Everett Koop to educate the public about AIDS. An
evangelical Presbyterian, Koop had become a hero to the evangelical
movement for his role in coauthoring an antiabortion, antieuthanasia
book titled *Whatever Happened to the Human Race?* with Francis
Schaeffer in 1977, accompanied by the release of a film by the same
name.[32] After surviving confirmation, though, Koop not only declined
to use his post to advance his antiabortion views, he also took a deep interest in stopping the spread of AIDS, which he saw early on as a looming public health crisis.[33] The virus was unheard-of at the time of
Reagan's election. But by the end of his first term, the Centers for Disease Control reported that 5,527 people had died from the disease.[34]
Some prominent Christian Right leaders proclaimed the virus God's
retribution for homosexual behavior and called for quarantine.[35] Koop
refused to join them. Stymied by the White House from speaking out in
public during Reagan's first term, he released a thirty-six-page report on
AIDS in 1986. With its recommendations for people having sex outside
marriage to use condoms and for early sex education, the report incensed social conservatives, triggering denunciations even from some
White House officials.[36] But when Congress allocated funds in 1988 to
send an abridged version of Koop's report to every household in the
country, it came to constitute the largest mailing in American history.[37]

As Falwell's Moral Majority continued to publicly support the administration, many Christian Right activists grew disillusioned. Some
saw Falwell as a victim of White House seduction. "I do not think we
were easy on President Reagan," Falwell said. "I rather think we were
trusting." Reagan continued to make symbolic gestures toward the
movement, addressing the National Religious Broadcasters' convention
in 1984 and letting James Robison and Jerry Falwell deliver the opening
invocation and closing benediction at that year's Republican National
Convention.[38] And in the 1984 election, evangelicals and fundamentalists found little solace in the Democratic Walter Mondale–Geraldine
Ferraro ticket.

But by the time of Reagan's second inauguration, the movement that had been born just over five years before already appeared to be waning. In 1986, Falwell changed the name of his flagging Moral Majority to the Liberty Foundation. In 1987 and 1988 the evangelical world was rocked by the Jim and Tammy Faye Bakker and Jimmy Swaggart scandals. A year later, in 1989, the Liberty Foundation shut its doors for good.

—ᴍ—

As early as the Sandra Day O'Connor nomination in 1981, Paul Weyrich realized that the grassroots movement he'd finally managed to launch after a decade and a half of trying would be more or less impotent through the Reagan years. In fact, Jerry Falwell never came close to realizing Weyrich's vision for Moral Majority. Rather than operating as a grassroots machine that could inundate Congress with letters and phone calls or mobilize against a Supreme Court nominee, Moral Majority aimed simply to make pastors politically conscious. "I told Falwell that as far as these members of Congress are concerned, it's pay me now or pay me later," Weyrich recalled. "What we needed to do is set up an operation that is strong enough that we go into somebody's district or somebody's state and say, 'Okay, Senator X, we want your vote on this, and here are ten thousand people in your state that have signed up for this effort. And [Senator X] says, 'The heck with you, I'm not interested.' And we turn right around and we translate this into a political operation, and we go out to defeat Senator X. [Falwell] didn't grasp it. . . . His whole concept was just to rally people, and he did that beautifully, but they never translated that into real action. He never did what you have to do if you're going to have real political impact. The guy who did that was Robertson."

Pat Robertson's long and ever-growing record of bizarre public proclamations makes it easy to forget that his formidable academic and professional credentials jump-started Falwell's fading Christian Right in the late 1990s and infused it with a new and enduring level of political sophistication. Religious Right chronicler William Martin has noted that Jerry Falwell's father was an alcoholic who killed his own brother in a gunfight and that Falwell's postsecondary education was limited to attending a Baptist Bible college in Springfield, Missouri. Robertson's father, by contrast, was a thirty-four-year veteran of the U.S. Congress, the last twenty spent as a Democratic senator from Virginia. M. G. "Pat" Robertson himself graduated Phi Beta Kappa from Washington and Lee University and then from Yale Law School and New York Theological Seminary. Falwell may have been more responsible than anyone for recruiting evangelical and fundamentalist pastors into the fledgling Christian Right in the early 1980s, but in 1988, Robertson actually launched a serious bid to be president. And while Falwell's *Old Time Gospel Hour* enjoyed weekly national syndication, Robertson presided over an entire cable network that included his own daily hour-long program called *The 700 Club*.[39]

Robertson's broadcasting kingdom was born with his 1959 purchase of a dilapidated Virginia television station. In the mid-1960s, when he was on the air for several hours a day, he told viewers he needed seven hundred people to pledge ten dollars each to keep the station afloat. The ensuing *700 Club* program revolutionized Christian television. Breaking with the reigning Sunday-morning-preaching format—whose sermons were often of the fire-and-brimstone variety— *The 700 Club* offered interviews with popular Christian figures and performances by Christian artists on a set that just as easily could have hosted a daytime talk show on network TV.[40]

An ordained minister, Robertson is a charismatic evangelical, a group distinguished by the practice of speaking in tongues, faith healing, and prophesying. A central feature of *The 700 Club* is Robertson's invitation to viewers to call a Christian Broadcasting Network counselor to request prayers and report miracles, some of which are shared on the air. Callers are added to the mailing list for fund-raising solicitations. Another important component is Robertson's frequent receipt of a "word of knowledge," a supernatural message about some viewer, somewhere, who has just received a miracle, typically the healing of a medical ailment, ranging from cancer to hemorrhoids.[41] Robertson received tremendous public exposure for a 1985 episode of *The 700 Club* in which he commanded Hurricane Gloria to move away from the Virginia coastline "in the name of Jesus of Nazareth." The hurricane changed course, making landfall on Long Island.

By 1978, Robertson's Christian Broadcasting Network had amassed three hundred thousand donors, providing a monthly income stream of $1.4 million.[42] That same year, CBN opened a news department that utilized early satellite technology to launch New York and Washington bureaus. *The 700 Club* began to feature congressmen, senators, and White House officials.[43] The program carried news segments with a conservative, pro-Reagan bent. By 1985, CBN's annual budget had grown to almost $230 million, and *The 700 Club* was carried on two hundred U.S. stations and in sixty foreign countries.[44]

Shortly after Ronald Reagan's first election, Robertson had quietly launched the Freedom Council, an organization aimed at training religious Americans, primarily evangelicals, to be grassroots political activists. While Robertson claimed his goal was to train ten activists in each of the country's 175,000 precincts, the operation allegedly consisted mainly of funneling large sums of money from the Christian Broadcasting Network into Michigan. Because elections for delegates to Michigan's 1988 state Republican National Convention were to be held in summer 1986, the state was the bellwether for the 1988 presidential primary, in which Robertson planned to run.[45] In anticipation of the precinct elections, Robertson made frequent trips to Michigan, attempting to mobilize *700 Club* members, CBN supporters, and members of charismatic churches. He appointed a state field director, but the entire effort remained purposefully invisible to the state's Republican establishment. Robertson's foot soldiers shocked the presidential campaign of Vice President George H. W. Bush when thousands of them submitted petitions to run as delegates on the eve of the filing deadline.[46]

Bush's operatives and the state's party establishment devised a dubious redistricting scheme that wound up depriving Robertson of enough
Michigan delegates that he finished third, behind Bush and Congressman Jack Kemp.[47] But Robertson employed similar organizational tactics in advance of the 1988 Iowa caucuses, where he beat Bush and
Kemp. Kansas senator Bob Dole, who'd skipped Michigan entirely,
took first, but Robertson's victory over a sitting vice president generated
more headlines.

With little time to organize in states hosting the next important primaries, like New Hampshire and the Super Tuesday lineup of southern
and southwestern states, Robertson's fortunes sank quickly after Iowa,
and Bush took a decisive lead. But Robertson's failed presidential bid
did more to integrate evangelicals and fundamentalists into the GOP
machinery than any development during the Reagan years. Bush adviser Doug Wead, a committed evangelical and cofounder of the
famine-relief charity Mercy Corps International, earned respect within
the Bush camp for outmaneuvering Robertson in Michigan, ensuring
that the campaign continued to pay attention to evangelical voters.[48]
Bush selected Indiana senator Dan Quayle, a well-known social conservative, as a running mate. And countless evangelicals who got their first
taste of politics working for the election of Robertson in Michigan,
Iowa, and elsewhere remained a permanent and growing presence in
the GOP, rising to the party's top echelons. "There are three presidential campaigns in post–World War II history that refashioned the political parties from which they emerged," said Ralph Reed, who would be
tapped by Robertson to transform his losing campaign into Christian
Coalition, in an interview. "Goldwater in '64, McGovern in '72, and
Robertson in '88. All three were losing efforts, but when history is written, each defeat carried the seeds of ultimate victory. [They] created
farm teams at the grassroots for future candidates and party leaders.

"For a number of people in the pro-family movement, most particularly Pat Robertson, they learned by being a candidate, by going out
there and competing in twenty or thirty primaries and caucuses," Reed
continued. "As Pat said to me one time, 'Look, I ran against the incum-

bent vice president of the United States, against [top Bush political aide] Lee Atwater. I went eighteen rounds with the best in the business, and I got a Ph.D. in politics as it's practiced at the presidential level."

On the evening of his first long conversation with Robertson, Ralph Reed was finishing up his own Ph.D., in American history at Emory University. It was the final night of festivities for President George H. W. Bush's January 1989 inauguration. Robertson was accepting the "Man of the Year" award from Students for America, an organization of conservative evangelical college students, of which Reed was founder and president. Seated at the same table for dinner, Reed impressed Robertson with his analysis of what his presidential campaign had done right—and what it had done wrong.[49] The two agreed that with the arrival of George H. W. Bush—who despite his campaign's nods toward evangelicals never pretended to be a true believer social conservative— the time was ripe for the decade-old Christian Right to turn its attention from Washington to the grassroots, to school boards, city councils, and state legislatures.[50] With the dismantling of Moral Majority and the momentum from his presidential bid, Robertson saw an opening for a totally new political organization to mobilize and lead the evangelical grassroots; he asked Reed if he would write up a memo on how to build it.[51]

Reed was just twenty-eight years old at the time, but his elfin build and boyish face made him look even younger. A hard-drinking blowhard during his undergraduate years, Reed quit alcohol and rededicated his life to Jesus Christ after graduation. Before enrolling at Emory, he served for two years as executive director of College Republicans, an organization that was developing a reputation as an incubator for future GOP stars. Reed's mentors at College Republicans included future antitax crusader and conservative überstrategist Grover Norquist, who preceded him as executive director, and future superlobbyist Jack Abramoff, who was serving as chairman when Reed arrived. (In January 2006, Abramoff would plead guilty to charges of corruption and conspiracy to bribe public officials and pledge his cooperation in the ongoing federal investigation into his activities. While there was no evidence that Reed was a target in the inquiry, his records were subpoenaed by federal prosecutors. Document disclosures revealed that Reed's companies had collected at least $4.2 million from Abramoff to organize conservative Christian opposition to Indian casinos that threatened to compete with Abramoff's gaming clients.)[52]

In his memo to Robertson, Reed identified as the main obstacle to building an effective grassroots evangelical machine the fact that, more than six decades after the Scopes Trial, evangelicals remained largely withdrawn from political life: "we have now had two full generations of Bible-believing Christians . . . with virtually no hands on experience in the political decision-making process."[53] Moral Majority had employed what Reed called a "rally and direct mail strategy" that had eventually become a shell game, while Reed wanted to transform the Christian Right into a well-trained grassroots army with troops in every precinct. Rather than call Congress or write letters to the White House, Reed's Christian Coalition would encourage trainees to focus on races in their own backyards. "It is much easier to move a city council or a school board than to move the U.S. Congress," Reed said later. ". . . [A]s a matter of political strategy . . . the religious conservative movement had always gotten it backwards. It always tried to leapfrog over the preliminary steps to political influence with one long bomb: trying to win the White House. But if you win the White House and you don't control anything underneath it, it can be a Pyrrhic victory, as we discovered with Reagan. . . ."[54]

Starting from scratch in training evangelicals for political combat would be a daunting task, but Reed thought it could be done. And if done right, he said in his 1989 memo to Robertson, the organization stood to include three million members, 350 nationwide chapters, and a ten-million-dollar budget by 1992.[55]

Within a year of his conversation with Robertson, Reed and his wife relocated to the Virginia Beach environs where the Christian

Broadcasting Network was headquartered. Reed had encouraged
Robertson to adopt a secular-sounding name for his organization to
avoid charges of self-righteousness and sectarianism—as Reed had
done with Students for America—but the televangelist insisted on calling it Christian Coalition.[56] As Reed and his wife set up shop in the
grimy warehouse that had served as Robertson's campaign headquarters, the grand vision he had sketched out in his memo looked to
be a long way off.

But as the news media were writing the Christian Right's obituary
in the aftermath of Moral Majority's demise, Pat Robertson's failed presidential bid, and a rash of televangelist sex and money scandals, Reed
and a team of regional field directors were quietly crisscrossing the
country, planting state affiliates and local chapters and sponsoring
"leadership schools" for evangelicals and other conservative Christians.
The sessions opened with a motivational video of Robertson bewailing
the country's moral free fall. Then Reed or a surrogate would distribute
training manuals and offer detailed instructions for building local political organizations, from creating church and volunteer databases to
tips on how to avoid speaking in "Christianese" when lobbying lawmakers.[57] Workshop by workshop, Christian Coalition's trainers
reached tens of thousands. Paul Weyrich's dream seemed finally to be
coming true.

Besides doing the painstaking work of training grassroots activists,
Reed's other early breakthrough was triggered by a study that had been
left behind by Robertson's presidential campaign in what was now
Christian Coalition headquarters. Reed had stumbled across it shortly
after arriving in Virginia Beach. The study showed that the supporters of
Robertson's candidacy fell into two broad categories: middle-aged
empty nesters who had worried about the direction of the country since
the 1960s, and suburban couples in their twenties and thirties who
were raising children.[58] This latter demographic included tens of millions of Americans whom the Christian Right had never courted, and it
quickly became the primary target audience of Reed's recruitment efforts. "You appeal to where the demographic is," Reed said while still at

Christian Coalition. "You say, 'We're concerned about children, we're trying to strengthen the family, we're trying to reverse the coarsening of the culture.' . . . That's a totally different kind of marketing than saying, 'We're evangelicals and we're here to take over.' "[59]

Indeed, Reed was attempting to do nothing less than mainstream a movement that until then had been comfortable residing in the right wing of American politics. When recruiting activists to start state and local Coalition chapters, he looked for college-educated, upwardly mobile professionals: small-business owners, lawyers, doctors, and political consultants.[60] "I'm not denigrating any blue-collar people—my father shoveled coal for a living—but those were the kind of people that Falwell attracted," said Paul Weyrich, who acted as an informal adviser to Christian Coalition. "[Pat] Robertson attracted a higher caliber of people. They were better educated, they were more able, and they understood technology."

Christian Coalition abandoned Moral Majority's intensive outreach to pastors, knowing that an organization whose leadership ranks were filled with religious figures would be relegated to a political ghetto in the eyes of lawmakers, candidates, and the media.[61] Plus, Reed knew that pastors were already too overworked to take on the long hours required for serious political organizing. Moral Majority's first board of directors had been a who's who of prominent preachers, from D. James Kennedy, leader of the Fort Lauderdale–based Coral Ridge Ministries, to Tim LaHaye, who would later become famous for coauthoring the Left Behind book series. Christian Coalition, by contrast, had a single ordained minister on its board and among its fifty state chapter heads.[62]

Like any effective political organization, the Coalition also understood that elections and grassroots lobbying were numbers games. It began publishing its trademark voter guides early on, distributing 750,000 in North Carolina to help save Jesse Helms's seemingly doomed 1990 reelection effort.[63] Voter guides had been distributed by earlier Christian Right organizations, but the Coalition beefed up distribution into the tens of millions.[64]

But because the organization dispensed with the rallies and press conferences that had earned Moral Majority so many headlines, its early efforts were all but invisible to the press and to its political opponents. "I do guerrilla warfare," Reed famously said in 1991, around the time of Christian Coalition's first "Road to Victory" conference. "I paint my face and travel at night. You don't know it's over until you're in a body bag. You don't know till election night." But the Road to Victory's speaker lineup, which included Vice President Dan Quayle, showed that the Coalition had the GOP's attention. By the end of 1992, Christian Coalition boasted an $8.5 million budget, a quarter of a million dues-paying members, and a thousand chapters in all fifty states.[65]

As the Coalition continued to draw new and more rarefied blood into the Christian Right, George H. W. Bush continued to make the movement yawn.

While Bush was almost surely more authentically religious than Ronald Reagan—attending church every Sunday, for instance—and was avowedly pro-life, evangelicals looked on Bush with more suspicion than they had his predecessor. As a mainline Protestant with a New England lineage, Bush was uncomfortable making elaborate public gestures of his religious beliefs.[66] Like Reagan, he appointed few evangelicals to top positions. Doug Wead, the Bush campaign aide who helped thwart Pat Robertson's 1988 insurgency and who directed evangelical outreach from the White House Office of Public Liaison, was fired in 1990 after he was seen to be operating as a free agent.[67] That same year, gay and lesbian groups were invited to the White House for the signing of the "Hate Crimes" bill, apparently marking the first time those organizations had received such an invitation. The news set off a firestorm in the Religious Right. A few months later, members of a gay rights group were spotted among a large crowd that had assembled at the White House for the signing of the Americans with Disabilities Act. The development prompted the director of the National Association of Evangelicals to caution Bush that "many evangelicals believe you are sacrificing your claim to be a traditional values president."[68]

In an apparent attempt to counter that impression, 1992's Republican National Convention in Houston was a valentine to the Christian Right. Even before the convention opened, the platform committee fortified the pro-life document of earlier conventions with language that championed tougher pornography laws and that unequivocally opposed gay rights.[69] While Reagan's handlers had given the convention's low-profile opening and closing prayer slots to prominent Christian Right leaders in 1984, the 1992 convention featured a speech by Christian Coalition founder Pat Robertson and a prime-time address by Pat Buchanan. "There is a religious war going on in this country," Buchanan thundered. "It is a cultural war as critical to the kind of nation we shall be as the Cold War itself. . . . And in the struggle for the soul of America, Clinton and Clinton [Bill and Hillary] are on the other side, and George Bush is on our side."[70]

Some pundits suggested that Houston's fiery rhetoric cost Bush the election, but public polling data suggested that the recession and Bush's broken no-new-taxes pledge were bigger factors. The convention's strident tone nonetheless served as a lesson to future GOP candidates about the importance of shoring up what had become the GOP's evangelical base early on in the campaign season—and behind closed doors, as Reagan had done. Bill Clinton won a 43 percent plurality in a three-way race in which Ross Perot won almost 19 percent of the vote and George Bush got just over 37 percent. But there were signs that Christian Coalition was dramatically altering the electoral landscape. Evangelical turnout had jumped almost 10 percentage points from 1988, accounting for 37 percent of the Republican vote.

Within days of Bill Clinton's inauguration, Christian Coalition pounced on the president's plan to lift the ban on gays in the military, helping squelch the move by flooding the congressional switchboard with more than four hundred thousand phone calls.[71] But with Clinton in the White House, Reed redoubled his efforts to turn the Coalition's gaze away from Washington. "No more photo ops in the Roosevelt

Room or bill signing ceremonies in the Rose Garden," he wrote in a
memo to local leaders. "It will force us to do what we should have been
doing all along. . . . Returning to the state and local legislative issues
that are closest to where people live. . . ."[72]

So in 1992 the Coalition began sponsoring seminars for state legislative candidates and, in 1994, for school board candidates. By 1994,
according to a survey by *Campaigns & Elections* magazine, Christian
Right forces dominated eighteen state Republican parties and exerted
substantial influence in thirteen others, many under the auspices of
Christian Coalition.

But as the Coalition matured, Reed grew convinced that main-
streaming the Christian Right would require more than recruiting secular professionals into Coalition leadership, targeting young suburban
parents, and winning seats on school boards; it would take a wholesale
message overhaul. "Everyone knew what the religious right was
against; few knew what it was for," he wrote later, homing in on the
movement's fixation on homosexuality. ". . . [M]any Americans lacked
[evangelicals'] biblical worldview, making such appeals unpersuasive
to the general population, and the religious right never broadened this
concern by emphasizing a more positive agenda of strengthening the
two-parent family. The agenda thus tended to be perceived as narrow
and negative."[73]

So after the 1992 elections, Reed resolved to stop using military
metaphors. He ordered the Coalition's field staff to do the same, saying
that "such language had allowed the media and the organized left to
caricature our movement as intolerant and uncaring." Reed told them
to use sports metaphors instead.[74] The shift was more than window
dressing. Reed had come to believe that the righteous purity of the
Christian Right's agenda—or what detractors would call its
radicalism—had left it marginalized, unable to achieve legislative victories. In 1993, Reed published a manifesto for his new approach in the
Heritage Foundation's *Policy Review* magazine under the title "Casting
a Wider Net."[75] "The most urgent challenge for pro-family conservatives

is to develop a broader issues agenda," Reed wrote. Issues like abortion and homosexuality were surely important. "To win at the ballot box and in the court of public opinion, however," Reed wrote, "the pro-family movement must speak to the concerns of average voters in the areas of taxes, crime, government waste, health care, and financial security." Restoring the family, in this view, had less to do with battling abortion and gay rights than it did with reforming welfare and the tax code.[76] Up till that time, Reed was attempting to lift the Christian Right out of the political ghetto. Now he wanted to go much further. "[T]he cluster of pro-family issues," he wrote, "must now be expanded to attract a majority of voters."[77]

A special election for Georgia senator a few weeks after Election Day 1992 gave Reed the perfect opportunity to institute the new strategy. The race pitted Paul Coverdell, a pro-choice Republican, against the Democratic incumbent. Because Coverdell opposed federal funding for abortions and was conservative on other issues, the Coalition decided to put its machinery to work for him despite his stance on abortion rights, distributing two million voter guides and calling fifty thousand households, all in an effort to get evangelicals to the polls. As expected, the effort sparked denunciations from some Christian Right quarters, including Operation Rescue's Randall Terry. But it worked. Coverdell won the election by seventeen thousand votes out of more than a million cast, and in a state that had just been carried by Bill Clinton.[78]

The Georgia campaign was just the beginning of Reed's big-tent gambit. Later in 1992, Christian Coalition opened its first Washington office and declared that its mission would be working to unite religious and economic conservatives by pushing for non-hot-button legislation like welfare reform and a balanced budget.[79] Its top legislative priority for 1993 was increasing the standard tax deduction for children. The new agenda had fellow Christian Right activists whispering that their movement's most brilliant tactician was doing more to help the GOP's cause than Christ's. And the whispering grew louder in 1994, when

Christian Coalition launched its costliest lobbying effort yet: a $1.4 million national media campaign aimed at stopping President Clinton's universal health care plan.[80]

But Reed was undeterred. When Newt Gingrich, then House minority whip, phoned him to say that the Contract with America he was drawing up for the 1994 midterm elections excluded culture war items, Reed pledged his support anyway, on the condition that the Contract include the child tax deduction he'd been pushing. The chorus of voices accusing Reed of selling out was growing, but he was emboldened by the warm reception he was getting from the Republican establishment, typified by Gingrich's phone call. If he could be a team player on the Contract with America and help the GOP make gains in 1994, Reed reasoned, his movement would reap future rewards from party bosses on issues like abortion and school choice.[81] Plus, having earned his political stripes at College Republicans, Reed had been a partisan before he was a born-again Christian. He wanted to help his party. "I had come up through the party," he said in an interview. "These [Republicans] were my friends, people that I knew and worked with, in many cases, before I ever made a faith commitment, and certainly before I ever took a leadership role in the pro-family community."

And Reed seems to have genuinely believed that the true evangelical political agenda was not limited to hot-button issues. Citing a national poll of evangelical Christians that showed they cared about taxes, education, and crime more than about outlawing abortion, he claimed the numbers were on his side.[82]

The Republican Revolution of 1994, in which the GOP gained fifty-two seats in the House of Representatives—winning control of the lower chamber for the first time in forty years—and eight in the Senate, would appear to have vindicated Reed's go-along-to-get-along approach toward the GOP. Christian Coalition volunteers had been active in 120 congressional races. Exit polls suggested that religious conservatives accounted for a full third of the electorate, and 70 percent of those voters supported Republicans, helping fuel a nine-million-vote increase in GOP turnout over the last midterm elections in 1990.[83] When the returns came in, 114 newly elected and reelected House members and twenty-six senators had either received a perfect score on Christian Coalition's congressional scorecard or had run with the Coalition's strong backing.[84]

After the election, Paul Weyrich and Family Research Council president Gary Bauer took to publicly knocking new House Speaker Newt Gingrich's Contract with America for excluding social issues, a campaign the two had embarked on even before the election. But Reed pledged a million dollars to promote the effort, more than he would spend on pushing Christian Coalition's own Contract with the American Family the following year.[85]

In fact, when the Coalition unveiled its ten-point Contract in May 1995, the document was tame enough to provoke incredulity from both left and right. It mentioned homosexuality only with regard to how it should be treated by public school curricula. Instead of calling for a constitutional amendment to outlaw abortion, it proposed only a legislative ban on the procedure opponents call partial birth abortion. This was how Reed planned to spend the capital he had earned by supporting Gingrich's Contract with America and turning out the evangelical vote in 1994? Other Contract with the American Family bullet points called for more tax credits, the elimination of taxpayer-financed abortions, and a change in the tax code to allow stay-at-home moms to contribute to a retirement plan tax-free.[86] "Having been involved in the political process for nearly two decades," Reed wrote of his Contract, "religious conservatives now understand the difference between what is desirable and what is possible. . . ."[87]

Over the next couple of years, two Contract with the American Family items were signed into law: the child tax credit and tougher restrictions on Internet pornography. But grousing over Reed's inclusive vision for the Christian Right continued, even among the Coalition's state and local chapters. As the 1996 Republican presidential field began to take form after the 1994 midterms, Reed began to quietly assist the campaign of Senate Majority Leader Bob Dole, even as the evangelical base was clearly more excited about Pat Buchanan, an outspoken pro-lifer who'd delivered the rousing culture war speech at the 1992 Republican National Convention.[88] Fiery, divisive, and an undeniable long shot in a general election, Buchanan represented all the qualities Reed had tried to purge from the Christian Right. When Christian Coalition mailed invitations for its fall 1995 "Road to Victory" conference, Buchanan's face was missing from the pictures of invited speakers.[89] But as Reed continued to play the part of Dole's evangelical consigliore, Buchanan took second place in the 1996 Iowa caucuses, then won the New Hampshire primary outright, picking up far more evangelical votes than Dole.

The next big primary would be South Carolina, which had often determined the front-runner in previous elections. The state's Christian Coalition chapter was probably the nation's most powerful, and it and the national Coalition planned a "God and Country" rally in Columbia for two days before the primary. The Coalition coordinated with Dole in importing his supporters from across the state in order to dilute the expected thicket of Buchanan backers. With an endorsement from the state Christian Coalition director's husband—the director had to remain officially neutral—and from evangelical South Carolina governor David Beasley, Dole won the primary in a romp.[90]

But just as Reed and Christian Coalition top brass should have been celebrating, calls began coming in from evangelical activists who were distraught over Reed's embrace of Dole. Some were threatening to resign from the Coalition. After the calls kept up for two more weeks, Reed faxed state and local Coalition leaders denying that he or the Coalition was championing Dole.[91] Then, a couple of months later, *The New York Times* ran a front-page story headlined "Christian Leader Would Back Shift on Abortion Issue." Appearing roughly three months before the Republican National Convention, the story said Reed would reluctantly accept antiabortion laws that provided exceptions for victims of incest or rape or to save the life of the mother, a position at odds with the GOP platform, which called for a constitutional ban on abortion and said nothing about exceptions. The news coincided with reports that Dole would attempt to make the Republican platform more friendly to pro-choice Republicans at the San Diego convention. The Coalition's phones started ringing again.

Reed denounced the *Times* story as "totally inaccurate" and fired off another fax to the Coalition's state and local chapter leaders reaffirming the Coalition's opposition to incest or rape exceptions in antiabortion laws.[92] But the phones kept ringing. "There is no question," Angela "Bay" Buchanan, Pat Buchanan's sister and campaign manager, said at the time, "that [Reed] no longer represents those of us who feel very strongly about family values and life and the importance of the Republican platform."[93]

It would turn out to be a prophetic statement. While Reed activated the Christian Coalition machinery for Dole in the general election, evangelical turnout dipped from 55 percent in 1992 to less than 50 percent. Dole took only 41 percent of the popular vote. After the election, donations to Christian Coalition began to slide. In April 1997, after leading an unsuccessful campaign to draw African American churches into the Christian Right, Reed announced he was stepping down. The Coalition had become the subject of IRS and FEC investigations over whether it had violated rules governing its nonprofit status by coordinating with the Republican Party or endorsing candidates. It was eventually forced to reorganize and to pay back taxes along with other penalties for partisan political activities, including sharing its mailing list with Oliver North's unsuccessful 1994 Virginia Senate campaign. Two years after Reed's departure, the Coalition was in shambles, suffering mass defections of leadership and members and saddled with $2.5 million in debt.[94]

Just as in the wake of Moral Majority's demise a decade earlier, the news media began to wonder if Christian Coalition's tumble represented a fatal blow to the Christian Right. "Coalition's Woes May Hinder Goals of Christian Right" read a front-page *New York Times* headline in summer 1999. "[N]ow even its prior assertions to such widespread strength are in doubt," the story reported. "Former national leaders who have recently left the group said in interviews that the coalition, as critics have long suspected, never commanded the numbers it claimed."

Even some within the movement grew despondent. As the Christian Right turned twenty years old, its chief architect, Paul Weyrich, was feeling as though the movement had little to show for itself. Jerry Falwell's Moral Majority had succeeded in attracting the attention of the White House and the news media, but failed to build a true army of in-the-pews evangelical activists or get legislative results. Ralph Reed, meanwhile, had built such an army, only to subvert much of the Christian Right's core agenda to practical politics and to his mission of expanding the movement. Bill Clinton had survived impeachment, and, rather than being punished for the president's sexual misdeeds, the Democrats had picked up House seats in the 1998 midterm elections. It was the first time the party that held the White House had done so since the 1930s. In February 1999, Weyrich drafted an open letter to fellow conservatives in which he said, "I no longer believe that there is a moral majority," and that "we probably have lost the culture war."

The document stunned conservatives, helping trigger a *Christianity Today* cover story titled "Is the Religious Right Finished?" that featured an abridged version of Weyrich's letter. The crux of Weyrich's argument was that cultural developments, including the rise of sex-drenched MTV, the availability of ever more violent video games to children, and the triumph of political correctness had eclipsed the conservative movement's considerable political accomplishments, like Ronald Reagan's election and the Republican Revolution. What was most shocking about the letter was that Weyrich, who spent nearly two decades trying to convince evangelicals and fundamentalists to become politically active before he finally began to succeed, was now urging church folk to withdraw again: "We need to drop out of this culture, and find places where we can live godly, righteous and sober lives." The man who had been more responsible than anyone for conceiving the Christian Right was now questioning whether it had reason to continue.

5

The Beltway's Bible Belt

"Does the Republican Party want our votes—no strings attached—to court us every two years, and then to say, 'Don't call me. I'll call you?' . . . If it is, I'm gone, and if I go . . . I will do everything I can to take as many people with me as possible."

—m—

Almost a year before Paul Weyrich's letter ignited a debate about whether the Christian Right was doomed, James Dobson had come to Washington to save it. On the evening of March 18, 1998, Dobson convened a meeting with two dozen Republican congressmen in the basement of the U.S. Capitol to deliver an urgent message: He was considering leaving the GOP. In the audience were some of Dobson's most dependable House allies. Oklahoma representative Steve Largent, a former football star, was a volunteer speaker for Focus on the Family in the early 1990s. Missouri representative Jim Talent, raised in a Jewish home, had become an evangelical Christian after hearing a Dobson radio broadcast in his car.[1] But Dobson was upset, and he wasn't about to let polite company keep him from saying so. Noting that it had been more than three years since the Republican Revolution, he complained that the GOP-controlled House and Senate still hadn't moved to curb abortion rights. It hadn't ended funding for Planned Parenthood abroad. The National Endowment for the Arts, which had funded the artists Andres Serrano, of *Piss Christ* fame, and Robert Mapplethorpe, famous for his homoerotic photography, was still alive and well. And where was the outrage over President Clinton's overtures to gay rights groups?

Dobson told the House members that he had scheduled interviews for the following morning with *The New York Times* and *The Washington Post*, where he would lay out his ultimatum to bolt the Republican Party and to take as many evangelicals with him as he could unless the GOP gave him reason to believe that it would take up the Christian Right's agenda in earnest. For the next two hours, almost until midnight, the House members took turns defending themselves, reminding Dobson that major obstacles—like President Bill Clinton—still stood in the way of advancing his agenda. Some congressmen had brought their wives to the meeting, and one broke into tears while telling Dobson about how his recent public swipes at the GOP had triggered rude comments from friends of the family.[2]

If James Dobson had come to Washington to save the Christian Right, he'd also come to usher in a new era in its relations with the Republican Party. Christian Coalition, the movement's most powerful organization up to that time, had imploded with Ralph Reed's 1997 departure. Reed had transformed a fledgling movement into a true grassroots machine but rankled evangelical activists with his obse-

quiousness toward the GOP. Dobson, by contrast, was a purist. He
prided himself on being an outsider to the Republican establishment.
"Under Ralph's leadership, the Christian Coalition had the reputation
of being a wholly owned subsidiary of the Republican Party," said
Michael Farris, a prominent Christian Right activist. "It was a bit of an
exaggeration, but that was its reputation. That characterization is not
even remotely correct of Dobson. . . . [H]e does what he thinks is right."

As the 1990s wore on, the divergent political strategies of Reed and
Dobson had increasingly been locking horns. In a 1995 appearance on
This Week with David Brinkley, Reed was asked repeatedly whether he'd
support a presidential bid by the pro-choice General Colin Powell, who
was being courted by some GOP heavyweights. As host Sam Donaldson
repeatedly rephrased the question, Reed continued to artfully duck and
bob.[3] The performance triggered an angry letter from Dobson, who accused Reed of sending a dangerous message to the Republican establishment: that the pro-family movement might be open to compromise
on abortion. "Is power the motivator of the great crusade?" Dobson
wrote in a five-page dispatch. "If so, it will sour and turn to bile in your
mouth. . . . This posture may elevate your influence in Washington,
but it is unfaithful to the principles we are duty-bound as Christians to
defend."[4] With Dobson's deputies faxing the letter all over Washington,
Reed quickly wrote up a defense, arguing that it made little sense to attack a noncandidate whom he thought unlikely to run. Reed feared a
broadside from the Christian Right would do more to provoke Powell
than dissuade him. He would later write that the circumstances "required a delicate balancing act."[5]

Dobson was never one for delicacy. Most of the 1996 Republican
presidential field, including Bob Dole, Phil Gramm, Pat Buchanan,
Lamar Alexander, and Alan Keyes, had sojourned to Colorado Springs
to court Dobson's support. Rather than follow Reed's strategy of be-
friending each candidate so that the movement would have an ally regardless of who won, Dobson's backing would be an all-or-nothing
proposition. At a meeting between Texas senator Phil Gramm and

Dobson, Reed, and Family Research Council president Gary Bauer, Dobson told Gramm that he was turned off by the senator's emphasis on fiscal issues over social issues. "I am not running for preacher," Gramm replied. "I'm running for president. I just don't feel comfortable going around telling other people how to live their lives." Exiting Gramm's Capitol Hill office, Dobson's face went red. "I walked into that meeting fully expecting to support Phil Gramm for president," he said, according to Reed's recollection. "Now I don't think I would vote for him if he was the last man standing."[6]

After quietly helping Dole shore up his bid for the Republican nomination that summer, Reed put Christian Coalition to work turning out evangelicals for Dole on Election Day. But Dobson, angry over Dole's attempt to make the Republican platform more hospitable to abortion rights supporters and by his selection of fiscal conservative Jack Kemp as a running mate, cast his first ballot for a non-Republican presidential candidate: the U.S. Taxpayers Party's Howard Phillips.

As if to herald his own arrival as Ralph Reed's and Pat Robertson's replacement and to announce that Christian Coalition's accommodationist ways were a thing of the past, Dobson launched his campaign against the GOP in February 1998, less than a year after Reed had left the Coalition. It was at a meeting of the Council for National Policy, a little-known but powerful club of conservatives whose founders include Tim LaHaye and Paul Weyrich.[7] Dobson had attended the CNP's top-secret meetings almost from the group's inception but had stopped going in 1993 because he sensed that it, like the Republican Party, had lost its spine. The invitation to deliver the keynote address at the group's 1998 convention in Phoenix was a kind of homecoming.[8]

But instead of lambasting the conservatives' usual bogeymen — liberal Democrats, moderate Republicans, and President Clinton, then embroiled in the Monica Lewinsky scandal — Dobson's Phoenix speech laid squarely into the conservative Republicans who'd taken over the House in 1994. He charged the GOP with nothing less than having abandoned God's law. "[T]he universe has a boss," Dobson told the crowd of about 450, in an address that inspired standing ovations throughout.[9] "It has a boss who has a very clear idea of what is right and what is wrong. It doesn't matter a whole lot what you think or what I think."

If Ralph Reed's strategy of "casting a wider net" were to be turned on its head, this is what it would look like. And Dobson was just getting started.

Dobson ticked off a litany of congressional transgressions the GOP had failed to prevent since the Republican Revolution, which he'd echo in the Capitol's basement the following month: nine hundred million dollars to Planned Parenthood operations abroad, two hundred million dollars to safe-sex education—as opposed to abstinence-only programs—and the failure to require parental consent for minors seeking abortions. President Clinton had convened a hate crimes summit in the White House where he expressed solidarity with gay rights groups, Dobson reminded his audience, "and not one Republican had spoken up in protest. I wait for the echo. Where are the Republican leaders who stand up and say, 'This is outrageous! We will not stand for it!' There was not a peep of protest from a single Republican leader in the House or the Senate . . . they're so intimidated. They're so pinned down. It was just incredible.

"Does the Republican Party want our votes—no strings attached—to court us every two years, and then to say, 'Don't call me. I'll call you,' and to not care about the moral law of the universe?" Dobson thundered at the speech's climax. ". . . If it is, I'm gone, and if I go—I'm not trying to threaten anybody because I don't influence the world—but if I go, I will do everything I can to take as many people with me as possible."

The speech was a hit with the GOP's activist base, but in the Capitol's basement the following month, a pared-down version had brought a congressman's wife to tears. "Some of us, myself included, said, 'Look,

don't form a circle and open fire—you're shooting your friends here,'"
recalled South Dakota senator John Thune, then a congressman who
attended Dobson's March 1998 tongue-lashing. "We had a majority in
the House, but we didn't have a conservative majority. At that point, his
expectations were high. [Part of the problem was] on his part, not fully
appreciating what it takes to get things through the legislative process,
how complicated it is."

Late that night, Dobson canceled his appointments for the following morning with *The New York Times* and *The Washington Post*.

For Republicans, it was a temporary reprieve. In between his
Phoenix and Washington speeches, Dobson had sent a letter to every
Republican senator and congressman—and to the news media—
outlining his legislative priorities: defunding Planned Parenthood,
eliminating federal Title X funds for safe sex education and condom
distribution, requiring parental consent for minors seeking abortions
within federal programs, and five other specific items. Dobson also expected action on objectives "that are so obvious that they require no
elaboration, such as a ban on partial birth abortion, the defense of traditional marriage, and opposition to any legislation that would add 'sexual orientation' to any civil rights law, education program, or any
congressional appropriation. . . .

"Finally," Dobson wrote near the end, "I would suggest that you ask
the [House] Speaker [Newt Gingrich] to quit insulting the pro-family
and pro-moral community with his words and his actions. . . . I would
strongly recommend to all Republican leaders that they abandon the
use of the phrases 'Big Tent' and 'Litmus Tests.' These terms are only
trotted out when the beliefs of conservatives are about to be trampled."

In Washington, recalled Paul Weyrich, House Republicans "were
scared to death. I had a dozen members calling me and saying, 'What
could we do? How do we keep this guy?' Because he has enough of a
following that if he said 'A pox on both your houses, I'm going to go
with an independent,' he could tube a lot of Republicans. So they knew
at that point that they had to pay attention. They didn't have any

choice." There was little doubt that the 1996 election, when the socially moderate Bob Dole had watched evangelical turnout drop 6 percentage points from 1992, was still fresh in Republican minds—particularly as the 1998 midterm elections closed in.

The GOP wasn't facing just external pressure on social issues. The Republican Revolution had swept a wave of religious conservatives into the House, including Kansas's Sam Brownback and Oklahoma's Tom Coburn, both later elected to the Senate. These true believers had grown frustrated with Speaker Gingrich, a small-government conservative who was more interested in racking up victories on the House floor than in spilling blood in the culture war. "Leadership at that time was interested in winning, and if you didn't win, they didn't want to have the battle," said Coburn, who served in the House until 2000 and was elected to the Senate in 2004. "I had a different philosophy: that you don't always have to win, but you can't *not* fight for what you believe. You look through history and you see people who stood the high moral ground by continuing to lose until the public was awakened to the truth of what they were saying. The battle [in 1998] was not can you win or not; it was about whether or not the Republicans were fighting. Fighting and losing has value. Not fighting has no value."

Taking heat from outside pressure groups and from a growing segment of the Republican caucus, the top House Republican brass, including Gingrich, Majority Leader Dick Armey, and Majority Whip Tom DeLay, announced that a "values summit" would take place in Washington in May 1998. Held in one of the more ornate chambers of the Library of Congress, the meeting had a guest list that was a who's who of evangelical conservatives. Led by Dobson, it also included newly appointed Christian Coalition executive director Randy Tate, the Southern Baptist Convention's Richard Land, and officials from Concerned Women for America. "Newt came in and he was going to calm everybody down," remembered a House aide who attended the summit. "Dr. Dobson was blowing up, and Newt was saying, 'This is hard work! You're telling me to cut this, but you have a very difficult process to do that.'" Still, Gingrich emerged from the summit sounding enthusiastic about moving the religious conservatives' agenda forward. "On almost every major issue," he said at the press conference afterward, "the people who are meeting represent the vast majority of Americans."

Even as some activists suspected that Gingrich and company were giving lip service to their cause, the summit marked a turning point in the Christian Right's relationship with the Republican Party. "It was the first time that something like that had ever been done, where virtually all the key leaders in Congress sat down and talked to us in somewhat sequential order," said evangelical activist Michael Farris. "There were so many people that stayed all day, like Tom DeLay. It was the biggest deal up until that time, a coming of age." The era of conservative evangelical leaders rallying their troops to the polls on Election Day only to be brushed aside by Republicans during the legislative process appeared to be coming to an end. And the tension between the GOP and the Christian Right, which Ralph Reed's departure from Christian Coalition had laid bare, looked to be easing.

Of course, the GOP knew that appeasement was impossible. If white evangelicals constituted the biggest demographic chunk of the Republican vote on Election Day, they were nonetheless a minority within the GOP coalition, whose libertarian and pro-business wings feared the prospect of government regulation of morality. "Within the Republican Party, there is a fairly narrow band which defines our comfort zone, and it's the fiscal issues set," said Mark Rodgers, staff director for the Senate Republican Conference and an evangelical Christian. "It's either probusiness policy or more efficient government policy, less taxes, and social conservatives tend to agree with that issue set. What is *uncommon* to that issue set is the culture war items."

Because Dobson could care less about the Republican "issue set," his legislative program had made little progress. In the late nineties, for example, one of Dobson's top priorities was abolishing the National Endowment for the Arts, long loathed by conservatives for funding projects they deemed obscene or antireligious. Though there had been talk in Republican circles of zeroing out funding going back to 1994, the NEA was still up and running in 1998. "The problem was that moderate Republicans [in Congress] were coming under pressure from their constituents to keep NEA funding, because this was the perfect ladies garden club–type issue," said Mike Schwartz, chief of staff to then congressman Tom Coburn. But Capitol Hill offices were not hearing from social conservative activists who wanted the NEA dead. And even if they had, attempting to bulldoze an agency with widespread Democratic and moderate Republican support was a losing battle. Evangelical leaders "were looking at the wrong priorities, it seemed to us as insiders," said Schwartz. "And the [Republican] leadership was not getting its message effectively to its base."

In fact, it seemed to the GOP that the Christian Right's other big problem—besides setting unrealistic goals—was that it had no means of effectively communicating and coordinating with congressional Republicans. Despite unleashing the occasional torrent of phone calls to Congress, Dobson and other evangelical activists tended to package their public policy goals as threats shouted from press conference lecterns. "They had no way of taking the message to the Hill," said a top Republican congressional aide. "So [Republicans] said, 'We're going to try to move conservative legislation, but we need your help. You can't just stand at the podium and tell us to do stuff—you have to figure out how the legislative process works and you have to work the grassroots and you have to work the votes.'"

To make that happen, House Majority Whip Tom DeLay contacted Mike Schwartz, the chief of staff to Congressman Coburn, around the time of the May 1998 values summit. Before arriving in Congress, Schwartz was a conservative activist who acted as a kind of sidekick to Paul Weyrich during his weekly strategy sessions for Washington's conservative culture warriors. DeLay wanted Schwartz to replicate these weekly meetings inside the House of Representatives, opening an official and permanent communications channel between dozens of Religious Right groups and Republican lawmakers. "We said [to outside groups], 'We'll introduce this stuff and we'll bring this bill to the floor,'" remembered Schwartz, "'but the part that the outside groups provide is the support and the muscle to make it happen—and if either side fails it's not going to work.'"

Christened the Values Action Team, or VAT, the forum allowed socially conservative congressmen to leverage the huge mailing lists of outside groups like the Family Research Council in lobbying wavering fellow members on key votes. "I'll say [to the outside groups], 'Who will do letters?' 'Who will do radio shows?' 'Who will contact these members?' and we strategize about tactics," said Pennsylvania congressman Joe Pitts, the son of Christian missionaries, who has chaired the House VAT since its inception. "Working together we can be much more effective. In politics, it's not always the wisest or the strongest who wins. It's the most persistent. The [outside groups] have to stay at it long term, and never, never go away. And if they work together and are persistent, they can advance their priorities."

In the wake of Christian Coalition's demise, VAT taught the Christian Right what it could realistically hope to accomplish in Washington, and gave it an appreciation for the Byzantine, glacially paced world of Congress. "Part of the problem was that, in the pro-family movement, they don't have the lobbying outfits like the National Association of Manufacturers or the Chamber of Commerce—you don't cash out [of a Capitol Hill job] to go to the Family Research Council or Focus [on the Family]," said a former top Republican Hill aide present at the formation of the Values Action Team. "They can't afford that kind of talent, so their work on the Hill is less politically sophisticated. And that's the role of VAT, to educate on what's possible, what's achievable."

With the rise of the Values Action Team, the Christian Right abandoned long-shot gambits such as eliminating the National Endowment for the Arts and pushing for a Right to Life Amendment to the Constitution. It adopted a more incremental approach to pursuing its agenda, such as helping move legislation that gradually endowed personhood on unborn fetuses as a way to slowly chip away at abortion rights. "It's a much more typical approach of how America deals with social issues," said Senator Sam Brownback, chairman of the Senate VAT, launched a few years after its House counterpart. "It's rare that there's big, revolutionary-type change. It's much more of an evolutionary type of process."

Rather than chafing at having to temper their expectations, Religious Right groups saw the creation of the VATs as a sign that they were finally being taken seriously. "Up until the Values Action Team process, meetings with religious leaders tended to be show-and-tell," said Gary Bauer, president of the Family Research Council from 1989 to 1999. "You brought them into the White House or up to the Hill and you ask somebody to pray and you shared a few things on your heart and then everybody hugs each other and leaves. It's quite a contrast to meetings with the business community, where business lobbyists will walk in and say, 'Look, my Fortune 500 company has to see this happen.'

"The VAT ended up being a serious place," Bauer continued, "where instead of culturally stroking folks, you actually talked about real legislation and what could or couldn't be done. And the religious groups have to come into the room with more than just what's on their heart. They have to come into the room with real things they can bring to the table: 'We can turn out five hundred thousand phone calls in forty-eight hours, Congressman, if you're willing to bring that bill to the floor.' And outside groups get a venue to say [to lawmakers], 'Look, you need to understand that there's real nervousness at the base right now and you need to show some progress because it's getting really hard to hold people in line and to keep enthusiasm up.'"

The House and Senate Values Action Teams host a meeting with dozens of Religious Right groups each week Congress is in session, but it was clear from the beginning that the Family Research Council enjoyed a privileged status. In addition to the weekly VAT coalition meetings, FRC sponsors a private weekly lunch with staff from the House and Senate teams. Closely allied with Focus on the Family, FRC had been the Christian Right's primary hard-line rival to Christian Coalition in the 1990s, becoming the movement's premiere Washington lobbying shop after Ralph Reed left the Coalition.

FRC hadn't always occupied a lofty perch. Founded by James Dobson and a handful of other religious conservatives in 1983, the organization had three staffers and a two-hundred-thousand-dollar budget when Bauer, a Reagan domestic policy adviser, was installed as president in 1989. FRC was folded into Focus on the Family that same year, partly because it was in such poor financial shape. Focus's board of directors was initially skeptical of Bauer. Like Ralph Reed, he is an evangelical Christian but is known in Washington as a brass tacks partisan rather than as a religious figure. Bauer persevered, in part, by selling Dobson on his vision for transforming the Family Research Council into an advocacy powerhouse by using Dobson's radio show as a national platform for mobilizing in-the-pews evangelicals.

When he arrived at FRC, Bauer recalled, it "was a sort of sleepy little think tank operation that occasionally put out Heritage [Foundation]-like papers on family policy issues. Dr. Dobson had not really given it the kind of mass visibility that you need for a start-up like that in Washington. So very early after I came on board, Jim found many opportunities to put me on the radio show. We would give out the mailing address and in pretty quick order we built a fairly significant mailing list. . . . My view was that there were lots of individuals sitting in these churches who were frustrated that the country was continuing to move in a particular direction, that there was drift in the culture, and that all we had to do was let them know we existed, that we would fight in Washington for their values. If we could get that message out through Jim's show, we could build a pretty large mailing list of twenty-five- and thirty-dollar donors."

Bauer's plan worked. By 1992 the Family Research Council broke off from Focus on the Family to regain its stand-alone status. Even with

Clinton in the White House, the FRC managed a number of successes: helping thwart the president's plan to lift the ban on gays in the military, seeing passage of the five-hundred-dollar-per-child tax credit and, in 1996, the Defense of Marriage Act, the federal gay marriage ban. The more Bauer appeared on Dobson's daily *Focus on the Family* radio show, the higher it lifted FRC's profile. "There were frequent episodes [on Dobson's show] where we gave the Hill's switchboard number, and it would literally shut down the Capitol Hill phone system," Bauer recalled. "So early on, when members [of Congress] would get to their offices and all the phones are lit up and their staffers are looking harried and [the congressman is] like 'What in the world is going on?' and the staff says, 'Dr. Dobson says you voted the wrong way on this bill,' that leaves a lasting impression pretty darn quick."

In the mid-1990s, two wealthy Michigan families—including that of Amway cofounder Richard DeVos—financed the construction of the six-story Family Research Council headquarters in downtown Washington at an estimated cost of five to ten million dollars. By the time Gary Bauer resigned as FRC president in 1999 to run for United States president—after failing to convince Dobson to throw his hat in the ring—the Family Research Council had a fourteen-million-dollar budget, 120 staffers, and a mailing list of nearly half a million people. Only the evangelical group Concerned Women for America, founded by Beverly LaHaye, wife of Tim Lahaye, approached FRC in terms of budget, profile, and influence.

Throughout the 1990s, Bauer scheduled appointments for Dobson with lawmakers, congressional aides, and beltway opinion-shapers on his Washington visits. But Dobson seemed content to concentrate on Focus on the Family and leave the lobbying to his D.C. surrogate. "[Dobson] felt this might be a way to help him avoid having to be here more frequently," Bauer recalled.

Dobson's 1998 trip to Washington had been a fateful exception. And with the election of George W. Bush in 2000, the House still in Republican hands, and an evenly split Senate, the Christian Right was poised to reap the benefits of the groundwork that Dobson's '98 campaign had laid. The Values Action Teams now provided a forum for direct communication and cooperation with Republicans in Congress. And the GOP had gotten the message that its evangelical base would no longer abide being treated as the party's red-headed stepchild. It all made for a great sense of expectation.

Then September 11 happened. The war in Afghanistan and the buildup to the invasion of Iraq distracted Republican lawmakers from the Christian Right's agenda. And yet, just after the 2002 midterm elections, the GOP managed to find the time to reward the big business interests that had bankrolled that year's election gains, which included gaining control of the Senate. After a five-year lobbying campaign that ran into the tens of millions of dollars, banking industry leaders got word from the House Republican leadership that it was finally scheduling the vote they'd been pushing for. It was for a bill that would make it much more difficult for Americans to file for bankruptcy to avoid paying debts, representing the most sweeping overhaul of the nation's bankruptcy laws in more than two decades. Bill Clinton had vetoed similar legislation, but President Bush had pledged his support.

There was only one snag. New York Democratic senator Charles Schumer had attached an amendment to the bill that blocked pro-life activists who violated abortion clinic access laws from entering bankruptcy to duck court-ordered damages or fines. It was the kind of Capitol Hill maneuver that a few years earlier might have slipped under the Religious Right's radar. But the eagle-eyed Values Action Team was on constant patrol on Capitol Hill. House VAT chairman Joe Pitts and a handful of his VAT colleagues resolved to challenge the Republican leadership, which was bent on passing bankruptcy reform. "We were caught between our friends on one side in the business community and our friends on the other side [in the Religious Right] and the leadership just really pounded us to go along, to take a loss for the pro-life community," Pitts recalled. "There were just two or three of us who were willing to go against the leaders, who were really, really vigorous in their position. I'm putting it politely. . . . The leadership was working tremendously to pass this. . . . So [VAT] created handouts about exactly what the issue was. We worked the members on the floor. We worked the doors. If it hadn't been for the VAT members, these outside groups would have gotten rolled."

Tipped off about the Schumer amendment by Pitts, the Family Research Council and Focus on the Family sprang into action. "Some conservative friends in town said, 'We're going to leave that one alone,'" recalled chief FRC lobbyist Connie Mackey. "We said absolutely not. Leave a bunch of grandmothers with signs out in front of an abortion clinic more liable than the union guys? We took it on, and leadership wasn't wanting us to and were quite surprised that we were willing to weigh in." Dobson urged his radio listeners to call the House Republican leadership, including then majority Whip Tom DeLay, in opposition. "Dobson gave out the numbers of DeLay and the Speaker [of the House] and their phones shut down," recalled a top Republican House aide. "Dobson said it was those people who are responsible for putting the bill to the floor and you should call them and express your outrage. There was this comeback [from GOP leadership] of 'Why are you doing this?' Dobson was flexing his muscle. . . . That was the first time DeLay had put something on the floor where members had been forced to choose between the social and fiscal conservatives. It was ugly."

The banking industry was shocked as it watched Democrats who opposed the bankruptcy bill on its merits join with pro-life Republicans to defeat it on a procedural vote. "I can't recall a single piece of legislation our industry worked so hard on to have it go down in defeat," said the president of the National Retail Federation at the time.[10] Dobson was so incensed that the bankruptcy bill had been scheduled for a vote in the first place that he didn't speak with DeLay again for two more years.[11] "That was social conservatives defeating the House leadership and the White House," said a source close to FRC. "It was a pivotal moment. From then on, [Republican leadership] was much more sensitive to getting our opinion before moving a bill."

It took almost three more years for Congress to pass and President Bush to sign the bankruptcy bill—without the Schumer amendment.

Flash forward to 2003: When the White House announced it would spend fifteen billion dollars to fight AIDS in Africa and the Caribbean, putting a more humanitarian face on American foreign policy, the Christian Right was in the loop. Before reaching the president's desk, the spending bill would have to clear the House and Senate. "The Republican leadership [in Congress] was of the mind to get something through and have a signing ceremony," said one FRC source. "But the same crowd that defeated the bankruptcy bill the year before was now making noise about the global AIDS bill. [Leadership] said, 'Okay, what are your concerns? Let's see if we can deal with this *before* it gets to the floor.' "

Christian conservatives have traditionally frowned on AIDS relief efforts because they say such programs often condone homosexuality and sex outside of marriage. After the White House announcement, FRC lobbyist Connie Mackey raised concerns about the legislation becoming what Dobson called "a big windfall for Planned Parenthood and condom distributors."[12] Through VAT meetings on Capitol Hill, she coordinated a push for a handful of amendments that would ensure the money went to programs compatible with the conservative Christian agenda. An amendment sponsored by VAT chairman Joe Pitts earmarked a full third of the money for abstinence-only education, even as many AIDS experts objected. Mackey and the FRC also promoted amendments that would ensure that AIDS relief groups working with prostitutes would be ineligible for funding, and that religious groups that rejected condom distribution wouldn't be denied funds. In Washington to make preparations for the National Day of Prayer, James Dobson, Franklin Graham, Chuck Colson, and Cardinal Theodore McCarrick of the Washington, D.C., Roman Catholic diocese all personally lobbied for the amendments at the White House and on Capitol

Hill.[13] All three passed. "It was a very close vote in the Senate," remembered Senator Sam Brownback. "We would not have gotten it without the VAT group."

Bush's speech at the signing ceremony for international AIDS relief legislation brimmed with evangelical and pro-life language, calling the effort a "great mission of rescue" and affirming that "We believe in the value and dignity of every human life."[14]

Congressional votes scheduled under pressure from the VAT teams also ushered in the first federal curbs on abortion rights since *Roe v. Wade*. The Born-Alive Infants Protection Act, passed in 2002, endowed a fetus born after a failed abortion procedure with certain rights. The ban on the procedure opponents call partial birth abortion passed Congress in 2003, and though it was quickly struck down by federal courts, appeals to those decisions were granted review by the Supreme Court in early 2006. President Bush signed both bills into law, along with 2004's Unborn Victims of Violence Act, which made an assault on a pregnant woman two separate crimes.

While the passage of such laws marked true milestones in the history of the pro-life movement, they were mostly symbolic. Stronger antiabortion legislation, like the Unborn Child Pain Awareness Act, which would require doctors to offer anesthesia for the fetus of a woman who is seeking an abortion and is more than twenty weeks pregnant, hadn't been passed by the House or the Senate by late 2006. Neither had a human cloning ban, championed by the Christian Right and passed by the House in earlier sessions. The Child Custody Protection Act, which makes it a crime to transport minors across state lines to circumvent parental consent laws on abortion, had passed the House in 2005 and the Senate in 2006, but died because differences between the bills could not be resolved. And during his 2006 State of the Union speech President Bush made no mention of the proposed constitutional amendment to ban same-sex marriage, which became the Christian Right's top priority after Massachusetts started offering marriage certificates to gay couples in spring 2004.

Indeed, even following widespread recognition of the role so-called values voters played in the 2004 election, the Christian Right was feeling as marginalized as ever as the 2006 midterm elections approached. "There's a lot of frustration," said Family Research Council lobbyist Tom McClusky. "We feel like through those so-called values voters, we brought more influence and more pro-family senators to the table and helped reelect the president. Dr. Dobson going around doing these rallies before the election [was] highly influential, and a number of people are still waiting for a payoff. . . . I don't know if Washington has gotten it yet. It's a frustration that we're fighting to keep the status quo. We can't even increase fines on indecency on the airwaves, something that Congress voted overwhelmingly for, the president says he'll sign, the FCC says they want, yet we have nothing."

Christian Right leaders began grousing publicly about the inaction in spring 2006. Dobson came to Washington to meet with Karl Rove and the House and Senate majority leaders and told FOX News that Republicans were "just ignoring those that put them in office. . . . [T]here's going to be some trouble down the road if they don't get on the ball." The complaints spurred Congress to pass higher fines for broadcast indecency. Around the same time, the Senate held a vote on a constitutional amendment to ban gay marriage, with President Bush delivering a televised speech endorsing it. Otherwise, though, Bush did nothing to build support for the amendment in the Senate or the public, rankling evangelical activists. In a Focus on the Family interview taping with White House Press Secretary Tony Snow shortly before the president's speech, Dobson's frustration was palpable. "Is he working the Hill, is he calling?" Dobson asked Snow about the president. When Snow responded that he didn't know, Dobson pounced. "That's unfortunate," he snapped, "because when Lyndon Johnson wanted the civil rights legislation, he didn't have the votes . . . and he made it happen. . . . [H]e used the bully pulpit to make it happen. President Bush has not done that yet."

Why did the Christian Right continue to see relatively little legislative progress despite its considerable political gain, even before Democrats reclaimed control of Congress in November 2006? The Senate, with a handful of moderate and pro–abortion rights Republicans and rules that require sixty votes to break a filibuster in order to bring proposed legislation up for a vote, had emerged as a roadblock. Senate Values Action Team chairman Sam Brownback has been seen as less effective than his House counterpart because his presidential ambitions make his colleagues suspicious of his motives.

Perhaps more important, the GOP knows that enactment of the conservative evangelical agenda continually threatens to scare off the big business wing of the party, along with swing voters and libertarians. Some Republicans blamed their 2006 midterm losses on the party's strategy of playing to its base rather than reaching out to moderates. "The issue of gay marriage is a lot harder as an issue to suggest to be on the Senate Republican agenda because it's controversial in the culture war," said Mark Rodgers, staff director for the Senate Republican Conference. "It's a lot easier to suggest reducing the tax burden on the family, making sure we have a strong defense. Even within our party, there is a discomfort at a certain level with the cultural stuff being definitional. . . . Look at what we actually did on the floor [in 2005]. It's class action and bankruptcy reform. We've done very little on the floor that is in the nature of these cultural issues. The irony is that what you hear from the business community is the Republican Party is *only* defined by those issues. I mean, good grief, it's the Supreme Court and judges and Terri Schiavo."

—ɯ—

The Terri Schiavo ordeal, and the extraordinary congressional intervention it provoked, had everything to do with timing. The episode came to a head just over four months after Election Day 2004, when evangelical and other religious voters were credited with delivering victory to

George W. Bush and with helping Republicans pick up seats in the House and Senate. Evangelicals had constituted the same portion of the electorate as in 2000, about 25 percent, but had turned out in higher numbers than in any presidential election for which statistics are available. White evangelicals supplied two of every five Bush votes and generally supported Republicans up and down the ticket. The media had created a new demographic category to describe them—values voters—and the GOP was intent on keeping them satisfied. Senate Majority Leader Bill Frist, a Presbyterian, was eyeing a 2008 presidential run and looking for opportunities to prove himself to the GOP's evangelical base. House Majority Leader Tom DeLay was fighting accusations of corruption in Washington and in his home state of Texas. He knew the Christian Right provided one of his last reserves of loyal support.

But by spring 2005, James Dobson and other Religious Right leaders were already griping over White House inaction in pressing for a constitutional amendment to ban gay marriage.

A perfect storm was brewing.

And yet, had it not been for a handful of activists associated with James Dobson's national network, particularly current and former officials at the Family Research Council, Congress might have never intervened in the Schiavo affair. The case illustrates the remarkable power of those advocates to leverage the clout of tens of millions of evangelical and other religious Americans in prodding Washington to take historic action, even as the constituency those advocates purported to represent opposed congressional intervention by wide margins. But the Schiavo affair also showed the cost of victory. It was another example of the Christian Right's agenda being subverted by activists and lawmakers for the sake of symbolic action. The Schiavo legislation was crafted on behalf of a single woman and ultimately failed to affect even her plight. And the episode triggered a backlash in American public opinion toward Republican leaders and toward the Christian Right.

Since going into cardiac arrest in 1990 at the age of thirty-six, Terri

Schiavo, of St. Petersburg, Florida, had been comatose and kept alive
by feeding and oxygen tubes. Terri's husband, Michael Schiavo, attempted to get a court order authorizing the removal of her feeding
tube in 1998, saying she wouldn't want to continue living in her condition. That set off a bitter legal dispute between him and Terri's parents.
After five years of litigation, and a long string of court rulings that sided
with Michael Schiavo and denied appeals from Terri's parents, Florida
governor Jeb Bush signed "Terri's Law" in fall 2003. The law allowed
him to grant a onetime stay in certain cases before state courts. When
Michael Schiavo challenged its constitutionality, Governor Bush hired
a Washington-based attorney to defend "Terri's Law."

The attorney was Ken Connor, who had succeeded Gary Bauer as
president of the Family Research Council and had recently left the organization after a rocky three-year tenure. Connor was an accomplished trial lawyer and a former Florida gubernatorial candidate, but
the state supreme court unanimously declared "Terri's Law" unconstitutional in fall 2004. Connor, who lives on a Virginia horse farm outside Washington, D.C., decided he would try to bring Schiavo's case to
the nation's capital.

In February 2005, Connor placed an op-ed piece in *The Washington Times* assailing Florida's courts for denying the appeals of Terri
Schiavo's parents. He said the state courts had abdicated their historical
role as protectors of the rights of the weak. Noting that the Florida
Supreme Court's rejection of his appeal fell on the thirty-second anniversary of the *Roe v. Wade* decision, Connor drew a parallel: that "any
time 'personhood' is withdrawn from a human being, legal protections
are eroded."[15]

By the time the op-ed column appeared, Terri Schiavo's case had
been a cause célèbre in the pro-life community for years. Her brother
was featured as an honored guest at a rally for Catholics at 2004's Republican National Convention.[16] Pro-life activists had embraced Schiavo as a way to show that the movement was about more than stopping
abortion. She provided a human face for promoting a "sanctity of life"

over a "quality of life" approach to death and dying. But up until that point, the case had been viewed as a Florida matter, even within the pro-life universe. In Washington, "you couldn't get arrested with a story about Terri Schiavo—no one cared," said Colin Stewart, who had been executive vice president of the Family Research Council under Ken Connor and had recently taken a position with a new advocacy group Connor had started. The group was called the Center for a Just Society, and its mission was expanding the conservative Christian agenda beyond fighting abortion and same-sex marriage. It saw the Schiavo case as a golden opportunity.

A day after Connor's op-ed piece ran in The Washington Times, Florida congressman Dave Weldon, a Republican and a former physician, phoned him to discuss what he might do to help. In a matter of days, Connor was in Weldon's office, helping draft the Incapacitated Persons Legal Protection Act. The bill would grant federal appeals power and an independent counsel to Schiavo and others who were unable to speak for themselves.[17] Connor also contacted recently elected Florida senator Mel Martinez, who had been Connor's roommate at law school. Martinez agreed to introduce the legislation in the Senate in early March.

Time was running out. A Florida judge had ordered Schiavo's feeding tube to be removed on Friday, March 18. On the Wednesday before that, the House of Representatives passed a bill similar to Weldon's bill—providing federal court review for certain state court cases involving incapacitated persons—by unanimous consent, then adjourned the next day for a two-week Easter recess. In the Senate, a memo from Martinez's office called the bill "a great political issue" because Florida senator Bill Nelson, a Democrat up for reelection in 2006, had declined to be a cosponsor and because "the pro-life base will be excited."[18] But Senate Majority Leader Frist, unable to rush the broad House bill through the Senate, had his staff craft a "private relief" bill that applied solely to Terri Schiavo, allowing her parents to lift the case out of the state courts, where dozens of decisions had sided against them, and into the federal judiciary. The bill passed on Thursday, the day before Terri Schiavo's feeding tube was to be removed. The Senate adjourned for Easter break later that same day.

Connor and the group of Family Research Council alums who comprised his Center for a Just Society were incensed. As the clock was running out for Terri Schiavo, the House and Senate had passed irreconcilable bills that would leave her to die, then quickly closed up shop for Easter. Connor's political instincts told him that Republicans in the House and Senate would use the fact that both chambers had technically passed relief bills to claim credit for doing everything possible to keep Schiavo alive. Once again, the Christian Right would be suckered by the very lawmakers it had worked so hard to elect.

Figuring that was the case, Ken Connor called a lobbyist he knew at the Family Research Council just before the Senate passed its private relief act on Thursday, March 17. According to a top FRC source, who requested anonymity, Connor said, "Look—do you know anybody in [House Majority Leader Tom] DeLay's office? They're all going to go home, and the Senate is ready to vote." So the FRC lobbyist drove to the Willard Hotel in downtown Washington, where the Family Research Council was hosting a banquet as part of its annual meeting of top donors and activists. With the FRC's top leadership tied up at the event, the official raced to the Family Research Council headquarters and phoned DeLay's office. The official told DeLay's staff that the House leader should take the extraordinary step of reconvening the House—even though House members had begun leaving town—to pass the Senate's private relief bill for Terri Schiavo. There was no way, the FRC official said, that the broader House bill could be jammed through the Senate. The failure to reconvene the House, the FRC lobbyist told DeLay's staff, would be "something we will not forget."

Just before ten o'clock that Thursday night, DeLay's office announced plans to issue a subpoena for Terri Schiavo to testify before Congress. In theory, the subpoena would prevent the removal of her feeding tube the following day. But the Center for a Just Society's Connor and Stewart, along with the FRC lobbyist, rejected the plan as a Band-Aid approach. Trading on the credibility and influence they'd built while at the Family Research Council, Connor and Stewart pressed DeLay's office to reconvene the House to pass the Senate bill. But the staff wouldn't budge. "The turning point was a conversation with staffers in Congressman DeLay's office in which we rigorously made the argument that the [Republican] base would hold the Republican House leadership responsible," said Stewart. "They would not blame the Senate Democrats [for refusing to pass the House version of the bill]. The Republican leadership were the people who could fix this problem."

After midnight, DeLay's office sent word to the Center for a Just Society and FRC that he wouldn't leave Washington without reaching a solution. It sounded as if he might be open to reconvening the House.

The next morning, the day Schiavo's feeding was to be removed, Connor showed up at the Willard Hotel to brief the Family Research Council's annual meeting on the Schiavo case. Connor was merciless in his assessment of the job Republicans were doing on Capitol Hill. He compared the House Republican leadership to arsonists who had set a fire in failing to pass the Schiavo private relief bill and now, by promising to do everything possible to keep Schiavo alive, were trying to take credit for making a valiant attempt to extinguish it. Speaking to an audience of about 250, including the leaders of Focus on the Family's state-based Family Policy Councils, Connor urged all present to telephone DeLay's office immediately and turn up the pressure. "Principle plus prayer plus pressure equals progress," he told them.

Roughly one hour later, Tom DeLay himself walked into the Willard Hotel. He had not been previously scheduled to appear at the FRC event. "One thing that God has brought to us is Terri Schiavo, to elevate the visibility of what's going on in America," DeLay told the same audience that Connor had addressed, "that Americans would be so barbaric as to pull a feeding tube out of a person that is lucid and starve them to death for two weeks. . . . We have to do everything that is in our power to save Terri Schiavo and anybody else that may be in this kind of position."[19]

Vowing to remain in Washington until Schiavo's case was resolved, DeLay connected Terri Schiavo's plight to his own political struggles. At the time, DeLay was the subject of an investigation by a Texas prosecutor that by year's end would result in a criminal indictment on money laundering and conspiracy charges in connection with a fund-raising scheme. His name also continued to surface in connection with federal investigations into ties between lawmakers and disgraced former lobbyist Jack Abramoff. He would step down from his post as House majority leader and announce his resignation from Congress the following year. At the time, though, he was fighting for his political life. He compared what he called the campaign against Terri Schiavo to what he said was a liberal campaign to destroy his own career—and the whole conservative movement. "This is exactly the issue that's going on in America, of attacks against the conservative movement, against me and against many others . . . ," DeLay told the crowd at the Willard Hotel. "The other side has figured out how to win and defeat the conservative movement, and that is to go after people personally, charge them with frivolous charges. . . ."

DeLay's speech culminated in a denunciation of the 1954 law that prohibited tax-exempt organizations like churches from making political endorsements. The House leader claimed that the law and the liberal campaign against him were both part of the same organized effort to muzzle Christian voices. "It forces Christians back into the church," DeLay said, "and that's what's going on in America: 'The world is too bad, I'm going to go get inside this building and I'm not going to play in the world.' That's not what Christ asked us to do. . . . We have to fight back."

The next day, a Saturday, DeLay and others in the Republican leadership announced they were reconvening the U.S. House of Representatives to vote on a private relief bill that the Senate was expected to pass on Sunday and that closely resembled the Senate's earlier Schiavo bill.

They called the plan the "Palm Sunday Compromise." Barred from reconvening before Monday by parliamentary rules, the House was to vote just after midnight on Sunday. The bill passed 203 to 58, with broad Republican support and with the Democrats about evenly split, though only half returned to Washington for the vote. President Bush, who'd flown back a day early from his vacation in Crawford, Texas, signed it shortly after one o'clock Monday morning. When a federal district court and a federal appeals court ruled in favor of Michael Schiavo, and the U.S. Supreme Court declined to hear the case, Terri Schiavo's feeding tube remained disconnected. She died on March 31.

In the eyes of the American public, Schiavo's death did nothing to vindicate the congressional intervention into her case, or the Christian activists who pushed for it. Evangelicals, fundamentalists, and conservative Catholics who were interested in the case found it difficult to keep up with the lighting-fast developments in Washington, and they were just as shocked as the rest of the country by the congressional action. "This was not a case where the House switchboard was shut down by the grassroots," said former FRC president Gary Bauer. An ABC News poll in the days following the congressional intervention found that just 44 percent of evangelicals supported the move, and that only 38 percent of Catholics did. Critics dismissed the survey by alleging that it asked loaded questions. But a poll conducted by the Pew Forum on Religion & Public Life four months later found that 69 percent of white evangelicals, 68 percent of conservatives, and 65 percent of Republicans thought Congress should have stayed out of the matter.

As the poll numbers came in, Republicans grew nervous about the perception that they had kowtowed to Christian Right extremists. "The White House has been very smart about crafting a social and moral agenda that wouldn't put off swing voters, through partial-birth abortion and faith-based initiatives," said GOP pollster Tony Fabrizio at the time. "Now the question [for swing voters] becomes, 'What are these guys really about?'" According to Paul Weyrich, a close monitor of Congress, Republican senators were so upset over the performance of

Senate Majority Leader Bill Frist, a heart and lung transplant surgeon
who had publicly questioned whether Terri Schiavo was really in what
doctors call a "persistent vegetative state," that they would have ousted
him as leader if he hadn't already announced plans to retire from the
Senate in 2006. A few months later, Frist, widely expected to make a
presidential run in 2008, distanced himself from the Christian Right in
announcing support for federal funding of expanded embryonic stem
cell research. The move drew a sharp rebuke from James Dobson, who
compared stem cell research to experiments conducted by the Nazis.

In Terri Schiavo's aftermath, there were predictions that the public
backlash to the Christian Right would spell the movement's demise.
Some political observers saw the dramatic Republican losses of 2006 as
confirmation of that theory. Such forecasts seemed to discount the
number of times the movement's epitaph has already been written—
after Moral Majority folded in the late eighties and following Ralph
Reed's departure from Christian Coalition in the nineties, to take the
two most obvious examples—only for it to come back stronger than before. (In the case of 2006's GOP losses, exit polls showed that white
evangelicals and other "values" voters constituted the same share of the
electorate as in 2004, but that many were simply punishing Republican
incumbents for their party's ethics scandals.) They also seemed to ignore the sheer number of white American evangelicals—roughly seventy million, or about a quarter of the U.S. population—and the extent
to which the community and the narrower Christian Right movement
have been integrated into the Republican Party. In Congress, the House
Values Action Team, which had fewer than a dozen Republican members when it started in 1998, counted about seventy by 2006, accounting for roughly one in every six members of Congress. Former Speaker
of the House Dennis Hastert, and former House Majority Leader Tom
DeLay, along with current House Republican whip Roy Blunt, are all
conservative evangelical Christians. So are Mitch McConnell and
Trent Lott, the number one and two Republicans in the Senate. (Ohio

representative John Boehner, reelected House Republican leader in November 2006, is Catholic but is not considered a religious conservative.) Jim Guth, a religion and politics expert at South Carolina's Furman University, has estimated that by the late 1990s, one in three Republican members of the House was an evangelical, up from about one in five in the mid-1980s. Over the same time period, evangelical Democrats saw their numbers decline in the House, from around one in four to one in ten. Evangelicals and other religious conservatives are filling more and more top Republican staff positions in Congress, including those in most leadership offices.

Little wonder, then, that while the Christian Right is perpetually frustrated by the slow pace with which its agenda is enacted in Washington, the movement is unquestionably meeting with much greater success than it did in the eighties or nineties. In the 1990s, religious conservatives in the House of Representatives complained that the Republican leadership would schedule votes for legislation only when victory was assured, keeping divisive culture war bills off the House floor. But until last year's Democratic takeover, GOP leadership in both chambers had gotten in the habit of pushing for votes on hot-button legislation it knew would lose, as part of a long-term strategy for victory and, in the interim, to reap political benefits. The repeated votes for a constitutional amendment banning gay marriage are the most obvious example. "Since I was elected to the Senate in '96, there has been an enormous shift," said Senator Brownback, an evangelical Christian who converted to Catholicism in 2002. "Those [hot-button] topics, it used to be you could hardly bring them up in the caucus without getting a lot of bad stares. Now they regularly appear on the core agenda."

The arc of Ralph Reed's career, from Christian Coalition executive director to top official in the Bush-Cheney 2004 campaign to 2006 candidate for lieutenant governor in Georgia, is a case study in the Christian Right's absorption into the GOP. "By working within the party and encouraging people to become leaders and candidates and legislative staff within the party, we're light-years ahead of where we were twenty

years ago," said Reed, who, plagued by his ties to lobbyist Jack
Abramoff, lost his July 2006 Republican primary race in Georgia.
"You've got Mike Gerson [a conservative evangelical] as chief speechwriter for the president of the United States. You've got people who are
chiefs of staff to leadership in both houses of Congress. You've got a
Wheaton College graduate [Dennis Hastert] as Speaker of the House.
It's irrefutable that working within the party and helping to advance a
pro-family majority has not only been successful but has been a historic
achievement on a par and scale with anything any social reform movement has ever achieved."

That evangelical and fundamentalist Christians generally frowned
on political activism until as recently as the 1970s makes that achievement all the more striking. "My grandparents and parents were not ter-
ribly engaged in politics," said South Dakota senator John Thune, an
evangelical Christian elected in 2004. "They voted and did their civic
responsibility, but it was never a subject at the kitchen table. There was
a perception in evangelical Christian circles that politics was sort of this
slimy, secular vocation, and you let somebody else do that. It wasn't
something you dabbled in."

Of course, the election of George W. Bush, a self-described born-
again Christian, has taken the integration of evangelicals into the GOP
to a new level. The role of Bush's personal faith and that of others in his
administration in shaping policy, from the Food and Drug Administration's decision to delay approval of over-the-counter "Plan B" contraception, to Bush's vision for spreading democracy around the globe and
his decision to invade Iraq, to his selection of Supreme Court appointments, has been one of the biggest sources of controversy in his presidency. The subject will not be examined at length here, though the
Christian Right's role in Bush's reelection, in lobbying the White
House to back a constitutional amendment banning gay marriage, and
in the Bush administration's promotion of its Supreme Court nominees
are examined at length in the following chapters.

It will be noted that the Bush White House has appeared to have

ripped a page from Ralph Reed's Christian Coalition playbook in marketing its religiously inspired policies as "compassionate conservatism,"
a term coined by an evangelical Bush adviser. Just as Reed worked to expand the Christian Right's issue set beyond issues of sexuality in an effort to mainstream the movement and give it more leverage in pushing
for controversial hot-button policies, the Bush White House has packaged its faith-based initiative as the softer face of social conservatism. After legislation failed in Congress that would have provided church and
religious-based charities with easier access to federal funds, Bush issued
executive orders early in his first term that set up faith-based offices in
ten federal agencies.[20] By the end of 2005, the program had distributed
more than three billion dollars to religious charities aiding prisoners,
drug addicts, the poor, and other vulnerable segments of the population. (It has also funneled tens of millions to conservative evangelical
organizations led by prominent Bush supporters, like Pat Robertson,
which oppose abortion rights and promote abstinence-only education.)[21] Bush's work in pressuring the United Nations to do more to
combat human trafficking, his advocacy on behalf of stopping genocide
in Sudan, while criticized as too little too late by many activists, and his
signing of the Prison Rape Elimination Act in 2003 were all developments for which evangelical Christians lobbied and which were framed
by the White House as examples of compassionate conservatism in
action.

Bush has also moved on issues important to hard-line social conservatives, appointing staunch conservatives to the federal judiciary; refusing to allow increased federal funding for expanded embryonic stem
cell research; imposing the so-called Mexico City Policy, which pro-
hibits family planning centers abroad that receive U.S. funds from providing or promoting abortion; and increasing funds for abstinence-only
education. He has also signed into law the abortion-related legislation
mentioned earlier in the chapter.

But as evangelicals have risen to the upper echelons of the government, many have grown frustrated with what they consider the outsized

expectations of Christian Right leaders. It's the same way Republicans felt toward the movement during James Dobson's 1998 crusade. "Outsider evangelicals attribute lack of total victory with lack of courage," said a top Republican Hill aide who is an evangelical Christian. "[Evangelicals] who are here know how Washington works, and they can be most influential as opposed to being in Colorado Springs questioning those in Washington." Some inside-the-beltway social conservatives complain that the Christian Right has come to see Washington as the solution to social problems, just as big-government liberals do. "We have to understand something which I preach all the time but nobody seems to get: Politics follows culture, not the reverse," said Paul Weyrich. "People thought that by electing enough conservative Republicans . . . you would be able to affect the culture, but you'll never be able to do it, because every time you get to a point that's close, the culture overwhelms things. We are losing the culture war more than ever, and unless we affect the culture we will never get anything of substance accomplished in politics."

Maybe so, but it hasn't stopped a handful of training programs for young evangelicals planning to pursue careers in politics and public policy from springing up in the last decade. The Family Research Council's Witherspoon Fellowship, founded in 1997, may be the most prestigious. Accepting roughly fourteen students each semester, the FRC provides housing, an eighteen-hundred-dollar stipend, and weekly seminars and field trips, along with in-house internships for each student. It intends to nearly double the size of the Witherspoon Fellowship in coming years, expecting to graduate more than three thousand students by 2025. FRC wants it to become the conservative Christian equivalent of the famed Heritage Foundation summer internship program, which pays twenty-five hundred dollars and boasts a cushy on-site dorm, along with famed alumni like *National Review* editor Rich Lowry. By the end of 2006, there will be nearly 350 alumni, with about four in ten graduates of the program landing public policy jobs.

Similar programs keep sprouting up. In 2000, evangelical activist Michael Farris opened Patrick Henry College, the first undergraduate institution to focus specifically on training home-schooled evangelicals for careers in government and politics. Located in Purcellville, Virginia, an hour's car ride from Washington, Patrick Henry's students major in government, journalism, or liberal arts, while interning at the White House and in more than a dozen congressional offices. By 2010 the college is expected to have produced more than three hundred graduates. In numbers not previously seen, evangelical and fundamentalist Christians are transitioning from lobbying Washington's policymakers to becoming them. It helps explain why, in the nearly ten years that have transpired since his 1998 trip to Washington to discipline Republican lawmakers, James Dobson hasn't felt the need for a repeat performance. And why, even after Dobson is gone—and regardless of the fate of Focus on the Family—the evangelical and fundamentalist influence on Washington is likely to keep growing.

6

Dobson's D-Day

"It's the hardest thing in the world to do.
It would be easier to elect a president than
to amend the Constitution. . . ."

—m—

The Terri Schiavo affair was a new high-water mark for the Christian Right. Never had the White House and Congress moved so quickly and transparently to satisfy the movement, and on an issue as unpopular with a broad majority of the American people.

Less than two years earlier, though, some of the Christian Right's leading lights feared that the air had gone out of their movement again.

It was summer 2003, a full twenty-five years after Paul Weyrich's earliest success in enlisting evangelical and fundamentalist Christians in a political crusade. On the surface, everything seemed fine. Evangelicals and fundamentalists were actually meeting with considerable success in Washington, particularly on antiabortion rights legislation.

Having the Values Action Teams in Congress, the House and Senate in Republican hands, and the most openly evangelical president in memory in the White House were developments the movement had fought for, and they were savoring the benefits, even as activists griped that progress was still too slow. The problem was that such success had a downside: With Bill Clinton's polices and sexual indiscretions no longer providing fodder for fund-raising letters and with the GOP in control of Washington, in-the-pews religious conservatives had grown complacent. Evangelical advocacy groups saw their revenue and membership lists flatline. For the first time in its twenty-six-year history, Focus on the Family announced cutbacks, laying off thirty-six employees, mothballing an additional sixty unfilled positions, and trimming twelve and a half million dollars from its budget.[1]

The malaise helped provoke American Family Association founder Don Wildmon, best known for spearheading boycotts against companies supportive of gay rights, to convene a June 2003 meeting of about a dozen high-profile Christian conservatives in Arlington, Virginia, just across the Potomac River from Washington. The group met in an apartment complex that was home to Sandy Rios, president of the evangelical group Concerned Women for America.[2]

As chance would have it, James Dobson had stepped down from the presidency of Focus on the Family, a perch he'd occupied since launching the ministry in 1977, just a few weeks earlier. After a few false starts in the preceding years, Dobson had finally jumped ship in May 2003, partly with an eye to stepping up his political activism. For the first time in Focus's history, he was unencumbered by the demands of managing the sprawling organization's day-to-day operations. He could also worry a bit less about running afoul of IRS restrictions on political advocacy by nonprofit groups, even as he retained the title of Focus chairman and continued hosting its daily flagship radio program, *Focus on the Family*. For Don Wildmon, meanwhile, having Dobson attend his June summit in Arlington gave it instant gravitas, ensuring that the Christian Right's most prominent leaders would show up. Actually, Wildmon would have preferred that Dobson host it. "Nobody knows Don Wildmon," Wildmon said in an interview. "Everybody knows Jim."

"To be honest with you," another of the summit's attendees said, "I think people came because Dobson was there."

The first topic to surface among the Christian Right leaders in Arlington was what to do about the proposed amendment to the U.S. Constitution that would ban same-sex marriage. At that point, the existence of such an amendment had received little national attention. Most Americans had never heard of it. But a small band of conservative scholars had been asserting for years that U.S. courts were quietly but inextricably moving toward the legalization of gay unions. Wildmon's summit attendees viewed the prospect of gay marriage not only as a genuine threat, but also as a likely catalyst for rousing the evangelical grassroots from their slumber. Besides viewing homosexual activity as sinful, evangelical and fundamentalist Christians believe the marriage of one man and one woman is an institution ordained by God in the Book of Genesis. The expectation that gay marriage would be legalized by judges rather than by elected lawmakers could be counted on to stoke the antipathy many evangelicals and fundamentalists had long felt toward the judiciary, over rulings that legalized abortion and outlawed school prayer. In the process, the activists in Arlington knew, their own ailing organizations stood to be revived. By the end of the meeting, the group resolved to focus exclusively on the question of how to stop gay marriage before it began.

But if the attempt to pass a constitutional ban on gay marriage held the promise of reinvigorating the Christian Right, much as the successful effort to kill the Equal Rights Amendment had in the late seventies and early eighties, it also threatened to drive a huge wedge through the movement. A good number of Christian Right activists opposed the amendment strategy because of the huge outlays of time and resources such a campaign would require. Many suspected that such a project would ultimately fail, as had the long crusade for a Right to Life

Amendment. Instead, they backed more practical strategies to stop gay marriage, like prodding Congress to strip courts of jurisdiction in gay marriage cases and redoubling efforts to get the most conservative judges appointed to the judiciary. Conservative Catholic activists, meanwhile, worried that an amendment push would distract from the fight to limit abortion rights, an issue much closer to their hearts than stopping gay marriage.

A conservative family feud over a constitutional amendment was brewing, and it would divide even the sprawling organizational empire that Dobson had spent decades constructing. The Family Research Council, Focus on the Family's Washington proxy, would zealously oppose the amendment at first, even though the chief architect of the campaign to pass it was an alumnus of Focus's Family Policy Council network. Such early fissures suggested that the amendment threatened to totally splinter the Christian Right at a moment when it had already fallen on hard times. On the other hand, a unified campaign to pursue a constitutional amendment banning same-sex marriage could not only revive the Christian Right, but also unite its key advocacy groups as never before. A political cause of such magnitude, and the sides it would require parties and politicians to take, held the potential to influence future elections, including presidential contests. Whether it would bring ruin or rebirth, the movement had a choice to make: to amend or not to amend. And no one would have more influence in shaping the decision than James Dobson.

The campaign for a constitutional amendment barring same-sex marriage really began in the 1990s, after a court in Hawaii ruled that denying homosexuals the right to marry was discriminatory under the state's constitution. The ruling drove Hawaiian voters to amend the state constitution to ban same-sex marriage through a 1998 ballot initiative. It also inspired a handful of conservative scholars to begin meeting at Washington, D.C.'s Ethics and Public Policy Center—a conservative think tank whose mission is "to clarify and reinforce the bond between the Judeo-Christian moral tradition and the public debate over domestic and foreign policy issues"—to draft an amendment to the U.S. Constitution that would ban gay marriage. The group included Princeton's Robert George, one of the country's most prominent conservative legal scholars, failed Supreme Court nominee Robert Bork, and law professors from Harvard and Notre Dame. "People involved in those early discussions thought same-sex marriage in the courts was going to happen soon," George recalled in an interview. "But we had a lot of trouble convincing other people to take it seriously. It seemed too distant and unlikely. And politicians weren't going to cross that bridge until they'd come to it."

But the Ethics and Public Policy Center group had no trouble convincing a young lawyer named Matt Daniels, who in the late 1990s was serving as president of the Massachusetts Family Institute, to take the prospect of same-sex marriage seriously. The Massachusetts Family Institute is one of Focus on the Family's Family Policy Councils, the state-level organizations that lobby legislatures to enact a Christian Right agenda. Like many executives employed by Focus and its affiliated organizations, Daniels came from a broken home. He was abandoned by his father at the age of two. His mother later suffered a broken back, lost her job, and fell into alcoholism. When Daniels returned home to New York City after college to care for her, he began volunteering in shelters and soup kitchens run by black churches. The experience led him to become a born-again Christian.[3]

While heading the Massachusetts Family Institute, Daniels was also pursuing a Ph.D. in politics. His specialty was the U.S. courts, and his dissertation research convinced him that liberal scholars were building a legal case for same-sex marriage. Though the passage of 1996's federal Defense of Marriage Act and dozens of state-level Defense of Marriage Acts would seem to preclude such a scenario, Daniels was sure that it was only a matter of time before activist courts began striking down such laws. Based in part on studies he was commissioning through the Massachusetts Family Institute on the harms of raising kids in fatherless homes, Daniels was convinced that legalized gay unions would deal a fatal blow to the family.[4] Though still in its infancy, scientific research on the subject has shown that children with same-sex parents often develop different views of gender roles than other children, but that they do not exhibit the troubling or risky behavior associated with children of single-parent families. But Daniels was less concerned with the potential harm of gay couples raising kids than he was with the message that legalized gay marriage would send to heterosexual couples. If marriage were open to everyone and were seen to be an evolving institution, his thinking went, it would lose allure for straight people. More heterosexual couples would begin having children out of wedlock, destabilizing the family structure. "Kids do best with a mom and a dad," Daniels said in an interview. "That's not a statement of animosity toward anyone. It's an affirmation of a social norm." He thought the norm would be undone sooner rather than later.

In 1999, around the time he met with the scholars affiliated with the Ethics and Public Policy Center, Daniels relocated to Washington and launched a group called Alliance for Marriage. In its first year of existence, Alliance for Marriage promoted welfare reforms to provide incentives for marriage and tax credits for couples that adopted children. Then, in 2001, the group introduced what quickly became known as the Federal Marriage Amendment, or FMA, an amendment to the U.S. Constitution to ban gay marriage. Daniels became Washington's chief amendment advocate. The text of the amendment was shaped not only by scholars, but also by a group of congressional aides that Daniels had convened to assess what kind of amendment could reasonably be expected to be passed by Congress. At first, his quixotic campaign received little attention. Five years later, a top Republican Senate aide would marvel at Daniels's ability to "see around corners and into the future."

As he built support for the FMA, Daniels was careful to avoid giving the impression that his was a Christian Right campaign. In assembling Alliance for Marriage's board of advisers, he enlisted an ecumenical

group of clergy, along with civil rights movement leader Walter Fauntroy and law professors from Ivy League universities. He crafted a
positive-sounding sales pitch built around promoting traditional marriage rather than denigrating homosexuality. As Don Wildmon, James
Dobson, and other Christian Right leaders convened in Arlington, Virginia, in spring 2003 to discuss how to wake up in-the-pews evangelicals
and fundamentalists, Daniels was predicting that the movement would
be revived only after some court somewhere legalized gay marriage. "I
don't think the bomb has gone off yet," he told a reporter. "It will go off
and go off soon. It's the marriage bomb."[5]

Like many right-wing activists and organizations at the time, the Family
Research Council was alarmed by the Federal Marriage Amendment.
Not long after arriving in September 2000 to replace Gary Bauer, who'd
left to run for president, new FRC president Ken Connor ordered a
handful of executive staffers to send him their analyses of the FMA. He
synthesized their findings into a ten-page position paper issued in May
2002, entitled "Why the Family Research Council Cannot Endorse the
Proposed 'Federal Marriage Amendment.'" The memo began defen-
sively, asserting that the Family Research Council viewed the prospect
of same-sex marriage as a real threat. "Literally thousands of years of legal, moral, and religious tradition will be thrown on the trash heap," it
read, "if 'gay marriage' or its counterfeits—'civil unions' or 'domestic
partnerships'—gain legal recognition in a growing number of America's
towns, cities, and states."

But Ken Connor's memo charged that the FMA protected only the
semantic definition of marriage. To be sure, the amendment clearly
prohibited state and federal courts from interpreting the U.S. Constitution, state constitutions, or state or federal law to require marital status
or the "legal incidents thereof" to be conferred upon same-sex couples
or other groups. But Connor said it left state legislatures free to enact
Vermont-like civil unions, domestic partnerships, and other legal
arrangements for gay couples.

Some of the amendment's drafters, including the scholars affiliated with the Ethics and Public Policy Center, argued that it actually did prohibit state legislatures from assigning legal rights to couples based on a conjugal relationship. But that was almost beside the point. The scholars were all but certain that legalized gay marriage and civil unions would come via the courts, as they had in Vermont in 2000. They felt that any attempt to straitjacket state legislatures, in addition to meeting with strong resistance from states' rights advocates, was unnecessary as a practical matter. "If, in the long run, people are opposed to the conjugal concept of marriage, then the courts are not going to save you," said Princeton's Robert George, one of the amendment's authors. "We should have to make our case to our fellow citizens and let the chips fall where they may. It wasn't just a matter of insulating marriage. . . . It should be the fruit of democratic deliberations, and not the deliberations of the courts."

Matt Daniels, for his part, believed the amendment clearly left state legislatures free to confer benefits on gay couples outside of marriage. In fact, he insisted on it. He argued that language that stripped legislatures of such power would never survive the rigorous amendment ratification process. In order to pass, constitutional amendments require two-thirds support in the House and Senate and approval by three quarters of the states, via state legislatures or state conventions. "Our starting point was viability," Daniels said. "An amendment that would strip states of legislative authority over benefits would be a good fundraiser, but it would result in defeat."

In its ten-page memo, the Family Research Council proposed an alternative Federal Marriage Amendment that would go further than Matt Daniels's version. It would not only bar the courts from legalizing civil unions, domestic partnerships, and similar arrangements for gay couples, but would also prevent state legislatures from doing so. Beyond attacking Daniels's particular version of the amendment, however, the FRC's memo noted that history showed the amendment game in general to be a losing one. "The long effort to amend the Constitution to protect unborn human life has thus far been unsuccessful," it read. "This experience should serve as a caution flag for any who believe that a proposed amendment will be a panacea for the protection of marriage."

In an interview after he'd left FRC, Connor was more emphatic. "Two thousand constitutional amendments have been proposed and we have twenty-seven on the books," he said. "So we're going to invest years of efforts, millions of dollars, and all you're protecting is the definition of marriage and not the institution? Then some state legislature is going to come along and pass civil unions, and all the people that worked for years and spent millions, they're going to say, 'But I thought we had a silver bullet.'"

To Connor, Daniels's version of the amendment had no guts, and a version that did could never muster enough support for ratification. Connor thought the Christian Right would do better to press for the appointment and confirmation of conservative judges and to pressure Congress into using its constitutionally granted power to limit the jurisdiction of the courts. Otherwise, Connor thought, congressional Republicans were being permitted to bewail the "runaway judiciary" while washing their hands of responsibility. A bill proposed by Representative John Hostettler, an Indiana Republican, to strip the federal courts of their jurisdiction on same-sex marriage cases would go on to pass the House in summer 2004. While highly controversial, the bill hewed closer to the incremental approach that the Christian Right had adopted toward enacting its agenda since the birth of the House Values Action Team in the late 1990s. The amendment route, meanwhile, was clearly a reversion to the movement's pre–Christian Coalition tactics, when it shot for the moon and risked accomplishing nothing.

Still, the pro-amendment forces saw the Hostettler bill as a Band-Aid that was likely to be found unconstitutional. An amendment was the only foolproof way to preclude the courts from legalizing same-sex marriage.

But Connor had another reason to doubt the scheme. He suspected that the GOP, smelling an opportunity to champion an amendment that would appeal to its evangelical base without having any real shot at passing, was using the Christian Right for political gain, as it had so many times before. Connor said that he and Matt Daniels attended meetings with the House Values Action Team in which some Republican lawmakers said, "We don't care about the issue, we just want to get the Democrats on the board on this." "The political types didn't care about it other than its utility for the upcoming election," Connor recalled. "I was concerned they'd manipulate us."

James Dobson, meanwhile—who if not technically Connor's boss nonetheless held tremendous sway over the FRC—was standing squarely behind the Federal Marriage Amendment. Six months after the FRC released its May 2002 memo opposing Matt Daniels's effort, Dobson invited Daniels onto his show and encouraged his listeners to call Congress in support of the FMA. Apart from believing that the Bible proscribes gay marriage and homosexuality generally, Dobson was convinced that legalized same-sex marriage was a ruse by gay activists whose ultimate goal was wiping out marriage entirely. "[M]ost gays and lesbians do not want to marry each other," he wrote in a 2003 Focus on the Family newsletter. "That would entangle them in all sorts of legal constraints. Who needs a lifetime commitment to one person? . . . the legalization of homosexual marriage is for gay activists merely a stepping-stone on the road to eliminating *all* societal restrictions on marriage and sexuality." The victims of this homosexual plot, in Dobson's view, would be the children who'd grow up with two moms or two dads, or in an ever-changing multiple-parent arrangement that he predicted would be the inevitable result of legalizing gay unions. Nothing less than the survival of Western civilization was at stake, and its best hope, Dobson insisted, lay with the Federal Marriage Amendment. "This effort," he wrote in the newsletter, ". . . is our D-Day, or Gettysburg or Stalingrad."

Until that point, major rifts between Focus on the Family and the Family Research Council were all but unheard-of. Dobson had helped launch FRC and sat on its board of directors. According to Connor, Focus also controlled two additional FRC board seats. Focus saw FRC as its Washington embassy. To FRC, meanwhile, its ties to Dobson, Focus, and their vast constituency were what distinguished it from the Christian Right paper tigers that inhabited Washington. "I would try to stay in very close contact with [Dobson] on a day-to-day basis. . . . I didn't want him hearing reports that would throw him off as to what I was doing," said Gary Bauer, FRC president through the 1990s. "A disaster would be to go out and criticize a senator and then have Dr. Dobson say publicly, 'Well I don't know what Gary's doing here, we love what Senator So-and-So is doing.'"

With the split over the Federal Marriage Amendment, though, that disaster scenario was actually playing out. To paper over the rift, the Family Research Council's lobbyists tried to steer clear of the amendment issue entirely. "We basically adopted a 'don't ask, don't tell' policy," Connor recalled. When asked about the organization's official position by a congressional office or by a journalist, FRC's Capitol Hill lobbyists would produce its antiamendment memo, but, out of deference to Dobson and Focus, resisted actively lobbying against the amendment.

Dobson and Connor weren't the only ones divided over the amendment. While some congressional Republicans expressed early support for the amendment, many others thought it drastic and far-fetched. But a handful of Republican true believers in the Senate, including the offices of Majority Leader Bill Frist, Republican Conference chairman Rick Santorum, and Kansas senator Sam Brownback, actively worked to convince Christian Right groups that passing a constitutional amendment was feasible and worth fighting for. "There were a couple of well-placed people on the Hill who were encouraging the amendment and who were energizing Dobson," said a source close to the Family Research Council.

Their cause was helped by the Supreme Court's June 2003 *Lawrence v. Texas* decision, which struck down the few remaining state antisodomy laws. In his dissenting opinion, Antonin Scalia warned that the majority's "reasoning leaves on pretty shaky grounds state laws limiting marriage to opposite-sex couples." Within weeks, Frist announced his support for the FMA.

Momentum for the amendment was building, and the Family Research Council was standing in the way.

That was fine by Ken Connor. From the beginning of his tenure, Connor wanted to increase FRC's institutional strength and to establish its identity independent of Dobson and Focus. He set out to make FRC the "IBM of pro-family organizations." He saw Christian Coalition's implosion after Ralph Reed's departure as a lesson in the perils of the evangelical world's tendency to build organizations around charismatic leaders. But Connor failed to realize, before arriving in Washington, how closely FRC was linked to Focus and Dobson. "I viewed them more as sister organizations as opposed to a subsidiary of Focus on the Family," he said. "I was probably not nearly as aware of the history of the Family Research Council and its relationship [with Focus]. My exposure to Jim had been more in the arena of Christian family and less in the policy arena. . . . I had been on Jim's show and listened to his shows and read his books, so I didn't really associate him as much with the public policy dimension."

In early 2003, Connor suffered a near-deadly bout with pancreatitis that had him laid up in bed for months. According to FRC sources, his absence made it easier for Alliance for Marriage's Matt Daniels to lobby the FRC's board in support of the Federal Marriage Amendment. But some of its most powerful members, including Princeton's Robert George, who had become the FRC's first Catholic board member in 2001, and James Dobson himself, needed no convincing. The power struggle between Dobson, Focus, and the FRC's board on one side and Connor and the top FRC brass on the other ended in July 2003, when Ken Connor resigned.

—⁊⁊⁊—

In looking for a new Family Research Council president, James Dobson and FRC's board wanted to find someone who would not only abandon the organization's opposition to the Federal Marriage Amendment, but make supporting it FRC's top priority. In fact, they wanted someone who could turn the organization into the FMA's most powerful champion in Washington. Tony Perkins seemed like a providential choice.

Raised in an evangelical home, Perkins was a graduate of Jerry Falwell's Liberty University. After settling with his family in Baton Rouge, he'd been elected to Louisiana's state legislature in 1995. The day after his first term began, he sat down with two conservative advisers—a local judge and a Louisiana State University law professor—to discuss an important project: identifying a legislative goal that could advance the Christian Right's agenda but also help reverse the popular image of religious conservatives as bigots eager to legislate all the Old Testament's "Thou shall not" clauses. "What I was looking to do was to break with the stereotype of social conservatives and to go out and define what it was we were *for*, as opposed to being just against this and against that," Perkins said in an interview. "I thought, 'What's the most important thing we can do to have an impact on public policy?' And you know, marriage is most important."

At his meeting with the judge and the law professor, someone floated the idea of trying to repeal the state's no-fault divorce law. "I didn't like it because it was *against* divorce," Perkins recalled. Instead, the trio decided to draw up a bill that would introduce a new category of marriage in Louisiana that they would call "covenant marriage." The first of its kind in the nation, the covenant marriage law would attempt to strengthen the marriage bond by making it harder to enter into and get out of. The program would be strictly voluntary. Couples opting for a covenant marriage license would be required to attend premarital counseling with a therapist or a pastor. Once married, they'd need to separate for two full years and attend additional counseling before being granted a divorce. "I latched onto the covenant marriage idea because, number one, it was a choice—we weren't forcing anybody to do anything," Perkins said. "And number two, because it's all about being *for* marriage." For once, the Christian Right would have a cause that couldn't be described as *against* a type of behavior or a group of people, such as homosexuals.

In 1997, with Tony Perkins leading the way, Louisiana became the first state to legalize covenant marriage. Since then, it has been legalized in Arizona and Arkansas, though only a tiny fraction of the couples in states where it is available have opted for covenant marriages. Similar laws have been debated in more than a dozen state legislatures.

Perkins viewed covenant marriage as a way to give the Christian Right a kinder, gentler face, but he was also determined to combat Louisiana's gay rights movement. In 1997, as the Louisiana state legislature was debating a hate crimes bill that would increase punishments for attacks on gays—as well as for violence motivated by race, age, gender, or religion—Perkins introduced an amendment to change the definition of hate crimes to exclude sexual orientation. "I was on the floor of the [Louisiana] House arguing in favor of the amendment, and there was a full-time lobbyist paid for by the homosexuals," Perkins recalled. "He was pulling out legislators one by one to lobby them, and my amendment failed by one vote. There was not a single person there working on behalf of families. No Christian Coalition, nothing. So I determined that we needed a voice for families."

By that time, Perkins knew a thing or two about grassroots organizing. He'd hosted one of Louisiana's first Christian Coalition meetings in 1989. He'd become chairman of the Coalition's Baton Rouge chapter and was eventually offered a position leading the state chapter. But he'd turned it down. Rather than distribute voter scorecards and work to turn out evangelical voters on Election Day, Perkins wanted to open a permanent lobbying shop to advocate "pro-family" policies and to hold legislators accountable *after* Election Day. Focus on the Family, which had begun planting its Family Policy Councils in states across the country in the late 1980s, appeared to offer the perfect model.

Independently financed, and governed by their own boards of directors, the Family Policy Councils' ties to Focus on the Family and to

Dobson gave them instant legitimacy, particularly in the eyes of potential donors. "The Policy Councils were not overtly designed to replace the [Christian] Coalition, but the Coalition had been diminishing in Louisiana, and in many ways it had been marginalized," said Perkins. "I didn't feel like you could jump-start the Coalition again. This [Focus on the Family] model was much different, in that it had greater credibility. Dr. Dobson has a tremendous reputation and that carries so much weight and it opens doors. [To get donors to] make that kind of investment, it helps to have an organization like Focus behind it."

At the time Perkins was looking to launch his "pro-family" advocacy group, Focus's Family Policy Councils, or FPCs, had already begun to replace Christian Coalition chapters as the premier state-level Christian Right groups. Unlike the Coalition, a national organization governed by a top-down management structure, Focus's FPC network operated according to a free-market model, with each state council filling a distinct niche determined by local leadership. For instance, Alabama's FPC, the Alabama Policy Institute, is a think tank that has shaped state education policy and helped prevent the legalization of gambling there. Ohio's FPC, Citizens for Community Values, is an activist group that has focused on keeping strip clubs and adult bookstores out of Cincinnati. Tony Perkins's Louisiana FPC, the Louisiana Family Forum, would be closely allied with a network of conservative evangelical pastors. Rather than taking orders from Focus on the Family, FPCs tap Focus as needed, to raise funds or to collect signatures for a petition drive. "Christian Coalition changed at the top and everything underneath died," said Peter Brandt, Focus on the Family's senior director of public policy. "But Focus could go away and these state organizations would continue."

By the time many Family Policy Councils were getting off the ground in the mid-1990s, their leaders—including Tony Perkins—had already gained political experience through first- and second-generation Christian Right groups. So they were the most sophisticated activists the Christian Right had yet produced. "I'm not going to say that there is no idealism, because that would be wrong, but these people are really operatives," said a strategist familiar with White House thinking. ". . . They would be remarkable mechanics because they preoccupy themselves with how the engine is built. . . . The state [Family] Policy Councils know exactly what they're doing."

That certainly characterized the group Tony Perkins launched in 1998, after his failed attempt to eliminate protections against hate crimes for gays in Louisiana. In its first few years of existence, Louisiana's Family Policy Council helped pass a law requiring state-level executive departments to accompany policy proposals with "family impact statements," developed a Sunday school curriculum for training conservative activists, and helped institute Bible as History and Literature courses in public schools. During his years at the Family Policy Council, Perkins grew close to James Dobson. He appeared on Dobson's *Focus on the Family* radio broadcast to talk up covenant marriage and to discuss his opposition to gambling. When Perkins ran for the U.S. Senate in Louisiana as a Republican in 2002, Dobson issued an endorsement. In a crowded field of candidates, Perkins took just 10 percent of the vote, suggesting his limited appeal even in a state where more than one in five residents is a white evangelical.

But he seemed a perfect fit for the Family Research Council. Unlike Ken Connor before him, Perkins would arrive with an already close relationship with Dobson. His boyish good looks and polished speaking skills, honed in the Louisiana state legislature, on the campaign trail, and in the pulpit—Perkins is an ordained minister in a nondenominational evangelical church—promised to be good for media coverage. His rise from founder of Louisiana's Family Policy Council to his 2003 installation as Family Research Council president—like Matt Daniels's earlier jump from Massachusetts's Family Policy Council to founding Alliance for Marriage—would demonstrate how Focus on the Family's Family Policy Councils had become the new farm team for the Christian Right's national leadership. And Perkins, having just turned forty, had thus far defined his career on an issue that was now topmost in James Dobson's mind: marriage.

*   *   *

After Tony Perkins arrived at the Family Research Council in late summer 2003, supporting the marriage amendment shot to the top of the organization's priority list. "It turned into the main thrust of the organization," recalled Genevieve Wood, then vice president of communications for FRC. Colin Stewart, FRC's executive vice president at the time, said, "[Perkins] felt that for the next year, we'd be focusing on one issue and one issue only, the marriage amendment. It was not only one issue, it was the subset of the issue: the amendment." Some current and former FRC staffers said the change signaled Dobson's attempt to exert more control over the organization. "I felt more and more we were being a mouthpiece for Dobson, and Dobson was not in Washington, so our strings were being pulled by someone that was not politically astute," said someone close to FRC. "Tony was hired by Dobson and I think he felt that he had to answer to Dobson."

In an interview, Perkins insisted he was hired by FRC's full board, and that the marriage amendment was just one of many issues discussed during his job interviews. But Perkins also said that one of his top goals was bridging the gulf that had opened between the Family Research Council and Focus on the Family. "Under Ken [Connor], the two organizations got very separate," Perkins said. "We've been working to bring them back together."

In reality, the split between the Family Research Council and Focus persisted even after Perkins's arrival. Many FRC staff still felt that the amendment was a long shot and that it would protect only the semantic definition of marriage. "What will it take?" FRC's Alan Crippen, a vice president who left the group in 2005, remembered thinking about the amendment strategy. "Lots of money, lots of resources. The temptation will become for FRC to become a single-issue organization. From my perspective, Ken [Connor] looked pretty prescient." By that time, Vermont had been offering civil unions for more than three years. Other states and cities had introduced domestic partnerships that offered some of the same benefits as marriage. Many FRC officials felt that they were about to pour all their resources into a battle they'd already lost.

The amendment had also produced stress fractures between Catholics and evangelicals at the Family Research Council, whose staff is more denominationally diverse than the mostly evangelical Focus (FRC's board is overwhelmingly evangelical). Catholics active in the Christian Right have generally been motivated more by opposition to abortion rights than opposition to gay rights. Some Catholics joined the staffs of primarily evangelical outfits like the Family Research Council as an alternative to bureaucratic, Vatican-beholden groups like the U.S. Council of Catholic Bishops.

Conservative Catholics also tend to see the expansion of gay rights in Supreme Court decisions like 2003's *Lawrence v. Texas* as an outgrowth of the earlier Supreme Court decisions that first articulated a constitutional right to privacy with regard to access to contraception and abortion. In 1965, *Griswold v. Connecticut* struck down a state statute prohibiting the use of birth control on the basis of a marital right to privacy. In 1973, *Roe v. Wade* struck down antiabortion laws on the basis of a more general right to privacy. Conservative Catholics rejected both decisions, arguing that they invented a privacy right out of whole cloth. So conservative Catholics felt that fighting abortion rights would necessarily carry over into a fight against the gay rights movement. "Catholics were not as animated about the whole [marriage amendment] thing because there is a hierarchy of rights here," said someone close to FRC. "Catholics have a better appreciation of all things based on the right to life. *Lawrence v. Texas* was the result of *Roe* and *Griswold*, and I don't know if evangelicals appreciate that judicial consistency. If you want to stop *Lawrence* from happening, we need to attack the root."

Still, Tony Perkins's arrival at FRC cleared the way for getting Washington's most powerful evangelical advocacy group officially behind the Federal Marriage Amendment. But Dobson and his pro-amendment allies still faced opposition from within the Arlington Group, the name adopted by the coalition of powerful Christian Right activists who'd first gathered in Arlington, Virginia, in spring 2003. "I was probably the most adamant opponent of the FMA in the whole gang, opposed to it in substance and as a strategic move," said Mike Schwartz, who was then vice president of the powerful evangelical group Concerned Women for America and who attended the Arlington Group's early meetings. "It was one of the dumbest things I've ever seen my colleagues do. It's the hardest thing in the world to do. It would be easier to elect a president than to amend the Constitution, so why do you set a goal that high when you can win it by other means?

"While opposing it as strenuously as I could, I realized it would be even dumber to start a civil war over it," continued Schwartz, who became chief of staff to Oklahoma senator Tom Coburn after he was elected in 2004. "To a certain extent, I just stood by and said nonparticipation might be the best way. . . . I articulated that here's what [Concerned Women for America's] strategic position should be: We should not actively campaign against this in public; we keep our campaign against it in private, behind closed doors with our colleagues, so we get as few battle scars as possible."

After its inaugural June 2003 meeting, the Arlington Group continued to convene every six weeks or so in Washington. The meetings were intended to allow the major Christian Right groups who made up the coalition to quietly work out their differences away from the public eye. Early sessions were devoted to debate over whether to support an amendment at all or to pursue alternative strategies of stopping gay marriage; whether to support Matt Daniels's version of the amendment or to back a stricter version that outlawed civil unions and similar arrangements outright; and eventually, which allies on Capitol Hill and in the White House to lobby on the amendment and when.

As it continued to meet, the Arlington Group's membership grew from just over a dozen marquee activists to count representatives from about seventy Christian Right groups. Attendees came to include for-

mer Watergate convict and Prison Fellowship Ministries founder
Chuck Colson, National Association of Evangelicals president Ted
Haggard, and Ohio secretary of state J. Kenneth Blackwell, a conservative Christian who would run for governor in Ohio in 2006. The meetings were highly secretive, with no news media permitted and strict
bylaws forbidding participants to discuss Arlington Group proceedings
with the press. Its dull moniker notwithstanding, activists who participated in its early meetings immediately sensed that the Arlington
Group's formation represented a historic development for the Christian
Right. "It was the most effective coalition that I've ever seen," said
home-schooling advocate Michael Farris, who attended one or two
early Arlington Group meetings before backing out over his opposition
to the marriage amendment. "In terms of getting the principals there,
and the number and the breath of leaders, it was the biggest deal ever."

Before the Arlington Group began meeting, the universe of Religious Right organizations and activists was wracked by competition for
funds, media exposure, and government access. There was a fair
amount of suspicion and antagonism among the groups. "Many think
that the founding of Moral Majority and other such groups is part of a
vast right-wing conspiracy," former Moral Majority operative Ed Dobson (no relation to James Dobson) wrote in *Blinded by Might,* the book
he coauthored with Cal Thomas in 1999. "They think that people like
James Dobson, [Fort Lauderdale–based televangelist] James Kennedy,
Donald Wildmon, Jerry Falwell, and dozens of others get together on a
regular basis at some remote location as part of a secret society. . . .
Nothing could be further from the truth. Moral Majority was not the result of some high-level consultation between the power brokers of the
Religious Right. It was the idea of one man: Jerry Falwell."[6]

The Arlington Group, by contrast, *is* a secret society of the Religious Right's top power brokers, including Dobson, Wildmon, Falwell,
and Kennedy's top deputy, that meets on a regular basis.

The formation of the Arlington Group didn't vanquish the competition for resources among Christian Right groups, but it did permit the

movement's dozens of individual organizations to coordinate their efforts in an unprecedented way. For months, Arlington Group meetings were devoted largely to just getting the various groups comfortable with the idea of working with one another. To make the process less painful, the coalition resolved to operate strictly by consensus. All the groups that agreed with a certain course of action, such as lobbying a particular senator or congressman to back the FMA, could participate in the project. Coalition members that disagreed could simply sit it out. By working together, the groups could aggregate their constituencies into a block that represented tens of millions of people—as much as a fifth of the population—which could be mobilized to call Congress or to back certain candidates for office. The coalition allows "all the groups to reach their [individual constituencies] with a similar message, and then you turn on the single biggest voting block in the United States, and that's huge," said Don Hodel, who replaced Dobson as Focus on the Family president in 2003 and began attending Arlington Group meetings.

The White House took notice of its formation early on. "It's a group of heft because they represent real people," said a strategist familiar with White House thinking. ". . . You meet their constituencies and they are people who really read their [leaders'] materials and listen to what they say." It wasn't long before conservative Republican senators and congressmen were clamoring for a chance to address the Arlington Group.

From its very first meeting, it was clear that James Dobson occupied a unique position within the coalition. He sat on the Arlington Group's executive committee—along with Paul Weyrich, the Southern Baptist Convention's political chief Richard Land, and others—and was elected national chairman. And as the debate over whether to support the Federal Marriage Amendment and about how best to promote it wore on, Dobson's opinion carried more weight than anyone else's. "A lot of those people knew me from my Reagan days, and I had personal connections among conservatives in Washington, but I must say my clout was enhanced because now I was working with Dobson, who was a real power in the culture," said Hodel, the former Focus president, who'd served as energy secretary and interior secretary in the Reagan administration. "People would work very diligently to get [Dobson] to support their position because he offered a great deal of influence once he said, 'I'll support that.' He was the guy people would turn to. The feeling in the meetings was if Dobson supported something, you had a great deal of people supporting it and if he didn't, the people wouldn't support it either."

Some Arlington Group members felt that Dobson wielded too much power. "Dobson saw [the Arlington Group] as a vehicle to move his policies forward," said a source close to the Family Research Council. "He was the giant in the room. He was the one who people ceded the discussion to."

The Arlington Group also increased the power of Dobson's institutional network because the coalition is closely tied to the Family Research Council. The Arlington Group holds its meetings at Family Research Council headquarters, and FRC houses its two full-time staffers. Sources close to FRC said that it, along with Focus on the Family, also pays the lion's share of the staffers' salaries. By the end of 2004, the Family Research Council and the Arlington Group had grown so close that some FRC staffers felt as if the coalition was overtaking them. Around that time, FRC sources say, the Arlington Group adopted FRC's full list of legislative priorities as its own. "We were handcuffed a lot in making sure we were conforming to the policy of the Arlington Group," said a source close to FRC.

And yet, despite Dobson's sway inside the Arlington Group, its early meetings included opponents of the amendment strategy who were among the most powerful and respected figures in the Christian Right. One was Michael Farris, former Republican gubernatorial candidate in Virginia and founder of Patrick Henry College, the school for home-schooled evangelicals aspiring to careers in government and politics. Another was Concerned Women for America, which rivaled the Family Research Council as a Washington powerhouse. Both opposed the

Daniels amendment for protecting only the semantic definition of marriage. Still, Dobson was able to convince other skeptics that the amendment was worth fighting for. Short of Dobson's support, some Arlington
Group members said, the Daniels version of the Federal Marriage
Amendment wouldn't have survived the fierce opposition within the
Christian Right. "If it hadn't been for Dr. Dobson," said Schwartz, the
former vice president of Concerned Women for America, "the FMA
would have been discarded in the fall of 2003."

After nearly six months of internal debate, the Arlington Group decided
it would first push for a marriage amendment whose language went further than Daniels's, which had already been introduced in Congress.
The Arlington Group's amendment would bar state legislatures from
approving civil unions or domestic partnerships. Such language convinced Matt Daniels that the Arlington Group had been created with
the express purpose of drafting a rival Federal Marriage Amendment to
his own. In November 2003, Arlington Group members representing
about twenty Christian Right groups headed for the House of Representatives for a meeting with Colorado Republican Marilyn Musgrave.
The congresswoman had introduced Matt Daniels's amendment that
May (it had originally been introduced in the previous Congress by
Mississippi representative Ronnie Shows, a Democrat). Led by Sandy
Rios, then president of Concerned Women for America, the Arlington
Group pressured Musgrave to support a tougher version.[7] But Musgrave
was convinced that the more sweeping language would never muster
enough support for the required supermajorities in the House and Senate. She refused to budge. Pennsylvania Republican Joe Pitts, chairman
of the House Values Action Team, was also present. He reminded Arlington Group members that a Right to Life Amendment had failed after a decades-long campaign by Christian Right groups.[8]

At that point, some of the activists who'd insisted on a ban on civil
unions and domestic partnerships, including Michael Farris and leaders from Concerned Women for America, quit the Arlington Group. "I

don't care if you call it civil unions," Farris told *The New York Times*. "I
don't care if you call it domestic partnership. I don't care if you call it
cantaloupe soup, if you are legally spouses at the end of the day, I am
not willing to do that."[9]

But most Arlington Group members were convinced that the
Daniels amendment was worth fighting for, largely due to Dobson's influence. Around that time, in November 2003, the supreme court of
Massachusetts handed down a ruling that gave the state legislature six
months to legalize gay marriage. The decision put the Bay State on
course to become the first in the nation to offer same-sex marriage licenses. The pro-FMA forces who'd argued that legalized gay unions
would be a product of the courts rather than state legislatures—and that
a constitutional amendment therefore need not outlaw state legislatures
from legalizing civil unions and domestic partnerships—felt vindicated.
Dobson was among them. With the Massachusetts ruling, his once obscure cause was suddenly the object of massive media attention. A few
weeks later, the Daniels amendment was introduced in the Senate by
Colorado Republican Wayne Allard. Like Musgrave, the congresswoman who introduced the Daniels amendment in the House, Allard is
an evangelical Christian. In an interview, he said it was coincidence
that Focus on the Family is headquartered in his home state and that it
had no bearing on his being the amendment's chief sponsor. Musgrave,
who represents a northeastern Colorado district, declined requests for
an interview.

Following the Arlington Group's November meeting with Musgrave and the decision to proceed with the Daniels amendment, it was
time to start lobbying the White House. In the days leading up to President Bush's January 2004 State of the Union address, the Arlington
Group's most powerful members, including Dobson and the Southern
Baptist Convention's Richard Land, called White House political aide
Karl Rove. Their message: With the presidential election less than a
year away, evangelical voters needed a reason to go to the polls for
George W. Bush. Since the Massachusetts Supreme Court had ruled to

legalize gay marriage the previous November, the president had been deflecting questions from the news media about whether or not he supported the Federal Marriage Amendment. Bush kept saying that his lawyers were examining the matter and exploring all options. Then, in his 2004 State of the Union address, Bush said that "If judges insist on forcing their arbitrary will upon the people, the only alternative left to the people would be the constitutional process." The remarks prompted the Log Cabin Republicans, the most prominent gay Republican group in the country, to drop its support for Bush. But many Arlington Group members were also unhappy. Bush had been given a chance to clearly trumpet his support for the amendment before a national audience. Instead, he punted.

Over the next month, the Arlington Group set to tightening the screws on the White House. At one point, according to *The New York Times*, Arlington Group members huddled around a speakerphone as Richard Land grilled Rove on whether the president would publicly endorse the amendment—and if he would lobby as hard for it as he had the Medicare prescription drug benefit of 2003, an entitlement expansion that had rankled the GOP's conservative base. Rove assured them of the president's full support. He said Bush was just waiting for the right moment to make the announcement.[10]

The moment arrived quickly, in February 2004, when San Francisco began distributing marriage licenses to thousands of gay couples under the direction of Democratic mayor Gavin Newsom. A county in New Mexico quickly followed suit. "After more than two centuries of American jurisprudence, and millennia of human experience, a few judges and local authorities are presuming to change the most fundamental institution of civilization," Bush said in his televised five-minute address from the Roosevelt Room of the White House on February 24. "Their actions have created confusion on an issue that requires clarity." Bush's vow of support for the Federal Marriage Amendment soon became the most reliable applause line on the 2004 campaign trail. "I stand for marriage and family," Bush would say, "which are the foundations of our society." The language was vague, but everybody knew he was talking about the FMA.

—⁓—

Even as many Republicans played up their support for the marriage amendment on the 2004 campaign trail, the FMA didn't get very far in Congress. In a vote that fall, the House of Representatives backed it by a 227 to 186 vote, more than 60 short of the required two-thirds support. In the Senate, it got 48 votes, not even enough to cut off debate. Some Christian Right activists interpreted the timing of the votes, shortly before Election Day, as a sign that Republicans were more interested in using the amendment for political purposes than in building the necessary support to pass it, just as then Family Research Council president Ken Connor had warned more than two years earlier. "Congress sees it as a political issue," said Family Research Council lobbyist Tom McClusky. "If we're going to have a vote on it, let's vote on it every September, not just every September there's an election." Asked if he felt the Christian Right was being used, McClusky responded, "Well, that's the message it sends." Republicans defended the vote's timing as designed to produce the most favorable outcome, given that politicians would soon have to face voters.

In 2004, campaigning for the Federal Marriage Amendment helped reelect George W. Bush and helped the GOP widen its majorities in the House and Senate, an effort examined at length in the following chapter. But to some in the Christian Right, the 2004 election looked like a reprise of 1980, when Jerry Falwell worked tirelessly to deliver evangelical and fundamentalist votes to Ronald Reagan only to see little in the way of legislative rewards. After he was reelected, President Bush's enthusiasm for passing the marriage amendment quickly waned. "Part of this speaks to the virtue and innocence of Jim Dobson," said Mike Schwartz, the former official of Concerned Women for America who became chief of staff to Senator Tom Coburn. "I've been in and around politics for my whole career and he hasn't. . . . [H]e's really effective telling the truth to families on the radio but not as effective sometimes in telling it to politicians."

In June 2006, as conservatives grew more outspoken in their criticism of President Bush and Congress in advance of the midterm elections, the Senate held another vote on the amendment, rechristened the more benign-sounding Marriage Protection Amendment. It got just one more vote than in 2004. President Bush made a televised endorsement of the measure the day before the Senate began debating it, but conservative Christian activists grumbled that the White House had done little to build support for the amendment, either in the Senate or in the public. The president certainly invested nowhere near the personal capital he had in other controversial second-term priorities, like reforming Social Security and immigration. "If he truly believed the [gay marriage] threat is there, we are disappointed that he did not do more or even equal to what he did last time," said the FRC's Mc-Clusky. In 2004 the president had reportedly called some Republican senators who were uneasy about the measure, such as New Hampshire's Judd Gregg, and convinced them to support it. Conservatives said that Bush made no such calls in 2006, and Gregg declined to back the amendment.

Such failures left some leading religious conservatives more convinced than ever that a marriage amendment would never pass. "I told [Coburn] to endorse and cosponsor the Federal Marriage Amendment because his failure to do so would be misunderstood," said Mike Schwartz. "But it's not going anywhere. It's as dead as could be. But Dr. Coburn wants to be in the right place, and I said, 'The right place to be is as cosponsor of this because that lets the world know that we are in favor of defending the institution of marriage. And we're never going to have to cross any bridge beyond that.'" (Coburn said in an interview that he believes the amendment will eventually pass.)

Other amendment opponents within the Christian Right worried that the long-shot gambit squandered an unprecedented opportunity, with George W. Bush in the White House and Republican majorities in the House and Senate, to enact more of the agenda the movement had spent decades fighting for. Before endorsing the marriage amendment, said a source close to the Family Research Council, "The White House would give us something every couple of months to satisfy us, so we wouldn't go completely public against them." After the amendment push, the White House "didn't feel like they had to give us anything else . . ." the source continued. "It allowed the White House to define our issue. It distracted from some important things. This was the very moment when we had finally gotten some progress on the life issue. Many of us felt the momentum was lost to attending to marriage."

As was previously noted, the Christian Right celebrated passage of the first curbs on abortion rights since *Roe* during Bush's first term. The earliest victory was 2002's Born-Alive Infant Protection Act, which amended the legal definition of *person* to include a fetus that survives an abortion procedure; the fetus is then entitled to emergency medical care and other protections. The law was criticized by some doctors who said there was no evidence that surviving fetuses had been left to die and that the new law muddled the definition of a living person.[11] The law was essentially unenforced, however, under the tenure of Health and Human Services Secretary Tommy Thompson. "This was a tree falling in the forest that nobody ever heard about," said a source close to FRC. "For two years or more, we were asking the White House to enforce this, and they were not responding. When the marriage amendment came along, the pressure to regulate the law or to pass other legislation was off. . . . [The White House] felt we should be satisfied by marriage."

Thompson's successor at HHS, Mike Leavitt, sent guidelines on complying with the law to hospitals after his 2005 swearing in. But HHS still hasn't notified hospitals of the penalties for violators.[12]

There were other antiabortion rights victories before the FMA came along. In 2003 came President Bush's signature pro-life gesture:

signing the ban on the procedure critics call partial-birth abortion. The ban was struck down by federal judges in three states on the grounds that it didn't include an exception for when a woman's health is at risk, but the Supreme Court agreed to hear appeals in 2006. In early 2004, Bush signed the Unborn Victims of Violence Act, which made violence against a pregnant woman two separate crimes, even if the attacker is unaware of the pregnancy. It was nicknamed "Laci and Conner's Law," after the murdered California woman Laci Peterson and the son she was expecting.

While the three antiabortion laws of Bush's first term did virtually nothing to curb abortion rights, they did take real steps toward endowing fetuses with "personhood." But Christian Right activists hoped they presaged more substantial laws, like the Unborn Child Pain Awareness Act, which would require doctors to offer a woman seeking an abortion the option of administering anesthesia to her fetus if she is more than twenty weeks pregnant. Even NARAL Pro-Choice America announced that it would not oppose the bill. Though the Bush administration didn't block the measure, it didn't seriously lobby for it, and Congress has failed to pass it. Congress did pass the Child Custody Protection Act, which makes it a federal offense to transport minors across state borders to elude parental notification laws, in mid-2006. But that was because Republicans were nervous about their low poll numbers and desperate to rally their base before the midterm elections, not because of pressure from the president. In fact, the House and Senate versions of the bill were never reconciled, so it never arrived on the president's desk. "The major cost of the emphasis religious conservatives placed on the Federal Marriage Amendment in 2004 is that it's the only thing on their wish list that they got a commitment from President Bush on," said Mike Schwartz. "President Bush also gave them a commitment to constitutional judicial nominations, but that's not what Dobson and those folks demanded. They demanded endorsement of the Federal Marriage Amendment. They said, 'If you do that, we'll get our people to the polls.' And they could have asked for better things than that."

With Republican candidates and Arlington Group activists focusing more and more attention on the marriage amendment as Election Day 2004 approached, others in the Christian Right began worrying that the movement was pigeonholing itself. "It was obviously defining who we were as an organization," said Genevieve Wood, Family Research Council's vice president of communications from mid-2001 to late 2004. "But for me the concern was that it was becoming what the conservative movement was all about. The church has to be concerned about issues across the spectrum. I don't think Jesus Christ was a single-issue person, and I was concerned the movement was becoming known as a single-issue movement. There are definitely times you should focus on one issue more than another, depending on what's going on on the Hill, but this was more than a two-month or six-month thing. This was an everyday, all-day thing. We were putting all our energy and money toward it."

In mid-2004 the Family Research Council began sponsoring "Battle for Marriage" rallies to promote the marriage amendment. Staged at various megachurches on Sunday evenings, the events were syndicated live to hundreds of other churches nationwide and carried by Christian radio stations and cable networks. They featured James Dobson, Tony Perkins, Chuck Colson, and a rotating lineup of special guests, including videotaped messages from Senate Majority Leader Bill Frist and House Majority Leader Tom DeLay. Genevieve Wood, who had been a Republican National Committee spokeswoman and was a veteran media trainer, made the decision to quit FRC while attending the second "Battle for Marriage" rally, held at Bellevue Baptist Church in Memphis. "You had an issue like the homosexual marriage issue and it was being spoken from the pulpit," she said. "This was not a convention hall. This was a church, so would people struggling with [homosexuality] be comfortable in that church when there had just been a rally held there against their lifestyle? . . . Those types of events have the ability to come across as very harsh. I felt we were getting too much fire and brimstone and further and further away from the grace and the mercy. I'm not suggesting that Dobson or anybody else feels that way. But perception becomes reality."

*   *   *

If the Federal Marriage Amendment had stalled in Congress, alienated some major Christian Right advocacy groups and activists, and potentially sidetracked antiabortion rights legislation, it nonetheless solved the problem that had helped provoke Don Wildmon to convene the first Arlington Group meeting in spring 2003: It woke up evangelicals and fundamentalists at the grass roots in a way the Christian Right hadn't seen in a decade. From 2003 to 2004, Focus on the Family's annual revenue shot up more than $30 million, to nearly $147 million. Much of the jump was due to Focus on the Family Action, the political organization Dobson launched in spring 2004, which managed to collect nearly $9 million in contributions in its first six months of existence.

More significantly, the Federal Marriage Amendment provided a model for the successful efforts in thirteen states to pass state constitutional amendments banning gay marriage through ballot initiatives in 2004. The language of most state amendments went further than the federal amendment did, outlawing civil unions, domestic partnerships, and similar arrangements. Their passage marked a historic setback for the gay rights movement, unlikely to be undone for decades or longer. All but two of the efforts were led by Focus on the Family's Family Policy Councils.

Before passing the state marriage amendments, the Christian Right had developed a long record of landing antiabortion rights or anti–gay rights legislation on state ballots only to fail on Election Day.[13] The state amendments presented the movement with a tool to mobilize activists and actually win the popular vote. A decade earlier, Ralph Reed had implored the Christian Right to expand its issue set beyond curbing gay rights in order to find traction with the majority of Americans. But the amendments gave the movement a way to advance a narrow anti–gay rights agenda and still win broad support among mainstream voters. Even where the amendment fared worst, in Oregon—where it faced the most opposition from gay rights groups—it still carried 57 percent of the vote. In the South, the amendments passed by margins of up to six to one.

In Ohio, the presence of the amendment helped increase Republican turnout enough to hand the state, and therefore the national election, to George W. Bush. In the aftermath of the state amendment efforts, conservative Republican candidates across the country were given revitalized grassroots Christian Right movements to hitch their candidacies to. With Focus on the Family and their state-level Family Policy Councils again leading the way, eight more states voted on marriage amendment ballot initiatives in fall 2006. All but one passed. (Texas was the only state to pass a marriage amendment in 2005, an effort led by the state Family Policy Council.) The following chapter takes a closer look at how the Family Policy Councils are organizing the state efforts, and how the campaigns for the state amendments and the Federal Marriage Amendment have benefited Republican candidates, from the president on down.

If some Christian Right activists complained that the Federal Marriage Amendment provided yet another opportunity for the GOP to reap evangelical and fundamentalist votes without having to deliver legislative rewards, the amendment's backers were also sensitive to the risk. But the formation of the Arlington Group helped institutionalize a strategy that James Dobson had long championed: getting Republicans to pay attention by making them feel pain. Unlike Jerry Falwell or Ralph Reed before them, the Arlington Group's members would not be content with a seat at the Republican table. The Coalition's number-one priority was amending the Constitution, and they wouldn't let Republicans forget it. "Militancy for its own sake is no good—you don't accomplish anything and you look foolish," said Paul Weyrich, one of the Arlington Group's earliest members, describing the organization's strategy. "But militancy where there's a purpose and where by doing it you achieve something is an entirely different matter. The Arlington Group understands this. . . . We are an important element, and you either play ball or you're going to have a revolt on your hands. For the first time, these people [in the Arlington Group] are not saying, 'Well, you know, we have to be Republicans' and all that. They don't care."

So when President Bush appeared to downplay the impact of evangelicals at the polls and to reduce his enthusiasm for the Federal Marriage Amendment after Election Day 2004, the Arlington Group wasn't going to keep quiet. At his postelection press conference, Bush was asked about the apparently deep religious divide between red and blue America, particularly between evangelicals and the rest of the country. "I will be your president regardless of your faith," Bush said. ". . . . I appreciate all people who voted. I don't think you ought to read anything into the politics . . . about whether or not this nation will become a divided nation over religion." James Dobson read the remarks as a slight to evangelicals. "I think he made a mistake," he said in an interview two days after Election Day. "The president could have paused to thank all those good people who poured in and gave him power again. The GOP has been given four years to deliver on marriage and life and family, and if they fumble it . . . [we'll] stay home next time."

In the coming days, though, as President Bush outlined a bold second-term agenda, which included partially privatizing Social Security and overhauling the tax code, he was conspicuously mute on hot-button issues like the Federal Marriage Amendment. In an interview with *The Washington Post* a few days before his January 2005 inauguration, Bush suggested that, rather than use his bully pulpit to press Congress to pass the amendment, he'd hold off until a federal judge struck down the Defense of Marriage Act, the 1996 law that banned gay marriage.

That was the breaking point. Two days before President Bush's second inauguration in January 2005, the Arlington Group fired off an angry letter to Karl Rove. "We couldn't help but notice the contrast between how the President is approaching the difficult issue of Social Security privatization where public opinion is deeply divided and the marriage issue where public opinion is overwhelmingly on his side," it

read. ". . . When the Administration adopts a defeatist attitude on an issue that is at the top of our agenda it becomes impossible for us to unite
our movement on an issue such as Social Security privatization where
there are already deep misgivings."

Reminding Rove that Bush was reelected partly because of his support for the Federal Marriage Amendment, that thirteen states had overwhelmingly passed their own constitutional amendments banning
same-sex marriage the previous year, and that the Senate had gained a
handful of new votes for the amendment in the 2004 elections, the letter called for the appointment of a top-level White House official to coordinate the amendment push.

But the White House wasn't biting. The Arlington Group "had a
number of goals, and one of them was to have the president on board
and to make sure that his support was solid, and they have that," said a
strategist familiar with White House thinking at the end of 2005. "But
it's been a very, very momentous year and you have to make a determination as president of the United States as to when is the right time to
push and to speak, and when is the right time not to push and not to
speak, and right now the priority is very clear. The priority is seeing the
war through successfully, the strength of the economy, and the
[Supreme Court] nominations. We will get back to the marriage
amendment . . . at the right time. . . . A lot of these people have learned
from the Human Life Amendment. They saw what was possible and
what was not, and I think they have been more deliberate in that regard."

So the Arlington Group would have to be patient. After coordinating Christian Right support for the amendment, getting the White
House to back it, and helping to elect a handful of conservative Republican senators in 2004, there was little else its members could do before
Congress scheduled the next amendment vote. (Of course, the Arlington Group couldn't know then that the spring 2006 Senate vote for the
FMA would again fail to yield even a bare majority of supporters.) After
spending his first full year at the Family Research Council single-

mindedly promoting the amendment, president Tony Perkins prepared to devote 2005 to another big national issue: seeing that President Bush's conservative nominees to the federal bench got confirmation votes. Which meant that the Arlington Group would turn its attention to the same goal. Some Bush nominees had been held up by Senate Democrats for months, or even years. And word in Washington was that a string of Supreme Court vacancies wouldn't be too long in coming.

7

The Values Vote

"I call it the 'Passion Crowd. . . .' It was a
demographic group that was courted and
yearned for, just as soccer moms were in
2000 and NASCAR dads in 2002."

—⁂—

If not for Phil Burress's twenty-five-year addiction to porn, George
W. Bush might not be president.

The head of Focus on the Family's Ohio Family Policy Council,
Burress spearheaded an eleventh-hour campaign to put a state constitutional amendment banning same-sex marriage on Ohio's 2004 ballot,
driving up turnout among the conservative Republican voters who delivered Bush a razor-thin victory in the state. And because a Bush loss in
Ohio would have handed the White House to John Kerry, it's not hard
to see Burress as a linchpin in the president's reelection. His effort to

place the amendment on the ballot was such a long shot, and the stakes so high, that Burress keeps a sheaf of news clippings about the ordeal in his office. The one he calls his "trophy" is a *Boston Globe* story that ran shortly after Election Day. It traced Bush's reelection victory to a meeting of lawyers that Burress convened on May 18, 2004, to discuss how he might amend the state constitution to outlaw gay marriage. The meeting took place the day after Massachusetts, under orders from its state supreme court, became the first state in the nation to begin distributing marriage licenses to gay couples.

In Ohio and across the country, the introduction of gay marriage in Massachusetts in spring 2004 sparked a grassroots Christian Right resurgence the likes of which hadn't been seen since the rise of Christian Coalition in the early 1990s. The campaigns to pass state constitutional amendments barring gay marriage through ballot initiatives in 2004 gave in-the-pews evangelicals and fundamentalists vehicles for channeling their outrage at Massachusetts into action. The results were remarkable. The passage of thirteen state constitutional amendments banning gay marriage in 2004 would deal the gay rights movement the biggest setback in its twenty-five-year history. And the state efforts gave President Bush and conservative Republican candidates up and down the ticket a surefire way to turn out evangelical and other conservative Christian voters in droves.

No one could claim more credit for the state amendment campaigns than James Dobson, Focus on the Family, and the Arlington Group. It was the Dobson-led push for the Federal Marriage Amendment that provided a blueprint for the state efforts. All but two of the thirteen state amendment campaigns were led by Focus on the Family's state-level Family Policy Councils. And the Arlington Group, which had just begun to come together in mid-2003, acted as the national coordinating body for the individual state campaigns.

But nowhere would amending the state constitution prove more consequential than in Ohio, where switching fewer than sixty thousand votes would have given the national election to John Kerry.

Now in his mid-sixties, Phil Burress earned his political stripes as a union organizer for truck drivers in the 1970s. But his career as a Christian activist grew out of his addiction to hard-core pornography, which he said began when he was fourteen years old and which he blames for the dissolution of his first two marriages (Burress is now married to his third wife). "By age 16, I was driving to downtown Cincinnati, where you could find adult bookstores on every corner, and strip bars," he said. "If I didn't have the money, I'd steal it. I was totally obsessed."[1]

Burress's transformation from smut addict to antiporn crusader began in 1980, when he was born again during a sermon delivered by his son-in-law, a Columbus-based pastor. He took up the antiporn cause and, in 1991, took over a conservative Cincinnati-based advocacy group called Citizens for Community Values. Nine years later, CCV would be designated by Focus on the Family as Ohio's Family Policy Council. From his perch at CCV, Burress has spearheaded a remarkably successful campaign to keep adult bookstores and strip clubs out of greater Cincinnati. By pushing for strict zoning restrictions and for zealous enforcement of obscenity laws, his group has limited the city's adult industry to a single chain-owned strip bar called Deja Vu. The most graphic material carried by local gas stations is *Playboy*. Under threat of prosecution, local hotels have removed blue movies from their in-room viewing options.

Once a month, Burress presides over a Citizens for Community Values luncheon at a country club outside of Columbus. A typical meeting, in summer 2005, got under way with Burress's deputy, a former Proctor & Gamble middle manager named Ken Taylor, rising to give a brief history of the organization for the benefit of about a dozen newcomers. As his audience picked over chicken cordon bleu and marinated asparagus, Taylor rattled off two decades' worth of victories in battling the smut industry and the gay rights movement. "You could say we're experts in things of sexual sin nature," he said. "It's not exactly the kind of stuff that, when somebody walks up and says, 'Hey, Ken, what are you doing? I haven't seen you in a while,' you want to say, 'Well I work in the sexual sin business,'" he continued, prompting a round of chuckles. "It's not a good icebreaker. And yet that's what we do."

Burress's wife, Vickie, was next to speak, discussing her work ministering to strippers and to gays and lesbians who are interested "in walking away from that lifestyle." Then it was Phil's turn. He chided his guests for permitting adult bookstores and strip clubs to invade greater Columbus, and told them how he'd cleaned up Cincinnati. "Anything the industry calls X is prosecutable," he said. "You can go to court and let a jury of your peers look at the materials and determine whether or not it violates your community standards. In Hamilton County [which encompasses Cincinnati], we have obscenity trials every year, and we win some and lose some. But community standards are never set. They evolve. So if you never go to court and allow a jury to determine if something's obscene or not, guess who's setting the community standards? The pornographers."

If it sounds like the rant of a fire-breathing culture warrior, Burress hardly fits the part. Tall, with thinning white hair combed straight back, Burress dons a sports coat and French cuffs and looks perfectly at home at the Scioto Country Club. He spends his spare time rating golf courses for *Golf Digest* magazine. He's warm and outgoing, and has been known to hug ideological opponents. "We are certainly on opposite sides . . . but I have rarely seen anyone so civil," said one Democratic state representative in Ohio, describing Burress, a frequent political foe. "I consider him a friend."[2]

Burress's establishment bona fides and sterling reputation are no accident. He took over Citizens for Community Values shortly after Ralph Reed began building Christian Coalition in the late 1980s, and in some ways Burress went even further than Reed did in attempting to mainstream a Christian Right organization. CCV had been founded by a group of pastors who'd come together to organize a Billy Graham crusade outside Cincinnati in the late seventies. But Burress took pains to avoid flaunting the group's evangelical DNA. Its advisory board has included a pro-football hall-of-famer, Cincinnati's Catholic archbishop, a handful of retired judges, and a slate of well-regarded businessmen.[3] The group had a secular-sounding name from the start, and Burress stepped up efforts to project a secular image. "In our early newsletters, we quoted a lot of scripture," he said. "Then we thought, 'Wait a minute. We're marginalizing ourselves.'"[4]

Citizens for Community Values has gone to great lengths to project a moderate image, vigorously combating charges of extremism in creative ways. When it received negative media attention for pressing Cincinnati prosecutors to pursue obscenity charges against a city art museum for hosting a Robert Mapplethorpe exhibit in 1990, CCV struck back with television advertisements for its annual golf tournament. "The purpose of the commercials was not to recruit more golfers but to reinforce CCV's image as a mainstream organization," Focus on the Family vice president of public policy Tom Minnery explained in his 2001 book, *Why You Can't Stay Silent*, which used Burress's work in Cincinnati as a case study in effective Christian activism. "After all, extremists don't hold golf tournaments."[5]

But even as it attempted to forge a mainstream image, CCV nonetheless departed from Christian Coalition in one crucial regard: It never strayed from the core Christian Right agenda of opposing abortion, gay rights, and pornography. In 1993, Burress led a ballot initiative to repeal a recently passed Cincinnati ordinance that outlawed discrimination against gays. In addition to striking down the ordinance, Burress's initiative amended the city charter to prohibit any future gay rights legislation. It passed with 62 percent of the vote.

A much more ambitious gambit came in 1995, when Burress learned that Hawaii's supreme court was hearing a case through which it was expected to legalize gay marriage. He rushed to assemble a national coalition of conservative Christian activists to draft and promote a federal law called the Defense of Marriage Act (DOMA). It defined marriage as a union between one man and one woman and permitted individual states to disregard same-sex marriage licenses granted in other states. President Clinton signed DOMA in 1996, just before he faced reelection. The law rippled across the country, with thirty-six states adopting similar measures.

It wasn't long after Burress's success with the federal and state DOMAs that Focus on the Family made Citizens for Community Values its Ohio Family Policy Council. The partnership would prove particularly helpful in Burress's 2004 campaign to amend the Ohio constitution to ban gay marriage, when being plugged in to the Focus on the Family network would mean the difference between success and failure.

Six months before Massachusetts began distributing marriage licenses to same-sex couples in May 2004, the state supreme court handed down a ruling that gave the state legislature six months to legalize gay unions. But Burress, who'd been an Arlington Group member from early on and who was a proponent of the Federal Marriage Amendment, said he nonetheless felt blindsided by the sight of gays marrying in New England. When Hawaii's supreme court ruled that restricting marriage to heterosexuals was discriminatory in the 1990s, there had been enough time before the ruling took effect for voters to pass a ballot initiative banning gay marriage via a state constitutional amendment. In Massachusetts, however, such an amendment could not legally appear on the ballot until 2006. So the very development Burress had spent the past decade making sure wouldn't happen *would* be happening in the Bay State, beginning May 17, 2004. "The day after that," Burress said in an interview, "I called the attorneys into my office and said, 'Draft a constitutional amendment. We're going to have to protect Ohio.'"

In the weeks that followed, hundreds of similar phone calls went out across the country, sparking marriage amendment campaigns in more than a dozen states. (Two amendments passed via ballot initiative in 2004 prior to Election Day, and eleven on Election Day.) If Ohio's marriage amendment would have the most impact on the national election, it was also the nation's most draconian. Known officially as "Issue One," the Ohio amendment banned not just gay marriage, but also civil unions, domestic partnerships, and any other legal recognition for gay couples. Gay rights activists challenged it in court more than forty times.

But defending the legality of the amendment's language was the easy part. In order to meet the deadline for getting Issue One on the November ballot, Burress would have to collect 323,000 signatures in less than three months. With a few doubts as to whether it was even possible, Burress phoned Ohio secretary of state J. Kenneth Blackwell. The state's top elections official, Republican Blackwell was also cochair of the Bush-Cheney 2004 campaign in Ohio and a member of the Arlington Group. A conservative Christian, Blackwell had known Burress since Blackwell's days as Cincinnati's mayor in the early 1980s.

Burress was seeking his advice because Blackwell had organized successful signature drives to put antitax measures on the ballot in previous election cycles. "The call from Phil was simple," Blackwell said in an interview. "Phil said, 'Can I put together a network that can deliver the organizational effort necessary to put this on the ballot in relatively short order?' I thought there was enough concern within the network of churches that you could."

While Blackwell had relied on conservative activists to gather signatures for his antitax measures, Burress could tap into a much broader network of thousands of mostly evangelical churches to do the job. A massive organizational infrastructure was already in place. The effort increased the size of Citizens for Community Values' church contact list by 70 percent, to seventeen thousand churches. Burress hadn't seen such receptivity in his twenty-five years as an activist, and he chalked it up to Massachusetts. "Getting churches involved to fight pornography is very difficult, because unless a strip bar opens right across the street, they're not interested," he said. "What the marriage issue did is hit people so close to their belief system. This was attacking the core of who we are. We have people who say, 'I don't have a problem with homosexuals getting health benefits, but homosexual marriage, now that's going too far.' Massachusetts basically threw cold water in the face of the church.

It said to them, 'You're losing your culture.' And people began to say, 'I had no idea it was this bad.' "

At one point or other in his activist career, Burress had led nearly every one of the major conservative evangelical organizations in the state, including Christian Coalition of Ohio and the state chapter of the American Family Association. So he had those groups direct their members to a Web site he launched under the banner of the Ohio Campaign to Protect Marriage, where volunteers could download petitions and sign up to knock on doors. Within a few weeks, Burress's volunteer list had exploded to six thousand. Some pastors stepped forward, but it was in-the-pews evangelicals who took the lead, leaning on their pastors to sponsor church voter drives and to promote Issue One from the pulpit.

Accompanying the signature collection drive was a development for which Burress had long been praying: Bridges were going up between conservative white evangelical churches and traditionally liberal black ones. The most dependably Democratic voting bloc in the nation, many blacks are nonetheless socially conservative, largely because of their strong Protestant faith. One black church in Toledo sent Burress a thousand signatures to get Issue One on the ballot. When he notified the church that the signatures needed to be collected on special forms, its pastor interrupted Sunday services to distribute the petitions and wound up collecting two hundred additional names.

The black outreach effort around Issue One was aided by Secretary of State Blackwell, an African American. Ohio's Republican establishment, including its governor and two U.S. senators, opposed Issue One because they said it went too far in outlawing civil unions and domestic partnerships. But Blackwell taped radio spots promoting the effort, including advertisements for black radio. He preached in support of Issue One from pulpits of black churches across the state. And he led pastor briefings for Christian Coalition of Ohio, where ministers could learn what they could say from the pulpit about Issue One and the upcoming election without jeopardizing the tax-free status of their churches.

The black outreach appeared to have worked. On Election Day,

African American support for President Bush in Ohio leaped to 16 percent, up from 9 percent four years earlier. It was one of the most dramatic jumps in black support for Bush anywhere in the country. It accounted for almost half of Bush's margin of victory in Ohio.

The Roman Catholic Church also endorsed Issue One, and the typically apolitical Eastern Orthodox Church and the Amish, with large communities in rural Ohio, played active roles, even as white evangelical congregations provided most of the organizational muscle. But Burress didn't rely on churches alone.[6] Worried that he couldn't collect enough signatures in time for the deadline, he contacted Focus on the Family, which sent petitions to sixty-five thousand of its Ohio constituents. "When you get a letter from Focus on the Family, you're getting a letter from Dr. Dobson," Burress said, "so it's different than getting a letter from any other pro-family group out there. None of us have Dobson's credibility." Burress also enlisted the mailing lists of other evangelical groups, like Gary Bauer's Campaign for Working Families and Don Wildmon's American Family Association.

But it was the Family Research Council, Focus on the Family's Washington counterpart, that provided the most crucial aid. On top of mailing letters to thirty thousand Ohio supporters, FRC gave two million dollars to Citizens for Community Values, helping to underwrite Burress's contract with a professional signature-gathering firm. The firm sent more than fifty workers to Ohio, collecting a hundred thousand signatures. It was FRC's biggest investment in any state in 2004, and it was undertaken with an eye toward winning Ohio for Bush. "Politically speaking, I knew it was a swing state, and an important state in the election," said Family Research Council president Tony Perkins in an interview after the election. "It's all about turnout, and we wanted to encourage our people to turn out and vote because the results would be more votes for pro-family, pro-marriage, pro-life candidates."

President Bush, Perkins said, was the first among them. By coming out in favor of the Federal Marriage Amendment in early 2004, the president had positioned himself to capitalize on support for state marriage amendments like Issue One, even without taking a position on such efforts. John Kerry also said he opposed gay marriage. But he opposed the Federal Marriage Amendment, had voted against the 1996 Defense of Marriage Act, and happened to hail from Massachusetts, the very state that had provoked the national state amendment frenzy.

In the end, Burress's team collected upward of half a million signatures, more than enough to get on the ballot. In the process, it wound up registering almost fifty-five thousand new voters, mostly social conservatives. Once signature-gathering was through, Citizens for Community Values went all out promoting the amendment. It hired a firm to call every home in the state to identify the most enthusiastic Issue One supporters, generating a list of 850,000 households. Then it phoned each of those 850,000 numbers on the day before Election Day with a taped message from Secretary of State Blackwell that reminded them to vote. CCV distributed nearly three million church bulletin inserts for the Sunday before Election Day. It called ten thousand churches with electronic messages that encouraged congregations to go to the polls and support Issue One. It bought ads in newspapers and on TV and radio.

With as much as $150 million spent in Ohio by the presidential campaigns, parties, and outside groups, and with a spike in voter turnout second only to South Dakota's, it is impossible to isolate one factor as responsible for the 118,601-vote margin of victory that delivered the state, and the White House, to George W. Bush. But the raw election data suggest that Issue One was a crucial factor, and perhaps the deciding one. Ohio's white evangelicals were Issue One's strongest supporters, supplying more than half its votes, and they backed Bush over Kerry by 75 to 25 percent, supplying one in three Bush votes. Eight in ten Bush voters backed Issue One, compared with just four in ten Kerry supporters.[7]

The statistics raise the question of whether Issue One drove up

Bush support or vice versa. But a handful of postelection analyses of Ohio found that Issue One was the driver, mobilizing conservative voters and focusing all voters on the gay marriage issue. A study by professors from Western Washington University, Kent State, and the University of Florida found that voters nationally who thought gay marriage was a "very important" issue were 9 percent more likely to vote for Bush than other voters. But the study found that those same voters who resided in states with marriage amendments on the ballot were 20 percent more likely to vote for Bush.[8] To put that finding in perspective, voters citing the economy as "very important" were only 17 percent more likely to support Bush. Concern over gay marriage even rivaled concern over the Iraq war as a predictor of Bush support.[9]

What was particularly remarkable about Bush's 50.8 percent win in Ohio was that he had the state Republican Party weighing him down. Ohio's Republican governor Bob Taft had championed an unpopular tax increase, and the state's Republican Speaker of the House had been accused of embezzling campaign funds. With Republicans long in control of both houses of the state General Assembly, Ohio's economy was floundering; manufacturing job losses numbered in the tens of thousands.[10] "The state was in an economic death spiral, and if voters' decisions were just made on 'How do I feel about the state of the economy?' the president would not have won Ohio," said Secretary of State Blackwell. "He should celebrate seven judges in Massachusetts."

Apart from spearheading most of the state marriage amendment efforts through its Family Policy Councils, Focus on the Family played an unprecedented role in the 2004 campaign on a national level. It sent out "I Vote Values" kits that included voter registration forms and instructions on promoting conservative causes like the Federal Marriage Amendment to twelve thousand churches across the country, along with eight million voter guides. A joint project of Focus on the Family and the Southern Baptist Convention, the "I Vote Values" campaign also included a Web site and an eighteen-wheel registration truck that toured the country signing up new evangelical voters. Officials with the Bush-Cheney 2004 campaign said the project was the most visible evangelical registration and get-out-the-vote effort in the country.

In Focus's eyes, mobilizing evangelicals was simply doing God's work. "This is not just some sort of some good citizen project," said Brad Miller, a Focus on the Family liaison with Family Policy Councils. "To us, this is fundamentally theological. This comes straight out of Genesis. We believe God has mandated that his people be involved with the civil magistrate and that's especially true when the issues are marriage and the sanctity of life. Evangelicals have not engaged in the political process. We've been turning our backs on the cultural mandate given to us in scripture."

Focus on the Family's pastor outreach ministry encouraged more than one hundred thousand ministers on its mailing list to talk up conservative social positions from their pulpits in the months leading up to Election Day. Pastor outreach director H. B. London, Jr., a first cousin of James Dobson's, traveled to ten states ahead of the election and met with thousands of preachers. He said many pastors were reluctant to play an active part in the election, and not because they were afraid of violating IRS rules that bar churches from making political endorsements. "Repercussions from their congregations was the issue," London said in an interview in his Colorado Springs office. "Many said it's not worth the effort to be controversial politically when constituents are so difficult to recruit in the first place."

But London worked to convince pastors that avoiding controversial political stances was a dereliction of duty: "Every pastor has the responsibility to inform their congregation of the danger that lurks around the corner, whether it's gay rights, same-sex marriage, or partial birth abortion."

Focus on the Family was just one of dozens of organizations mobilizing evangelicals in 2004. *The Purpose-Driven Life* author and internationally known megachurch pastor Rick Warren activated his vast network of tens of thousands of pastors. Redeem the Vote, a new organization aimed at registering young evangelicals, taped a get-out-the-vote commercial featuring *The Passion of The Christ* film star Jim Caviezel that was widely circulated on the Internet. The group also set up registration tables at Christian rock concerts and appeared on Christian radio, mostly in Ohio.

But the most important evangelical mobilization efforts were those undertaken by tens of thousands of individual churches around the country. At the twelve-hundred-member Genoa Baptist Church, located just north of Columbus, Ohio, pastor Frank Carl organized two preelection conferences for more than a thousand pastors; the conferences included sessions on political activism and on what pastors could and could not say about the election from the pulpit. "One pastor told me that it was pastors like me who will cut our tax-exempt status and that our focus should be in the pulpit, not in the community," Carl recalled in an interview after the election. "I responded, 'My dear brother, I hope the reason you're in the ministry is not only to be in the pulpit—only 20 percent of our population attends church!'"[11]

But like H. B. London at Focus on the Family, Carl said an even greater fear among pastors was that voicing conservative political positions would incite their congregations to turn on them. "The great fear was that the pastors would get booted from their congregations," Carl said. "Small church pastors were especially scared. I would call them and say, 'This is not only your privilege, it's your responsibility.'"

Carl applied the same pressure to his own congregation. On the Sunday before Election Day, Genoa Baptist held a church rally that featured Fox News Channel host and AM radio personality Sean Hannity, retiring conservative Democratic senator Zell Miller—who spoke at the 2004 Republican Convention—Reagan education secretary Bill Bennett, and a videotaped message from Jerry Falwell. It drew nearly three thousand people. Because Carl had expected a huge crowd that would overwhelm the sanctuary, he outfitted the church's sprawling campus with fourteen Toshiba flat-screen TVs at a cost of more than ten thousand dollars. He reserved one church classroom just for Bush supporters, though no room was set aside for Kerry supporters. The rally was carried by Christian cable channels, where it was aired round the clock through Election Day.

—m—

Despite the unprecedented get-out-the-vote efforts on the part of evangelical groups like Focus on the Family and the spontaneous mobilization efforts of countless evangelical pastors, the Bush-Cheney 2004 campaign wasn't taking any chances. After the 2000 election debacle, Bush political don Karl Rove concluded that evangelical turnout had been much too low. In 2000 only 14 percent of voters who backed Bush identified themselves as religious conservatives, down from the 17 percent who backed Republican presidential nominee Bob Dole in 1996. What made the numbers particularly troubling was that President Bush is a born-again Christian, while religious conservatives had expressed deep reservations over Dole. Rather than support Dole, James Dobson had backed the U.S. Taxpayers Party's Howard Phillips.

As early as 2001, Karl Rove remarked that the polling data from 2000 suggested that evangelicals and fundamentalists were retreating from public life again, as they had after the Scopes Trial. "If this process of withdrawal continues," Rove said, "it's bad for conservatives, bad for Republicans, but also bad for the country." He estimated that four million white evangelical voters had stayed home on Election Day 2000, and he vowed to reinvigorate them.[12] No other demographic that size could be counted on to consistently pull the Republican lever.

But rather than blame the Bush-Cheney 2000 campaign for the depressed evangelical turnout that year, the Bush-Cheney 2004 reelection team pointed the finger at evangelical groups like Focus on the Family. In the eyes of the Bushies, Focus and other evangelical groups claimed to have huge followings but had failed to get them to the polls. "Because the ball was dropped so precipitously in 2000, [the evangelical mobilization] had to be brought inside," said one Bush-Cheney 2004 official, speaking on condition of anonymity to avoid offending Focus and other evangelical groups. "What campaign is going to count on people that they're not allowed to talk to and not allowed to coordinate with [by law]? It's too big a gamble. No Republican campaign will ever again count on groups on the outside to do the job alone."

Officials inside Focus on the Family's public policy shop said they had been much less gung-ho about mobilizing evangelical voters in 2000 than in 2004 because candidate Bush was something of an unknown quantity. Though during the 2000 presidential debates he cited Jesus Christ as the political philosopher who had most influenced him, Bush promoted "compassionate conservatism" and a "big tent" GOP rather than play up antiabortion and anti–gay rights themes. "We didn't really know George Bush till he was inaugurated for the first time," said Focus on the Family vice president of public policy Tom Minnery. "At that inauguration, he had Franklin Graham there with an evangelical message, and there were church hymns being sung. It was a Christian service was what it was. . . . [W]e realized this man had depth to his faith beliefs."

Focus on the Family officials also noted that in the 2000 election, Massachusetts hadn't yet legalized gay marriage, the Federal Marriage Amendment hadn't yet emerged as a key issue, and Bush hadn't yet signed abortion restrictions and appointed conservative judges to the federal bench, as he did during his first presidential term.

But Bush's 2004 reelection team had a different theory about 2000's depressed evangelical turnout. After the 1996 election, Ralph Reed had left Christian Coalition, and the organization had more or less collapsed. Membership dwindled, top leadership fled, and it fell into debt. But, the Bushies theorized, neither Republican strategists nor Christian Right groups had appreciated the vacuum in voter registration and mobilization efforts left by Christian Coalition's implosion until the exit polls came back in 2000. Up to that point, said one Bush-Cheney 2004 official, "people trusted that there was still a Christian Coalition getting out the vote. . . . But Christian Coalition had fallen apart, and no one else had picked up the slack yet. Focus [on the Family] hadn't. They were not at that level."

So in 2004, the Bush team vowed to take evangelical mobilization into its own hands. In 2000 the Bush campaign had outsourced evangelical outreach to Ralph Reed's Century Strategies, the consulting firm he'd launched after leaving Christian Coalition. In 2004 the campaign instead hired Reed to work from the inside. Officially, he was the Bush-Cheney chairman for the southeast region of the United States. But his more important assignment was to construct a vast volunteer infrastructure, extending into tens of thousands of voter precincts across the country, to get evangelicals to the polls on Election Day. "It was very new in terms of outreach and full-scale investment in this particular demographic," said Gary Marx, who worked under Reed as the Bush-Cheney 2004 national conservative coalition director. "I call it the 'Passion Crowd' . . . [because it's] emblematic of Mel Gibson's movie, which reached out not only to evangelicals but to Catholics in an unprecedented way. It was the first time in Republican political history that the presidential campaign was run in such a way that this was a formalized element in everything we did, from radio buys to direct mail to the grassroots ground game to phone work. It was a demographic group that was courted and yearned for, just as soccer moms were in 2000 and NASCAR dads in 2002."

More than a year before Election Day 2004, Reed appointed chairpersons for social conservative outreach—which essentially translated into evangelical outreach—in a dozen and a half battleground states. The state chairs appointed regional and county chairpersons, who in turn recruited volunteer foot soldiers. "It was a brilliant strategy to integrate the social conservative constituency into the campaign," Reed said in an interview after the election, "rather than rely on outside groups to identify and turn out that vote on Election Day. The Democrats did the opposite. Their ground game was outsourced to America Coming Together and MoveOn.org and labor groups."

Of the 1.4 million volunteers that the Bush reelection team signed up, Reed estimates that 300,000 to 350,000 were social and "pro-family" conservatives. "We made them part of our campaign," he said.

In Florida, Reed drafted Pam Olsen, the leader of a ministry called Florida Prayer Network, to be the state chairperson for evangelical outreach. In 2000, Olsen had staged a forty-day fast before Election Day and a second fast from Election Day till the presidential recount fiasco was resolved. After being tapped by Reed in late 2003, she quickly appointed a dozen regional coordinators around the state, along with chairpersons in each of Florida's sixty-seven counties. Each county chairperson signed up between thirty and fifty volunteers.

Just like Bush's evangelical outreach teams in other states, Olsen's network had two main objectives: persuading evangelical churches to host voter registration drives, and convincing evangelical pastors to speak from the pulpit on the importance of making voting decisions based on hot-button issues. "The two strongest biblical issues on which there is no debate are that the word of God says God is pro-life and that God is for marriage between a man and a woman," Olsen said in an interview after the election. "That's not debatable. With issues like education or poverty or the war in Iraq, Christians fall on both sides."

Armed with a database of five thousand evangelical Florida churches, Olsen stressed to pastors that voter registration drives needed to be nonpartisan. She made no attempt to discourage churches from registering Democrats or potential Kerry supporters. That's because the Bush-Cheney campaign had calculated that seven out of ten new white evangelical voters would support Bush. Olsen hosted pastor luncheons featuring Ralph Reed and Arkansas's Republican governor Mike Huckabee, who is a Baptist minister, to discuss what pastors could and couldn't say from the pulpit. "Quite often, the ACLU was trying to muzzle people in churches, saying they can't do anything political," Olsen said. "So educating people as to what's legal and not legal was really important."

Olsen's job was made much easier by Bush's immense personal appeal among rank-and-file evangelicals. "Bush is a born-again Christian and stands up for his pro-life stance," she said. "He's one of us. Some candidates, like Bob Dole, stick their finger in the air and decide what crowd you're talking to. Bush isn't afraid to stand up for his faith, and that makes a difference."

Efforts like Olsen's were replicated in battleground states across the country. Despite its enormous size, though, Ralph Reed's get-out-the-evangelical-vote machine was nearly invisible to the mainstream media and to those outside the evangelical subculture. In fact, the conventional wisdom was that Bush was connecting with white evangelical voters through coded rhetoric and conservative stances on social issues, leaving churches to mobilize their own congregations for the election. Feeding that perception was the bad press the Republican National Committee attracted in July 2004, when it was reported to have solicited church directories from Catholic supporters in Pennsylvania. Even Richard Land, president of the political wing of the Southern Baptist Convention and a staunch Bush ally, said he was "appalled" by the strategy. "To share the church directory with anyone outside the church body," he said, "is a violation of the sanctity of the body."[13]

But because there were virtually no follow-up accounts of the RNC continuing to seek church directories after the Pennsylvania incident, the widespread assumption was that the GOP had pulled the plug on the operation. After the election, the Southern Baptist Convention's Washington lobbyist said that "the Bush campaign backed off" after coming under fire in Pennsylvania and "pretty much let evangelicals mobilize themselves."

Nothing could be further from the truth. The Bush campaign continued to zealously pursue church directories to identify and sign up new evangelical voters even after being exposed in Pennsylvania. Careful to work through parishioners, as opposed to pastors—whose close coordination with a candidate's political campaign would violate the terms of their churches' nonprofit, tax-exempt status—Reed's national network collected directories from thousands of evangelical churches and funneled them to Bush-Cheney national headquarters. Campaign workers then checked the names in the directories against lists of registered voters. "We would input all the individual [church directory] lists, match them against the voter files, and find out—surprise, surprise— there are millions of people who attend church who are not registered to vote," said Gary Marx, the Bush-Cheney 2004 national conservative coalition director.

Bush-Cheney headquarters sent the names of unregistered churchgoers back to volunteers across the country, who would call their evangelical neighbors and urge them to register. The volunteers would even offer to deliver registration forms and absentee ballots. Asked how many new voters the Bush campaign registered this way, Marx couldn't produce an exact number. But he estimated that it was "in the range of millions."

While the Bush-Cheney campaign was enlisting hundreds of thousands of white evangelicals in its reelection effort, the Republican National Committee relied mostly on one: a Texas-based evangelical activist named David Barton. A graduate of Oral Roberts University and a former schoolteacher, Barton has built a full-blown industry around advocating for a greater recognition of Christianity's role in American history, particularly in shaping the philosophy and writings of the Founding Fathers. He argues that the Christian influence on the nation has been replaced by secular revisionism in school textbooks and among mainstream historians. Attempting to reverse the trend, Barton has published dozens of books, booklets, CDs, DVDs, and CD-ROMs, with titles like *America's Godly Heritage, The Role of Pastors and Christians in Civil Government,* and *The Spiritual Heritage of the United States Capitol.*

Though he lacks formal training in history, Barton has consulted with school boards and textbook publishers across the country, and has worked with an organization called the National Council on Bible Curriculum in Public Schools to introduce Bible literacy courses in hundreds of school districts nationwide. He has led thousands of visitors,

including many members of Congress, on "spiritual heritage" tours of
the U.S. Capitol. And Barton maintains a rigorous public speaking
schedule, giving four hundred lectures a year on Christianity's role in
American history to church, business, and military groups.

Barton was active in Republican politics long before the Republican National Committee hired him in 2004. As vice chairman of the
Texas Republican Party in the 1990s, he'd helped engineer victories for
then governor George W. Bush. In 2004, Barton was working for Bush
again, speaking to about a hundred pastor briefings across the country
on behalf of the RNC. He estimated that he reached upwards of ten
thousand pastors, each of whom, in turn, reached hundreds or thousands more through their congregations. Barton's message: Pastors
needed to reclaim their proper roles as shapers of elections and public
policy.

"Two hundred years ago, John Adams was asked who was behind
American independence," Barton told a gathering of Independent Baptist pastors near Richmond, Virginia, in September 2005, in a presentation that he said closely mirrored those he gave for the RNC in 2004.
"The list of names that [Adams] gave is not the list of names we study
any more today. They were all Christian and a whole bunch were ministers. . . . You got to start with Reverend Dr. Samuel Cooper, and of
course there's the Reverend George Whitefield, and then you got the
Reverend Dr. Jonathan Mayhew. . . ."

Clad in black down to his cowboy boots, weighing about 145
pounds, and speaking not much slower than an auctioneer, Barton
ticked off the names of more Christian clergymen. Then he invoked a
verse from the Old Testament book of Malachi that identified the clergy
as the paramount source of knowledge for all of society's members, including lawmakers. He ran down a list of sermon titles from
seventeenth- and eighteenth-century America that illustrated the principle at work, citing sermons about current events of every sort, from the
execution of certain criminals, to the occurrence of solar eclipses, to
news of house fires. This, Barton said, was the legacy that evangelical

pastors had to reclaim. "There is no issue that the Bible doesn't address," he said, as the few hundred pastors in attendance sat in rapt attention. "Did you know that the Bible takes a very clear position on capital gains tax? It takes a very clear position on income tax. The Bible takes a clear position on the estate tax, and takes a position on minimum wage. All these are economic issues that we should be able to shape citizens' thinking on because of what the Bible says."

As he reviewed the biblical position on fiscal matters—anti–capital gains tax, pro–income tax, but only as a flat tax, anti–estate tax, anti–minimum wage—the relevant biblical verse numbers, from Proverbs to the Gospel according to Luke, flashed across a projector screen mounted above the pulpit.

Barton ended his ninety-minute talk by railing against the 1954 law that barred ministers from endorsing political candidates. "You know, in America, Jesus Christ could not stand behind this pulpit and say today what he said in the New Testament," he said. When his speech was through, Barton was swarmed by more autograph-seekers than the conference's keynote speaker, Republican gubernatorial nominee Jerry Kilgore.

Departing from the pastor briefings led by President Bush's surrogates, Barton's 2004 presentations for the Republican National Committee urged pastors to do more than simply talk up social issues from the pulpit. Armed with a six-page printout of IRS guidelines outlining what pastors could and could not say from the pulpit to maintain their churches' tax-exempt status, Barton told his audiences that they could indeed endorse candidates, just so long as they did it the right way. "I like to say, 'Push the envelope,'" Barton said in an interview after his presentation in Richmond. "Pastors have a tendency to always think worst-case scenarios. They have a tendency to hear what Barry Lynn does," he continued, referring to the president of the liberal group Americans United for Separation of Church and State, which monitors political activity in churches. "Throughout the election, [Lynn] kept sending tapes to the IRS whacking on pastors. And the IRS is going to do what they always do: They're going to drop those tapes in the trash, because what he turned in was no violation of the IRS code. It's an intimidation tactic."

In his 2004 RNC briefings, Barton told pastors that they had to fight back against such campaigns to silence them. "The IRS code prevents corporate machinery from being put into effect to alter an election," he said. "So if a pastor gets up and says the deacons' board has voted and we're endorsing this person for dog catcher, they're in trouble. If the deacons' board gives one penny of money to a candidate, they're in trouble. But if a pastor wants to get up and say, 'Look, the deacons' board has not voted about this, I'm just telling you my opinion, this is the guy we need for dog catcher and this guy isn't,' he's fine to do that. And that's one thing the pastors were completely unaware of."

Of course, Barton wasn't promoting nameless dog catchers in the 2004 election cycle. He was campaigning for George W. Bush.

Between the efforts of the Bush-Cheney campaign, the Republican National Committee, and outside groups like Focus on the Family and the Ohio Family Policy Council, Karl Rove nearly met his goal of turning out four million more evangelicals in 2004 than in 2000. Exit polls showed that 3.5 million white evangelicals who stayed home in 2000 cast ballots in 2004. Because of increased across-the-board turnout, white evangelicals constituted the same proportion of the electorate in 2004 as in 2000, about 25 percent. But evangelical turnout had nonetheless jumped 9 percent. All other demographic factors being equal, Bush might have lost the presidency to John Kerry were it not for the surge in evangelical voters.[14]

Bush also captured a larger share of the evangelical vote in 2004— 78 percent—than he had in 2000, when 68 percent of evangelicals backed him.[15] Between new evangelical voters and those who had voted for Al Gore in 2000, the president picked up nearly six million new evangelical votes in 2004, about twice his margin of victory. Evangelicals provided a whopping two in five Bush votes.[16] "That made the dif-

ference," said Gary Marx. "That's the whole game. It's why Bush increased from a 200-vote [margin of victory] in Florida in 2000 to 5
points in 2004. It was those values voters."

Indeed, an Election Day exit poll found that more American voters
cited moral values as their top priority in casting their ballots than cited
any other issue, including terrorism or the economy. But the survey
quickly came under attack for failing to define moral values. Conducted by a consortium of news outlets, the survey asked an open-
ended question about voters' top priorities, and grouped a wide
spectrum of responses—dealing with everything from social issues such
as same-sex marriage to the presidential candidates' trustworthiness—
under the "moral values" label. Critics also argued that combining similar issue categories on the survey, like "Iraq" and "terrorism," or "jobs"
and "healthcare," showed there was greater concern about the nation's
security and economy than about moral values.

But a poll conducted by the Pew Research Center in the week after
Election Day confirmed what the exit polls had found: that for a plurality of Bush voters, so-called moral values trumped all other concerns.
Responding to a multiple-choice survey, 44 percent of Bush voters said
moral values mattered most—more than the combined percentages of
those who cited Iraq, terrorism, or the economy. Asked to define the
term, nearly 80 percent of respondents who cited "moral values" as their
top concern said it referred to stances on social issues like gay marriage
or had to do with religion or "traditional values." Among voters who
backed John Kerry, meanwhile, only 7 percent said moral values mattered most. Many more Kerry voters cited Iraq (34 percent) or econ-
omy/jobs (36 percent).[17]

Even more striking than the divide between Bush and Kerry voters
over moral values was the split between the American electorate at large
and white evangelical voters. The general electorate assigned relatively
low priority to social issues such as same-sex marriage and abortion; 24
percent of all voters said social issues were most important, compared to
35 percent who cited foreign policy and 33 percent who cited economic

issues. But among evangelicals, 37 percent cited social issues as most important, more than cited foreign policy or economic issues.[18] For the traditionalist evangelicals—those attending church frequently and showing high levels of religious commitment—who constituted more than a quarter of Bush's vote, social issues took even higher priority. Nearly half considered social issues most important, about twice the proportion of those in the general electorate who felt that way.[19]

Traditionalist Catholics and traditionalist mainline Protestants were also more likely than the electorate at large to cite social issues as a top priority, and they, too, voted for Bush in lopsided fashion. The pattern prompted many political experts to suggest that the rift in the American electorate was more a "God gap" between more and less religious Americans than it was a religious identity gap between white evangelicals and the rest of the country. But even traditionalist Catholics and traditionalist mainline Protestants assigned less weight to social issues than evangelicals did in 2004.[20] And traditionalist evangelicals outnumber traditionalist Catholics and mainline Protestants combined, with most evangelicals identifying as "traditionalist" while most Catholics and mainliners do not, making them a much more potent voting block.[21]

Of course, to the true believers who built Bush's 2004 evangelical voter machine, there was more than demographics at work in the president's reelection victory. "To me, prayer was a hugely important part of the strategy," said Pam Olsen, the Bush-Cheney chairwoman for social conservative outreach in Florida. "I prayed over every battleground state every night. There was a very specific prayer strategy: I prayed that people not be persuaded by their pocketbooks [at the voting booth] but that people vote biblical Christian worldview, that they voted as if God was to come down and vote."

—◌—

When the Arlington Group first convened outside Washington just a year and a half earlier, the Christian Right appeared to be gasping for air. But the 2004 election suggested that evangelicals, the long-conjectured "sleeping giant" of American politics, had again been roused from their slumber. Newspaper headlines heralded the arrival of "values voters," and journalists scrambled to explore the role evangelicals played in the election and in American life more broadly. The campaigns to pass state constitutional amendments banning same-sex marriage and other legal arrangements for gay couples through ballot initiatives had forged new bonds among evangelical activists and had drawn new troops into their fold. With the election behind them, the activists realized they had a fleeting opportunity to parlay 2004's activism into a permanent grassroots movement. Otherwise, the giant might fall asleep again. "The doctor doesn't want to become Chicken Little, saying the sky is always falling," said John Fuller, James Dobson's cohost on the daily *Focus on the Family* broadcast, in an interview after the election. "But there is a sense with the election that the troops are mobilized, and we have to keep them active."

That sense provoked an Ohio-based pastor named Russell Johnson to launch an effort to get thousands of conservative pastors in his state more politically involved, and to register hundreds of thousands of new conservative evangelical voters in very short order. Claiming the effort was "the genesis of the Lord," Johnson called it the Ohio Restoration Project.

Hashed out with other activists and church staffers in the car ride home from President Bush's January 2005 inauguration, Johnson's vision for the Ohio Restoration Project was straightforward, ambitious, and had potentially election-shaping consequences for future Ohio political contests. Through word-of-mouth advertising, an e-mail campaign, and a series of big luncheons across the state, he would sign up two thousand conservative "Patriot Pastors" in Ohio. Each would be tasked with recruiting three hundred new "values voters" for the 2006 election. If successful, the plan would mint six hundred thousand new voters, mostly white evangelicals, in two short years. Almost all would be Republican. "We're grieved," Johnson said in an interview, "that the Democratic Party has become enslaved to gay activists and abortionists."

In Johnson's view, convincing pastors to use their influence in the
political realm was the best way to reverse the gains of America's "secular jihadists." During a 2005 visit to his office inside Fairfield Community Church in Lancaster, Ohio, southeast of Columbus, he produced a
textbook used by local public school students in 1923. " 'Dedicated to
the boys and girls of Lancaster public schools,' " he read, referring to the
book's inside cover. " 'That none of them may go astray and that all may
be led to a high and holy life.' " Johnson thumbed through the pages,
which featured passages for memorization culled straight from the
Bible: for first grade, The Lord's Prayer; for fourth, the Sermon on the
Mount; for sixth, a verse from Paul's Letter to the Galatians. Johnson
had stumbled across the volume in a local used bookshop, bought it,
and had it rebound, as a symbol of the kind of country he wanted America to be again. And with his comb-over hairdo, clenched grin, and
wide, fiery eyes, Johnson looked as if he'd just come from an old-
fashioned revival meeting. Holding the 1923 textbook in his office, he
sighed and, invoking the *Andy Griffith Show*, said, "Let's get back to
Mayberry."

After the 2004 election, Phil Burress—the Family Policy Council
director who'd led the Issue One campaign—caught wind of Johnson's
plans for the Ohio Restoration Project and drove up from Cincinnati to
meet him. The two hit it off immediately. "What Russell is trying to do
is take us back to the days when the separation of church and state is
corrected," Burress said. "Up until 1948, the Bible was used in most of
our schools as a textbook. People don't understand how this nation was
founded on Judeo-Christian principles, and how it's all slipped away
and how our culture's going with it. That's really the culture war. . . . It
starts with the separation of church and state, which does not exist."

At that point, Burress had already begun working to enlist Issue
One's most outspoken supporters into a permanent grassroots network.
After the election, Citizens for Community Values began reaching out
to the volunteers who'd collected Issue One petition signatures, enlisting them in a campaign to organize Christian conservatives in each of

the state's eighty-eight counties. To help county organizers get started, CCV offered them names from a list of 230,000 hard-core Ohio social conservatives whom it had identified through its massive preelection telephone effort.

Like his Issue One campaign the previous year, Burress's postelection organizing efforts targeted primarily in-the-pews evangelicals; he saw Russell Johnson and the Ohio Restoration Project as a portal into Ohio's network of thousands of evangelical pastors. "We're pretty much joined at the hip," Burress said of his relationship with Johnson. "Pastors respect pastors, so if I call them I won't get the reception Russell will get."

With Johnson's help, Burress began working to identify a contact person in each of the seventeen thousand Ohio churches that CCV was in touch with during the Issue One campaign. "We're trying to drill deeper," Burress said, explaining the strategy. "I'm talking about true grass roots. If you get down deep enough, like we did on Issue One, you can't spend enough money on radio and TV commercials to change an election [the way the grass roots can]. We want a contact person who the pastor approves of in every church. We're trying not just to send letters to these churches, but to build personal relationships with every one."

While Burress and Russell Johnson were working to organize pastors in Ohio, the Family Research Council lent assistance from Washington. Since arriving at FRC in 2003, president Tony Perkins had made stepping up pastor outreach a top priority. Perkins hired FRC's first director of pastor outreach, with a goal of reaching twenty thousand churches by 2008. Since his early days as FRC president, Perkins had been visiting evangelical churches across the country, addressing a different congregation from the pulpit almost every other Sunday. He launched FRC's "pastor briefings," annual conferences aimed at introducing conservative pastors to Washington's world of politics and public policy. It was at the 2003 briefing that Perkins met Russell Johnson. At Johnson's invitation, Perkins attended the first major organizing meeting for the Ohio Restoration Project after the 2004 election.

Perkins and the Family Research Council would be the eyes and ears of the Ohio Restoration Project in Washington, alerting the group to legislative victories and defeats, and issuing calls to action. Around the same time, Perkins began working with similar pastor groups in Washington State, South Carolina, Pennsylvania, and elsewhere, many formed in the aftermath of the 2004 state amendment campaigns and other election-related efforts. Rather than brand such projects with the Family Research Council name, however, Perkins wanted to ensure that they remained self-sufficient, much as Focus on the Family's Family Policy Councils were. The model attempted to avoid the fate of Christian Coalition, whose state affiliates imploded in the late 1990s after the shakeup at national headquarters. Perkins called it a "cell concept in which the cells are interdependent."

By allowing pastor groups like the Ohio Restoration Project to maintain their autonomy, Perkins could also position himself and FRC more as a support team than taskmasters, which he cited as another of Christian Coalition's mistakes. "I don't say [to pastors], 'You've got to make this call,'" he said in an interview in late 2005, after addressing an Ohio Restoration Project luncheon in Dayton. "If in your first exchange you ask for something, then you're perceived as political. [Instead] you say, 'Pray for this and pray for this.' And as the relationship deepens, they say, 'I'm already praying. What else can I do?'"

Indeed, because they were made up of pastors and led by pastors, state-level evangelical "cells" like the Ohio Restoration Project could make the case that they were driven more by religion than by politics. When a pastor involved in such efforts returns to his congregation to promote conservative causes, his advice is taken as that of a religious authority rather than an activist. Working through such groups, advocacy groups like Family Research Council and Citizens for Community Values could have a much more effective channel for influencing tens of thousands of in-the-pews evangelicals than would be possible through direct mail or newspaper advertisements. "Focus doesn't come close to having the impact on the average evangelical as the local pastors, and that's the way it should be," said Brad Miller, Focus on the Family's liaison to Family Policy Councils. "So if we could move pastors to say something from the pulpit, then we've replicated our efforts one hundred, five hundred, a thousand times."

In fact, while they worked with secular Christian Right organizations like the Family Research Council and the Family Policy Councils, pastor-driven groups like the Ohio Restoration Project resurrected the model of Jerry Falwell's Moral Majority. "The key to maintaining an outreach to moral America is through the pastor," said Rick Scarborough, a Texas-based evangelical pastor turned political activist who coined the term "Patriot Pastor" in the late 1990s, when he pioneered pastor outreach for the Christian Right. "Christian Coalition circumvented the pastor. They put together a model that could live or die without the pastor. Pastors were intimidated by the fact that their people were going down to some neutral setting to meet with members of other churches and denominations. A Baptist preacher doesn't necessarily want his people to spend a lot of time with Catholic members. So while [Christian Coalition] was motivating many Christians to go out and take part in elections, they almost had to keep it a secret from their pastors."

Groups like the Ohio Restoration Project, by contrast, empowered pastors to be political leaders. "If I go to the pastors," Scarborough said, "and say, 'I want you to create what is effectively a cell within your congregation, to register them to vote, give them the truth about moral issues, and preach a sermon every now and then about the need to be salt and light,' then that pastor is in total control."

The Ohio Restoration Project's inaugural luncheon, in August 2005, was held in the ballroom of the Kings Island Resort and Conference Center outside Cincinnati, with the roller coasters of the nearby Paramount's King Dominion looming in the background. The ballroom was hung with banners emblazoned with the words "Patriot Pastors," a crucifix taking the place of the t in "Pastors." More than five hundred pastors and laypeople showed up, forcing Johnson to turn some away.

The program opened with a suite of patriotic and religious numbers performed by a choir from Russell Johnson's church, with the female singers in bright red sweaters and the men in black tuxedos. The set list included "God Bless America" and a song called "The Battle Belongs to the Lord": "In heavenly armor we'll enter the land . . . /No weapon that's fashioned against us shall stand." As the troupe belted out the song's apocalyptic lyrics to a booming brass-and-drums soundtrack, a photograph of U.S. soldiers helping children in Iraq flashed across a big projector screen. Then a picture of machine gun–wielding troops silhouetted against a Middle East desert landscape. Then jets taking off from aircraft carriers. The juxtaposition of images and lyrics created the impression that the United States was engaged in a Holy War.

Approaching the podium to open the speakers' portion of the event, Johnson held up a newspaper he'd recently helped launch, called *Citizen USA*. He explained that it featured local, national, and world news from a conservative evangelical perspective. The lead of one front-page story was that "America has been blessed by the nightly stand for traditional family values on FOX TV."[22] Johnson encouraged pastors from other churches to begin distributing the paper, and for each church to insert its own "B Section" featuring local community news. He told a story about talking to the owner of a local cement company who was frustrated over negative news coverage of U.S. progress in Iraq. Johnson struck a deal to run positive Iraq stories in exchange for a few ad buys. "Iraq is not just a geopolitical skirmish," he told the Patriot Pastors. "It's about whether or not there'll be a foothold for Christ in a country whose people have been enslaved."

Johnson then called the afternoon's two honorees—Citizens for Community Values president Phil Burress and Secretary of State J. Kenneth Blackwell—to the stage to present them with awards for their work promoting Issue One in 2004. At that point, Blackwell had launched a campaign to be governor of Ohio, and he was locked in a heated three-way contest for the Republican nomination. He made sure to shake hands with each guest at each of the dozens of tables inside the ballroom. After receiving his bronze eagle statuette from Johnson, Blackwell implored the pastors in the audience to reengage the culture, quoting a half dozen Old and New Testament verses from memory.

Blackwell was a featured speaker at all but one or two of the eight Patriot Pastors luncheons before the May 2006 gubernatorial primary, and each time he appeared, the awards ceremony was reenacted. (Burress also attended most of the luncheons, each time taking to the stage to receive his bronze statuette.) The lunch events featured no other political candidates. But, like Russell Johnson, Blackwell rejected the suggestion that the Ohio Restoration Project was promoting his candidacy. He noted that nonprofit groups are legally barred from making political endorsements. "This organization's reason for being is not to advance my candidacy," he said in an interview after his speech. "There will be many issues and many races where these people will make a difference. Do I respect their power to move numbers in my race? Yes."

In early 2006, a coalition of dozens of liberal Ohio religious leaders filed a complaint with the IRS alleging that Johnson had violated his church's nonprofit status by endorsing Blackwell through the Ohio Restoration Project. As of this writing, the IRS has declined to rule on the complaint.

But as the 2006 primaries approached, the perception of Blackwell as the Christian Right's candidate made even many in Ohio's Republican establishment cringe. One of Columbus's top lobbyists said that he and other Republicans were worried that Ohio was "going back to the Stone Ages of Salem."[23] But primary elections are won by appealing to hard-line party activists, and Blackwell, along with the growing organizational muscle of Ohio's Christian Right, forced his opponents rightward. One of them was Jim Petro, then state attorney general. Petro burnished his Christian credentials by airing a commercial featuring him with a Bible. And he took the unusual step of naming a running mate during the primaries, a Cincinnati county commissioner named Phil Heimlich. An evangelical Christian, Heimlich had recently been working as a consultant for Phil Burress at Citizens for Community Values.

Heimlich was not invited to attend the first Ohio Restoration Project luncheon outside Cincinnati. He suspected, of course, that that was because he was the running mate of Blackwell's most formidable challenger. But Heimlich had come to the Convention Center ballroom anyway, as an audience member. In an interview after the event, he said he was troubled by what he'd seen. "We are creating the impression that Christianity is a political movement, as opposed to God wanting a personal relationship with us," Heimlich said. "We're sending the message that unless you agree with us on certain issues, you're not eligible for the Kingdom of God. You may be pro-abortion, pro–gay rights—which I am not—but that doesn't disqualify you from a relationship with Jesus Christ. . . . Anybody who has a requirement to enter the Kingdom of God other than accepting Christ the Savior and asking forgiveness for sin is essentially doing what the Pharisees did."

By the time Ohio's May 2006 primary arrived, Russell Johnson had signed up eighteen hundred Patriot Pastors. Heimlich had dropped his bid to run for lieutenant governor two months earlier. The third Republican gubernatorial contender had also dropped out, leaving a two-way race between Ken Blackwell and Jim Petro. Blackwell took the Republican nomination with nearly 56 percent of the vote. November, however, vindicated the Ohio GOP establishment's fears about Blackwell, who lost in a landslide. With a rash of corruption scandals plaguing top state Republican officials, Democratic gubernatorial candidate Ted Strickland, an ordained Methodist minister, managed to win half of the state's weekly churchgoers. Had John Kerry fared so well among Ohio churchgoers two years earlier, he would have won the presidency.

Ohio was hardly the only place to see a Republican candidate lash his candidacy to a Christian Right revitalized by a state marriage-amendment campaign. The same thing happened in a handful of other states, with the efforts frequently connected to the Family Research Council and to Family Policy Councils. Just as the Ohio Restoration Project was getting off the ground in early 2005 and boosting Ken

Blackwell's candidacy, for example, Texas governor Rick Perry was hitting some strong political headwinds. Having failed to deliver on promises to reform the state's school finance system and to push a property tax cut through the Republican-controlled legislature, Perry, a Republican, watched his poll numbers wilt. He'd inherited the governorship when his predecessor, George W. Bush, was elected president in 2000, and had been voted back into office with nearly 60 percent of the vote in 2002. But almost two years before Perry would face reelection in 2006, U.S. senator Kay Bailey Hutchison, a Republican, began to weigh a primary challenge to him.

Hutchison began taking swipes at Perry's broken promises in the news media. Her aides cited internal polls that showed her beating Perry, and noted her 67 percent job approval rating. But Perry knew Hutchison's weak spot in a Republican primary: She had a somewhat moderate stance on abortion rights, opposing an outright ban. So naturally, the governor began looking for a way to shore up the Texas GOP's conservative evangelical base.

A ballot initiative to amend Texas's constitution to ban same-sex marriage presented the perfect opportunity. Called "Proposition 2," the marriage amendment was the only one in the nation to land on a state ballot in 2005. Drafted by the Texas Family Policy Council, Proposition 2 had passed in the Texas House and Senate, and, though it wasn't required by law, Governor Perry had taken the unusual step of signing it, to show his fervent support. Then, in May 2005, six months before the amendment was scheduled to appear on the ballot, Perry began appearing at a series of pastors' briefings across the state. The meetings were organized by a new group with a familiar-sounding name: the Texas Restoration Project. "One of the great myths of our time is that you can't legislate morality," Perry told the first pastors' briefing, in Austin. "If you can't legislate morality, then you can neither lock criminals up or let them go free. . . . I say you can't *not* legislate morality."[24]

Over the next few months, Perry addressed thousands of mostly evangelical pastors at Texas Restoration Project briefings in Houston,

Dallas, and San Antonio, building support for Proposition 2 and, in the process, for his own reelection. By the end of June, Kay Bailey Hutchison announced that, rather than challenge Perry, she would run for reelection to the U.S. Senate. She was already the fifth highest-ranking Republican in the Senate, Hutchison explained in announcing her decision to forgo a Perry challenge, and there was a good chance she could jump to the number three spot after the election.

But some political insiders, and many Christian Right activists, said Hutchison had been scared off by the Texas Restoration Project. "In April, Kay Bailey Hutchison already had an office set up in Texas—she's going to run for governor," said an Ohio political strategist who helped export the Ohio Restoration Project to Texas and who requested anonymity. "Rick Perry has some challenges, his numbers are weakening. We just said to him, 'Organize a summit for Patriot Pastors at the governor's mansion.' They had over six hundred pastors show up. A few weeks later, Kay Bailey Hutchison recalibrates and says, 'Maybe I don't need to do this.' It was more than a coincidence. This is not rocket science. You get pastors involved, and you move the map." Perry would go on to win reelection in 2006.

It's impossible to tell how many new evangelical voters the Texas Restoration Project signed up before Election Day 2005, when Proposition 2 appeared on the ballot. But most of the roughly one hundred thousand voters to register between the 2004 and 2005 elections resided in the conservative exurban and rural counties of Texas, where the group had been most active.

The leader of the Texas Restoration Project was Laurence White, a pastor whose Houston church includes fifteen hundred members. White encouraged the Patriot Pastors to designate the Sunday before Election Day "Reclaiming Texas Sunday" and to use their sermons on that day to frame the same-sex marriage ban and stopping abortion as their top political priorities. "These church people may have been voting in the past," White said in an interview in his Houston office, sitting beneath a framed photo of himself and Ronald Reagan, "but they were voting as conservative or liberal or Democrat or Republican. We want to begin a pattern where evangelicals vote as Christians first and foremost."

As he did with the Ohio Restoration Project, Family Research Council president Tony Perkins attended early organizational meetings for the Texas Restoration Project. It was partly his connection to Perkins that landed White an invitation to attend his first Arlington Group meeting just a couple of days after Election Day 2005, when Texas's marriage amendment passed with overwhelming support. At the meeting, held in Family Research Council headquarters in Washington, White discussed the success of the Texas Restoration Project and asked the Arlington Group to help him execute a bold new plan: to export his organization to any number of states on an as-needed basis in order to promote conservative candidates and causes. Such an undertaking could capitalize on the influence of hundreds of thousands of evangelical pastors, and White already had a name for it: the American Restoration Project.

In addition to Laurence White, the Arlington Group's November 2005 Washington summit included an important presentation from Kelly Shackelford, president of Focus on the Family's Texas Family Policy Council. A lawyer whose victories in a string of landmark religious liberty cases won him national attention, Shackelford was Phil Burress's Texas counterpart. And like Burress in Ohio, Shackelford was more responsible than anyone for getting Texas's same-sex marriage ban on the ballot in 2005. Governor Rick Perry and the Texas Restoration Project provided the brawn for promoting Proposition 2. Shackelford was the brains behind the operation.

Unlike Burress in Ohio, Shackelford didn't need to collect hundreds of thousands of signatures to get Proposition 2 on the Texas ballot. Instead, the Republican-controlled state legislature simply voted the amendment onto the ballot in spring 2005. (Ohio's Republican-dominated state legislature could have done the same thing in 2004, but declined.) Just as Ohio's signature drive played to the strengths of

Burress, a former union organizer, the process in Texas matched Shackelford's skills perfectly. "Once we started this, we said, 'We're going to
need some good legal advice,'" said Republican representative Warren
Chisum, chief sponsor of the gay marriage ban in the Texas House of
Representatives. "So Kelly [Shackelford] and I got together and worked
very closely."

Shackelford drafted the amendment's sweeping language, which
barred not only gay marriage but also arrangements similar to marriage,
understood to include civil unions and domestic partnerships. Then,
working closely with the state legislature, he revised it repeatedly with
an eye toward averting potential legal challenges. When Proposition 2
came up for its public hearing at the Texas House of Representatives in
April 2005, Shackelford was the only person to show up to testify on its
behalf. More than one hundred fifty gay rights activists flooded the
hearing room to rail against it, pushing the afternoon session to past two
in the morning.

Because it was the only marriage amendment on the ballot in the
country in 2005, and because Congress was expected to vote on the
Federal Marriage Amendment in early 2006, Shackelford wanted
Proposition 2 to pass in a landslide, to send a strong message to Washington about the public's overwhelming support for banning gay marriage. But since 2005 was an off-year election, which typically see
dismal turnouts, he worried that liberal activists would rally their troops
to the polls. Shackelford was less concerned about losing the vote than
he was about the amendment passing by a much tighter margin than it
had in other states the previous year. Such an outcome, he feared,
would be interpreted by Washington as a sign of flagging support for the
Federal Marriage Amendment.

Because Proposition 2 hadn't required a signature drive, however,
Shackelford lacked a grassroots volunteer network that could promote
the amendment and mobilize evangelical voters. The Texas Restoration
Project was working with pastors, but Shackelford wanted to reach in-
the-pews evangelicals, as well as the many pastors who were either too

busy or too timid to join the Texas Restoration Project but who nonetheless wanted to help pass Proposition 2. So he phoned the chiefs of the eleven Family Policy Councils who'd spearheaded marriage amendment bans the previous year and asked what he should do. They told him not to worry, that he could run his amendment campaign almost entirely online.

Under the auspices of a political action committee called Texans For Marriage, Shackelford quickly set to work building his Web site. Sleek and simple, it featured everything a conservative activist or pastor could possibly need to promote Proposition 2: downloadable inserts for church bulletins; ready-to-print newspaper ads; dozens of videotaped endorsements from pastors of different denominational and racial backgrounds; additional videotaped endorsements from officials at Focus on the Family and the Family Research Council; a list of dos and don'ts concerning what pastors could say from the pulpit; and a handful of field-tested sermons on the topic of opposing gay marriage.

With Christian Coalition of Texas totally dismantled, it also fell to Shackelford's Family Policy Council, called the Free Market Foundation, to distribute three million voter guides about Proposition 2. And just when he thought he had it all under control, Shackelford's fear about gay rights activists mobilizing against the amendment was realized. Just two weeks before Election Day, a group called No Nonsense in November began placing automated "robocalls" to millions of Texas homes. The calls employed a novel tactic, alleging that the amendment was written so broadly that it threatened to undo heterosexual marriage. The calls were taped by a Presbyterian minister, invoked the writings of two well-known Texas Republican figures as being against the proposition—even though both vigorously insisted they were not—and ended with the salutation "God Bless You," allegedly giving the impression that the Republican and religious establishments opposed Proposition 2. "We are making a horse race out of [an anti–gay marriage amendment] for the first time in any state," boasted the gay rights activist who led the effort.[25]

Shackelford, of course, saw the robocall campaign as a dirty trick. But he lost little time in taping his own calls to counter it. Knowing that the state Republican Party—where David Barton, the Republican National Committee's liaison to the evangelical community in the 2004 campaign, was still vice chairman—could be depended on to get its evangelical base to the polls to support Proposition 2, Shackelford instead targeted his calls to swing voters. He tapped one of the state's Catholic archbishops to tape a bilingual call to Hispanic voters, a black megachurch pastor for a call to African Americans, and state representative Warren Chisum, Proposition 2's chief sponsor in the Texas House and a longtime rancher, for a call to rural households. Costing nearly a hundred thousand dollars, the effort reached four million Texas homes.

When the polls closed a few days later, on the evening of Tuesday, November 8, Kelly Shackelford knew his plan had worked. Proposition 2 passed with 76 percent support, with 18 percent of registered voters turning out to vote. While hardly soaring, off-year turnout for constitutional amendments in Texas had rarely cracked 10 percent before.

As he watched the returns come in over the TV screens at the Proposition 2 victory party at a megachurch outside Austin, his wife and three young children beside him, Shackelford breathed a sigh of relief. He could hold his head high going into that week's Arlington Group meeting; he had authored 2005's sole state marriage amendment and helped pass it in a landslide. A long-standing Arlington Group member, Shackelford was in the habit of flying to Washington every six weeks to attend its powwows. But he would have to deliver his presentation on Proposition 2 via videoconference from Texas. He had spent so many long hours on the amendment campaign, his wife wouldn't let him leave town.

It would be an important presentation nonetheless, with dozens of Christian Right activists in Washington looking for guidance on how to wage their own state amendment campaigns in 2006. Shackelford offered them plenty of legal, political, and tactical advice from the Proposition 2 campaign, but he stressed that the "key thing was the reliance on prayer." Shackelford told the Arlington Group how, on the day the anti–Proposition 2 robocalls started going out from the gay rights group, his political action committee had just six hundred dollars left in its bank account. He knew that an automated call effort to combat No Nonsense in November would require roughly a hundred thousand dollars. With less than two weeks to go till Election Day, Shackelford sat in his office, bowed his head, and prayed.

Two hours later, the phone rang. A Dallas businessman was offering to wire a hundred thousand dollars to the political action committee's account the following morning. "The other side is doing strategy, our side relies on prayer," Shackelford said, recalling his Arlington Group presentation. With that, the baton was passed to the Family Policy Councils that would lead most of the eight state marriage amendment campaigns of 2006. All but one would succeed.

8

The Bench Press

"If you believe that God meant a particular

thing by what is in the Bible, . . . you will

be much more open to the idea that those

who made our Constitution meant a partic-

ular thing. And that the judge who is the

reader of the Constitution does not have the

freedom to make it mean something else."

—𝔪—

It didn't look like the kind of place where a Supreme Court nominee's fate could be sealed. Manuel Miranda's office consisted of a lap-
top nestled atop a slender desk tucked behind the couch in his Capitol
Hill living room. Floor-to-ceiling built-ins held biographies of Pope

John Paul II and a copy of Robert Bork's *The Tempting of America*, along with a shoebox-sized television set tuned to MSNBC. A small toy car belonging to Miranda's not quite two-year-old son peeked out from the cushion of the loveseat. Miranda, a chubby, Cuban-born lawyer who two years earlier was working as counsel to Senate Majority Leader Bill Frist, picked up the phone to assume his new perch as commander of America's conservative activist army. Their mission: defending President Bush's Supreme Court nominees from the liberal attackers who'd sabotaged Robert Bork's nomination eighteen years earlier.

It was nine-thirty on a typically sultry July night in Washington in 2005, and George W. Bush had just announced the nation's first Supreme Court nomination in over a decade on prime-time television. The moment for which conservatives had been planning for more than a decade, the moment that had helped drive tens of millions of evangelical Christians to the polls the previous November, the moment that had spurred James Dobson to hit the campaign trail to assist in toppling Democratic titan Tom Daschle and to work for a handful of Republican Senate candidates, had finally arrived. Hunched over his desk, receiver pressed to his ear, Miranda introduced himself as the host of the evening's conference call. The rapid-fire clicks of more than seventy of the country's most powerful right-wing activists piling onto the line ricocheted through his living room.

Miranda had assembled his network, which he called the Third Branch Conference, over the course of the previous six months. It included lawyers, pro-life advocates, and, most outspoken of all, dozens of influential evangelical pastors and activists. The evangelical contingent included representatives from the Arlington Group, Focus on the Family, the Family Research Council, and Focus's state-level Family Policy Councils. Many of the callers were jumping in straight from a teleconference organized by the White House, on which administration aides delivered a pep talk about John Roberts, the federal appeals court judge who'd just been nominated by Bush to take Justice Sandra Day O'Connor's place on the Supreme Court.

As luck would have it, Miranda had handled Roberts's file during his nomination to the District of Columbia's Court of Appeals two years earlier. At the time, Miranda was working as a high-ranking staffer for the Senate Judiciary Committee. Roberts's was the last file he'd supervised before joining Senator Frist's staff to head up judicial nominations for the majority leader in early 2003. Miranda's brief tenure on the Hill had basically consisted of shepherding Bush's judicial nominations through the often tumultuous Senate confirmation process.

Opening the July conference call, Miranda stressed the president's bravery in forgoing a female or minority candidate to fill the vacancy left by O'Connor, the high court's first female justice, who'd announced her retirement a few weeks earlier. Miranda also reviewed Roberts's sterling legal credentials. He was a two-year veteran of the Court of Appeals for the District of Columbia, whose power is second only to that of the Supreme Court. Roberts earned his conservative bona fides clerking for Supreme Court Justice William Rehnquist, who'd later become chief justice, and by serving in the Reagan and first Bush administrations. And he'd ingratiated himself with Washington's power circles through a more than decade-long tenure at Hogan & Hartson, one of the capital's top firms, where he'd argued dozens of cases before the Supreme Court. In his opening remarks on the conference call, Miranda referred to Roberts repeatedly as a "lawyer's lawyer."

But judging from Miranda's responses during the call's twenty-minute Q&A portion—the call itself was closed to the press—and from interviews with participants afterward, the Third Branch activists were much more interested in learning whether Roberts was predisposed toward overturning *Roe v. Wade* and about his religious background. By the end of the call, it was clear that they had established that the nominee was a committed member of a Catholic parish in suburban Maryland whose priest had attended pro-life rallies, and that Roberts's wife was legal counsel for a small and relatively obscure group called Feminists for Life.

More impressive than such crackerjack fact-finding, the July conference call revealed a remarkable level of political sophistication among a crowd often perceived as having knee-jerk reactions. Rather than come out swinging for Roberts—tripping alarm bells for their opponents on the left, like People for the American Way and NARAL Pro-Choice America—the activists on Miranda's call were plotting to lie low so that expected opposition from the left would come through in the news media as more shrill. "Being sober . . . is always a good idea," Miranda told his Third Branch compatriots, reminding them that the Democratic National Committee trolled the Web sites of right-wing groups in search of outlandish comments. "Everyone should keep their powder dry, and we'll defend [Roberts] in due course." One participant later said the strategy devised on the call boiled down to a single word: restraint.

This was grown-up strategy for a grown-up conservative movement that was less comfortable taking marching orders from the White House than it was taking matters into its own hands. Back in 2003, the White House had handpicked four allies to sell Supreme Court nominees to conservatives and fend off the liberal attack dogs. Dubbed the "four horsemen," the group included Reagan-era attorney general Ed Meese, George H. W. Bush's White House counsel C. Boyden Gray, Federalist Society executive vice president Leonard Leo, and Jay Sekulow, an evangelical legal advocate and talk radio host. Each adviser had a clear constituency that he would try to sell Bush's high court nominees to. Miranda had met with the four horsemen in 2003, when he was a Senate staffer. The following year, Miranda was pressured to resign his Senate post because of his role in "MemoGate," a beltway scandal in which Republican Senate aides were accused of improperly accessing confidential Democratic memos from an unsecured Judiciary Committee computer server. Miranda admitted to reading the memos, but denied any wrongdoing.[1]

From his new vantage point on the outside of official Washington and inside the conservative activist network, Miranda viewed the four horsemen with skepticism. He thought they were likely to be better at telling the White House what it wanted to hear than they were at coordinating with "grasstops" leaders, powerful state-level activists who commanded battalions of grassroots activists to shore up vital conservative support for Bush's Supreme Court nominees. Because the horsemen reported to the White House, Miranda thought they lacked credibility with conservative activists. A case in point was Sekulow, the White House point man on evangelical outreach for judicial nominees. Sekulow had won historic religious liberties cases before the Supreme Court and claimed an e-mail list of more than eight hundred thousand names for his group the American Center for Law and Justice, which was founded by Pat Robertson. But Sekulow had little contact with evangelical activists in the field. Most of those activists were instead plugged in to Focus on the Family's web of organizations. "There's a French cuff crowd in Washington who would love nothing more than to control the message," Miranda said. "That's a misguided attempt to do what the left does. The weakness of the left is their vertical formation."

Even before Miranda's call had gotten under way on the night of the Roberts nomination, the White House was working to line up evangelical support for the nominee. It reached out to top activists through Karl Rove and his deputy, Tim Goeglein, deputy director of the White House Office of Public Liaison. Since the beginning of Bush's first term, Goeglein had been the president's chief envoy to the evangelical community. "'He said, I wanted you to hear it from the White House first,'" then-National Association of Evangelicals president Ted Haggard said in an interview on the evening of the Roberts nomination, shortly after hanging up with Goeglein. "Our confidence is high because he indicated that this was a man who would adhere to the Constitution, who would have respect for precedent, but that precedent would not have the same weight as the Constitution itself."

Asked if he took Goeglein's remark as a suggestion that Roberts was likely to vote to overturn *Roe v. Wade*, Haggard said, "That was the thought that came to my mind as he was going over it."

The White House offensive, which sources close to James Dobson said included a call to him from Karl Rove, worked beautifully. In a rare conference call with reporters the next day, Dobson gushed over Roberts. "I don't think there's any evidence that he's going to be another [David] Souter," he said, referencing the George H. W. Bush Supreme Court appointee who was sold as a conservative but who turned out to be a moderate and voted to uphold *Roe*. "Justice Souter was what's called a black box. No one knew what was in it. We know a lot about Judge Roberts from his life, from his record, and from the things that he has stood for, and we feel much more comfortable with this nomination." Indeed, Dobson said, "This is a man who we could get very excited about."

Family Research Council president Tony Perkins, also on the call, struck a triumphant tone, claiming that the Roberts nomination fulfilled Bush's campaign promise to appoint justices in the mold of the Supreme Court's two most conservative jurists, Antonin Scalia and Clarence Thomas. Perkins vowed that FRC would "do all we can to mobilize concerned citizens."

Less than forty-eight hours after the Roberts nomination, Manuel Miranda was invited to address the Arlington Group coalition, which had gathered at the Family Research Council's downtown Washington headquarters for a previously scheduled two-day meeting. The Roberts nomination had knocked all other business off the Arlington Group's agenda, and Miranda joined a strategy panel moderated by Paul Weyrich. According to Miranda, Arlington Group members pressed him on why he was confident that Roberts was pro-life and would, given the opportunity, vote to overturn *Roe*. Some were concerned that Roberts's brief stint as a judge made it difficult to draw conclusions about where he stood on such controversial issues. Miranda gave the usual lines about the nominee's conservative, if thin, record of judicial rulings and about Roberts being well known and highly regarded within Washington's conservative circles. "As my grandma used to say, he's hung out with all the right people," Miranda said in an interview after the meeting.

Ultimately, though, Miranda told the Arlington Group that supporting Roberts required a "leap of faith" that was made easier by Roberts's Catholicism. The "single most important thing" about Roberts, Miranda said, was his wife's affiliation with Feminists for Life.

The Arlington Group discussion then turned to strategy for helping to ensure that Roberts survived the expected assault from the left. As on

Miranda's conference call, the general agreement was to lie low. "I've been here since the [Abe] Fortas nomination fight, and I've seen a lot of it," Weyrich said in an interview shortly before his Arlington Group presentation. "We'll tell them what to look for and what not to get involved in. We don't want people out there making foolish statements . . . and we may not have to expend that much energy."

In the two months between John Roberts's July 2005 rollout and the beginning of his Senate confirmation hearings in September, the Christian Right's enthusiasm for the nominee waned considerably. It began in early August, when *The Los Angeles Times* reported that, as a lawyer with Hogan & Hartson in the mid-1990s, Roberts had given pro bono assistance to a group of gay rights activists. The activists were preparing to go before the Supreme Court to challenge a Colorado law banning the passage of any gay rights legislation. They wound up winning their case, with the Court striking down the Colorado law in its 1996 decision *Romer v. Evans.* Focus on the Family found the disclosure of Roberts's role in the case particularly unnerving, since Focus had actively promoted the 1992 Colorado ballot initiative that enacted the law. Without James Dobson's personal involvement, the initiative probably would not have appeared on the ballot in the first place.

Unease about Roberts's short rulings record as a judge also continued to grow. His brief tenure on the federal bench had allowed him to pen fewer than fifty published opinions, very few of them on controversial cases that could provide clear insights into his judicial philosophy. Roberts's thin record was particularly worrisome to conservative activists based outside Washington who, unlike those on the Beltway's conservative circuit, didn't know Roberts personally and didn't have colleagues who could personally vouch for him. "This wasn't someone like a Scalia or Thomas, where you know where they're coming from" by examining their judicial records, said chief Family Research Council lobbyist Connie Mackey in an interview. "Nobody has a claim to make on how he'd see a *Roe v. Wade.* It's anybody's guess about what he thinks about precedent."

And yet the Family Research Council and other evangelical advocacy groups could not actively oppose Roberts; his legal credentials were iron-clad. "It's just a big fat question mark," Mackey said, "and we'd like the White House to find as good a candidate with less of a question mark."

In retrospect, it became clear that the initial outpouring of Christian Right support for Roberts's nomination was owed largely to the fact that, in the forty-eight hours leading up to its announcement, the Washington rumor mill was running full tilt with reports that Bush's pick would be someone wholly unacceptable to the movement. The news media were reporting that Bush would most likely choose Judge Edith Clement, who sat on the U.S. Court of Appeals for the Fifth Circuit in New Orleans. Social conservatives saw Clement as a wild card because she hadn't ruled on any hot-button cases and lacked the long conservative résumé of a nominee like Roberts. The speculation provoked a frenzied conference call among the Arlington Group, which had sent out a thirty-six-page analysis of Clement's record to its members. The call was marked by hand-wringing over how to respond. "The elation you sensed on Roberts came on the heels of the rumor that we spent the day with Edith Clement," said the FRC's Mackey. "The White House fakes left and then goes right, and then we're all elated."

When the Arlington Group reconvened in Washington for its September 2005 meeting, some of its members were much more skeptical about Roberts than they had been in July. The Federalist Society's Leonard Leo, one of the White House's four horsemen, arrived at the meeting to talk up Roberts and was peppered with tough questions. According to a participant in the session, one of the most skeptical of all was James Dobson.

—⁂—

Ambivalence over the first Republican-selected Supreme Court nominee in fourteen years was not what the White House or the GOP wanted its evangelical base to be feeling. On the campaign trail in

2004, Bush made the crowds roar with his vow to appoint federal judges who would "faithfully interpret the law, instead of legislating from the bench" and who "know the difference between personal opinion and the strict interpretation of the law." In the South, where Republican candidates had picked off all five Senate seats held by retiring Democratic senators in 2004, railing against the "runaway judiciary" was a staple of GOP stump speeches. "If you were to divvy up the United States and say what is the biggest percentage of the population, what are you going to come up with?" asked a top Republican aide in an interview after Roberts was nominated. "Evangelicals." The aide rose and walked toward a map of the United States that showed all the southern states where a Senate seat had gone from blue to red in 2004—North Carolina, South Carolina, Georgia, Louisiana, and Florida. "We took every one!" the aide bellowed. "And why do you think that was? Judges!

"Southerners can't understand," the aide continued, "why they can't say prayers at high school football games: 'I can't say a prayer at the football game where my son is going to be the quarterback? For 240 years in the United States people could do and say whatever the heck they wanted, and I want to say a prayer and you're telling me I can't? And you want me to vote for you?'"

In the decades-long conservative campaign to turn judicial appointees from a concern among wonky Republican insiders into a campaign issue, evangelicals had been pioneers. The Christian Right didn't emerge until the late 1970s, but 1973's *Roe v. Wade* retroactively became its bête noire. As the movement grew, it began tracing the decline of religion's role in public life to earlier Supreme Court decisions, like the 1960s-era Supreme Court rulings that struck down mandatory school prayer and devotional Bible reading in public school classrooms. In the 1980s, Supreme Court rulings banning public prayer at graduation ceremonies and stopping the mandatory posting of the Ten Commandments in public schools reinforced the Christian Right's view of the nation's high court as an unaccountable oligarchy.

More recently, the Christian Right has come to see the courts as the final impediment to legislative victories. Federal judges struck down the Partial Birth Abortion Ban Act of 2003 and have ruled against a handful of state-level Defense of Marriage Acts, the legislative gay marriage bans. The primary catalyst for jump-starting the Christian Right in the twenty-first century, the 2004 legalization of same-sex marriage in Massachusetts, also came at the hands of judges. "All the issues . . . boil down to the one simple issue, which is the Supreme Court," James Dobson said after Election Day 2004. "When the Supreme Court makes all the great moral decisions of our time, they are overriding the will of the people . . . and I believe there is a backlash coming."

Conservative strategists who have worked to popularize judicial activism as a political issue among rank-and-file conservative voters have seen evangelical Christians as perhaps their most important target constituency. Not only are evangelicals particularly sensitive to court rulings on abortion, gay rights, and the place of religion in public life, they also espouse a literal reading of the Bible that comports well with the conservative ideal of constitutional "originalism." Holding that the Constitution is a static document that means only what its drafters intended, originalists call on judges to practice restraint. They chafe at the notion that the Founding Founders envisioned a right to abortion or a right to practice homosexual sex, and view decisions recognizing such rights as exercises in judicial activism. "I don't draw many parallels between the Constitution and the Bible," said one strategist familiar with Republican thinking on judges. "But if you believe that God meant a particular thing by what is in the Bible, and that I as a reader of the Bible do not have the freedom to make it mean whatever I jolly well please, you will be much more open to the idea that those who made our Constitution meant a particular thing. And that the judge who is the reader of the Constitution does not have the freedom to make it mean something else."

"It's almost as if religious people generally but evangelicals in particular," the strategist continued, "are tailor-made to better understand the kind of principles that the Founders established as our political system. They come with the right wiring."

Evangelical activists haven't fought to reverse the court-ordered gains of liberal groups like the American Civil Liberties Union and women's rights and gay rights groups just by increasing pressure for "strict constructionist" court appointments. Realizing that they were winning political battles only to be stymied in court, Christian Right groups in the late 1980s and early 1990s began opening public interest law firms to fund and litigate religious liberties, antiabortion, and antigay rights cases. Jay Sekulow, the evangelical White House "horseman" working on Supreme Court nominees, was drafted by Pat Robertson to open the American Center for Law and Justice (ACLJ) as a counterweight to the ACLU in 1990. In the decade that followed, Sekulow, a Brooklyn-born Jew who became a Messianic Jew—meaning that he believes Jesus is the Messiah—won a series of landmark Supreme Court decisions, including one that permitted religious groups to meet on public school property outside school hours. The ACLJ now has a budget of around thirty million dollars.[2]

At about the same time, in 1994, James Dobson and a handful of other top Christian Right figures launched a nonprofit law firm called Alliance Defense Fund (ADF). It helped fund the Terri Schiavo litigation for Schiavo's parents and successfully fought to revoke the nearly four thousand marriage licenses granted by San Francisco mayor Gavin Newsom to same-sex couples in 2004. Based in Scottsdale, Arizona, the firm has a seventeen-million-dollar budget and a hundred-person staff, including twenty in-house lawyers. In addition, ADF has trained a national attorney network of 850, with each lawyer pledging 450 pro bono hours over three years.[3] When Phil Burress needed a team of lawyers to draft an amendment to Ohio's constitution banning gay marriage and to protect it from dozens of legal challenges in 2004, it was ADF that stepped in to help.

*   *   *

With George W. Bush's victory, the gain of four Republican seats in the Senate, and an expected string of Supreme Court vacancies, the Christian Right's dream of shifting the Supreme Court's ideological composition finally seemed within reach following the 2004 election. After thirty years, *Roe. v. Wade* stood to be overturned. Laws denying gays the right to marry or to enter civil unions or other legal arrangements would be safe from judicial activists. Religion could make more inroads into public life. So it came as a major alarm to the movement that Senator Arlen Specter, the pro–abortion rights Republican from Pennsylvania who was in line to assume the chairmanship of the Senate Judiciary Committee, chose the day after his 2004 reelection victory to fire a shot across the bow to the White House on judicial appointments.

Earlier in 2004, Specter had come within less than 2 percentage points of being knocked off by an archconservative in Pennsylvania's Republican primary. His primary challenger had been aided by an endorsement from James Dobson. Specter probably owed his survival in the primary to President Bush's repeated visits to Pennsylvania on the senator's behalf. He was also greatly helped by support from Pennsylvania senator Rick Santorum, one of the country's most powerful and popular social conservatives. But on Wednesday, November 3, the day after Election Day, Specter warned the White House against nominating anti–abortion rights judges. "When you talk about judges who would change the right of a woman to choose, overturn *Roe v. Wade*, I think that is unlikely" that they would be confirmed by the Senate, Specter said at a Philadelphia news conference.

The remarks set off a firestorm in the Christian Right, which called for Republican senators to block Specter's ascension to the Judiciary Committee chairmanship. James Dobson urged his listeners to phone their senators to insist that they do so. Some congressional offices logged more than a thousand calls from angry pro-lifers.

Even as they were publicly calling for Specter's head, however, Christian Right leaders were facing the political reality that blocking him from the chairmanship was a long-shot gambit at best. In an Ar-

lington Group conference call shortly after the news media reported
Specter's comments, Paul Weyrich and a top aide to Senate Majority
Leader Bill Frist convinced the Christian Right's top leadership that it
would be better to neuter Specter than to derail him. According to one
participant on the call, the thinking went like this: "It was better to have
[Specter] tied down with a series of very clear statements of what he
would and wouldn't do, as opposed to toppling him. If he were toppled,
he would be out there accountable to no one, and he could work with
Democrats and help tie up any number of the president's nominees.
Specter is smarter than most of his colleagues, and most are fearful of
him. Having him out there on his own would have been a nightmare."
No one on the Arlington Group conference call objected to the plan.

National Association of Evangelicals then-president Ted Haggard,
meanwhile, in Washington for an Arlington Group meeting, said he
"coached" Specter for over an hour on how to deal with the pressure he
was getting from conservative evangelical groups. "I did not want the
chairman of the Judiciary Committee," Haggard said in an interview,
"to think that evangelicals are his enemy."

Within a couple of weeks, Specter, still trying to shore up the support of fellow Republicans who would have to ratify his appointment to
the Judiciary Committee chairmanship, called a press conference. He
announced that he had drawn up a pledge that, were he appointed
chairman, he would not apply a "litmus test" to President Bush's
Supreme Court judicial nominees, which meant he would not block
President Bush's appointments just because they threatened to overturn
Roe, as he had implied he would in his post–Election Day remarks.
The announcement secured the backing of Specter's conservative Republican colleagues, some of whom had been coordinating with the Arlington Group. And Specter's pledge included two additional victories
for the Arlington Group. One was a vow not to use the committee to
hold up the Federal Marriage Amendment, which Specter was on the
record as opposing. The other was a promise to consider changing Senate rules to overcome Democratic filibusters of judicial appointments, a
change that had been dubbed "the nuclear option."[4]

Immediately following his November press conference, Specter met with three members of the Arlington Group's executive committee: Paul Weyrich, Tony Perkins, and Gary Bauer. Dobson was in Washington and was invited to participate but, according to a source familiar with the situation, didn't want to lose face after opposing Specter so adamantly. "We are disappointed by the announcement that Senator Specter will become the Judiciary chairman," Dobson said in a statement at the time. "However, he will assume his new position on a very short leash."

At the meeting with Specter, Weyrich said that he and his colleagues extracted another promise from the senator: He would allow the Judiciary Committee's more conservative members to hire some committee staffers, who are key to preparing for judicial confirmation fights. (An aide to Specter denied the deal but said that Specter was "open to hiring good conservative candidates.")

In the minds of the Arlington Group members, their success in reining Specter in was a direct result of the huge role that evangelical voters, and groups like Focus on the Family and Ohio's Citizens for Community Values, had played on Election Day, which at the time was still a very fresh memory. "Absent the results of the 2004 election, what happened with Specter would not have occurred," Weyrich said afterward. "It was the recognition by the majority leader and many other senators on the Judiciary Committee that you simply cannot give our coalition the finger."

Indeed, after the 2004 election, Senate Majority Leader Frist, widely expected to run for president in 2008, began to march more in step with conservative evangelicals. After the Specter flap, Frist and the GOP's other Senate leaders appointed two of the chamber's most socially conservative Republicans, Sam Brownback of Kansas and newly elected Tom Coburn of Oklahoma, to the Judiciary Committee.

As 2005 opened, the Christian Right increased pressure on Frist and Senate Republicans generally to invoke the nuclear option, the suspension of the filibuster rule in voting to confirm the president's judicial nominees. The movement especially wanted to see confirmation of religious conservatives such as California Supreme Court justice Janice Rogers Brown and Texas Supreme Court justice Priscilla Owen, both nominated to the federal bench. Focus on the Family Action spent approximately one million dollars on radio and newspaper ads pressuring a handful of moderate Republicans to support the nuclear option. And in April, the Family Research Council sponsored a televised church rally that it called "Justice Sunday: Stop the Filibuster Against People of Faith." The event featured live appearances by James Dobson, Tony Perkins, and Chuck Colson, and included a videotaped message from Bill Frist.

"The filibuster was once abused to protect racial bias," read a flyer for Justice Sunday, "and it is now being used against people of faith."

Held at Highview Baptist Church in Louisville, Kentucky, the Sunday evening rally was broadcast live to hundreds of churches and on Christian cable TV and radio networks. Justice Sunday allowed the nation's top Christian Right leaders to circumvent the mainstream media and speak directly to a potential audience of tens of millions. It was an extension of the series of rallies sponsored by the Family Research Council to promote the Federal Marriage Amendment in the run-up to the 2004 election.[5]

Allegations of religious discrimination against the Senate Democrats who were holding up some of President Bush's judicial nominees were raised throughout the Justice Sunday rally. Dobson inspired a righteous cheer from the audience in proclaiming, "We *do* have a right to participate in this great representative form of government." Raising a Bible, Tony Perkins said, "As American citizens, we should not have to choose between believing what is in this book and serving the public."

A few weeks later, President Bush was asked at a press conference whether he agreed with the Justice Sunday speakers that Democratic stonewalling on some judicial nominees was an attack against people of faith. "I think people are opposing my nominees because they don't like [their] judicial philosophy," Bush responded. ". . . I don't ascribe a person's opposing my nominations to an issue of faith."

A few weeks after that, a group of seven Democratic and seven Republican senators dealt the Justice Sunday crowd a more severe blow. The so-called Gang of Fourteen senators announced that it had struck a deal to avert filibusters against judicial nominees except in "extraordinary circumstances." The compromise tabled the threat of the nuclear option, at least for the time being. Upon hearing the news, Dobson immediately took to the airwaves to mourn, taping a broadcast with Gary Bauer and Tony Perkins. "I was at home with my family . . . when I got a phone call," said Bauer. "I felt like someone had punched me in the stomach." Tony Perkins said that when he heard the news about the Gang of Fourteen compromise, he and his coworkers "began to pray about the situation, but I'll tell you what, I wanted to cry."

"I went home and hugged [my wife] and pulled the covers up over my ears and went to sleep," Dobson offered.

In response to e-mailed questions about the Senate compromise, Dobson said that the Senate Gang of Fourteen "will use the filibuster to prevent any pro-life, pro-marriage, pro-moral nominee from being confirmed." But the deal actually represented something of a victory for conservatives. It granted three of Bush's most controversial nominees — including Janice Rogers Brown and Priscilla Owen — up or down Senate votes, and all three were confirmed.

In the view of many conservative Christian activists, however, Senate Republicans had enough of a majority to invoke the nuclear option. And yet seven of them had snatched defeat from the jaws of victory. The Christian Right had again been shrugged off by the GOP, its supposed ally. So when Sandra Day O'Connor announced her retirement on the first day of July 2005, the Family Research Council wasn't going to be shy about telling the White House exactly what it was expecting in her replacement.

Or rather, what it wasn't expecting. The FRC said simply that it wanted President Bush's first Supreme Court nominee to be someone other than Attorney General Alberto Gonzales. A longtime Bush pal who had served on the Texas Supreme Court, Gonzales was widely rumored to be on Bush's short list for the U.S. Supreme Court. But he was tainted in the eyes of Christian conservatives because, as a Texas jurist, he had ruled to allow minors seeking an abortion to forgo parental notification in certain circumstances. "Our position on Attorney General Gonzales," Perkins said at a Family Research Council press conference held on the same day that O'Connor announced her retirement, "is that he holds great promise as attorney general."

On a trip to Europe the following week, Bush appeared visibly rankled by such swipes at Gonzales. "Al Gonzales is a great friend of mine," the president told USA Today. "I'm the kind of person, when a friend gets attacked, I don't like it." Senate Republicans called Christian Right activists to the Hill to urge them to cool their rhetoric.

Of course, the nomination of John Roberts a few weeks later allayed the Christian Right's fears. Roberts was elevated to fill the Chief Justice slot after William Rehnquist's death in September, and with substantial Democratic backing, he was confirmed later that month, 78 to 22. The apocalyptic fight between the left and right that many court watchers predicted would accompany George Bush's first Supreme Court appointment never materialized.

And yet many in the Arlington Group were far from satisfied. At the Family Research Council's televised Justice Sunday II event in August, this time featuring an appearance by embattled House Republican leader Tom DeLay, pledges of support for Roberts were more cautious than enthusiastic. Dobson, appearing via videotape, said that while it appeared that Roberts was a strict constructionist, "Only time will reveal his judicial philosophy and how it relates to the issues that we care about most."

—∞—

When the Family Research Council suggested in spring 2005 that Democrats were filibustering some of President Bush's judicial nominees because of their religious faith, the White House refused to get on board. But in the weeks after Chief Justice William Rehnquist's death in September 2005, the White House began hinting that Democrats might oppose Bush's next Supreme Court nominee for that very reason.

Three days after John Roberts's confirmation, the president shocked nearly everyone with his announcement that the next Supreme Court nominee would be White House counsel Harriet Miers. Many conservatives gasped. Miers had not been among the dozens of federal and state-level judges and legal scholars whom the conservative movement had been floating for the Supreme Court and whom the Bush White House had reportedly been considering. Conservatives had spent decades cultivating a deep bench of qualified Supreme Court candidates to compete with the surfeit of qualified liberal contenders. And now the White House was spurning the entire system with the selection of Harriet Miers, who had been neither a judge nor a scholar. Having spent much of her career in private practice, she had little in the way of a paper trail. Conservatives had seen this movie before: a Republican White House pushing an appointment with dubious conservative credentials, like Reagan's selection of Sandra Day O'Connor and George H. W. Bush's nomination of David Souter.

The White House emphasized Miers's evangelical Christian faith from the start. If John Roberts was sold through Washington's conservative elites, who were willing to see past his limited judicial record because he was a known quantity in the capital, Miers would be sold through evangelical activists, who would see past her complete lack of a judicial record because she was one of them.

By the time Manuel Miranda's eleven A.M. Third Branch conference call opened on the day of Miers's nomination—President Bush made the announcement at eight in the morning on the first Monday in October—a great deal about Miers's churchgoing habits was already known. The Web site of the evangelical newsweekly World had posted the details within ninety minutes of Bush's announcement. A former adviser to President Bush, World editor Marvin Olasky had gotten a phone call the day before from Harriet Miers's longtime friend—and sometime boyfriend—Nathan Hecht, a Texas Supreme Court justice. An evangelical Christian whose rulings had made him a hero to the pro-life community in Texas, Hecht told his old friend Olasky that Miers would most likely be named to the Supreme Court the following day. Olasky began rattling off questions and taking notes. He posted Hecht's responses on *World*'s blog the next morning, after the Miers announcement.

According to the *World*'s posts, Miers had a Catholic upbringing but didn't become a serious Christian until she started attending Hecht's nondenominational evangelical church around 1980, when she "made an abrupt change." "Look at her tax returns," Olasky quoted Hecht as saying. "She tithes." The posting also noted that Miers taught Sunday school at the church—Dallas's Valley View Christian Church—had sat on its Missions Committee for a decade, and had attended a pro-life dinner or two with Hecht. Asked by Olasky about Miers's stance on abortion, Hecht replied that "her personal views are consistent with that of evangelical Christians . . . You can tell a lot about her from her decade of service in a conservative church." The *World* blog also quoted Hecht as saying that Valley View was "in the vernacular, fundamentalist, but the media have used that word to tar us."

Before getting off the phone with Olasky the evening before Miers's nomination, Hecht gave him the phone number of Miers's longtime pastor, Ron Key. Olasky called Key that same evening and posted excerpts of the interview on *World*'s blog the next morning. According to Olasky's post, Key said that since Miers had first starting attending Valley View twenty-five years earlier, she had undergone a major transformation: "She came to a place where she totally committed her life to Jesus." Key also discussed Miers's politics. "Our church is strong for life, but Harriet and I have not had any conversations on that," he said. ". . . We believe in the biblical approach to marriage."

According to sources on Miranda's conference call, *World*'s posts about Miers's church life were a major topic of conversation. Rather than shoring up the support of the conservative activists, however, the revelations drove a sharp wedge between its evangelical and nonevangelical participants. Citing *World* blog postings that testified to her strong evangelical faith and considerable church involvement, the Third Branch Conference's evangelical participants were enthusiastic about Miers. Some were downright ecstatic. "I was very surprised by how much [Miers's evangelical faith] meant to them," Miranda said in an interview afterward. "It was remarkable how much it meant to them that she went to a particular church, that it said certain things on [the church's] Web site. I don't remember if it was that call or a subsequent call, but someone said she had had a total immersion baptism. And I was like, okay. . . ."

If evangelicals on Miranda's call were excited about Miers's nomination, Miranda himself, along with nearly all the Third Branch Conference's Catholic activists and its sizable contingent of lawyers and think tank scholars, expressed shock and disgust. To them, the White House had squandered a historic opportunity to reverse the legacy of Robert Bork. Bork's 1987 nomination had been derailed by Democrats who attacked the bold conservatism articulated in his voluminous writings and public remarks, including his view that *Roe v. Wade* was unconstitutional. Now President Bush had the opportunity to show that an unabashedly conservative nominee with a paper trail could survive confirmation. He had failed to do it with John Roberts, who had a thin dossier of judicial decisions, but had at least served for two years on the federal bench. For Miers, Bush's word and disclosures about her religious life would have to suffice as evidence of her solid conservative temperament. It was too much of a stretch.

To Miranda, Miers's nomination vindicated his fears that the four horsemen had insulated the White House from the conservative base they were supposed to be reaching out to. "The president has made possibly the most unqualified choice since Abe Fortas, who had been the president's lawyer," Miranda wrote in an e-mail to activists that morning. "The nomination of a nominee with no judicial record is a significant failure for the advisers that the White House gathered around it."

The split over Miers within the Third Branch Conference would not be easily contained. One source on the conference call said that an "interdenominational conflict" broke out when a well-known conservative Catholic activist warned evangelicals not to read too much into Miers's religious background. He reminded them that Supreme Court Justice Anthony Kennedy had been sold to the Christian Right as a conservative Catholic by the Reagan administration in 1987 but that he turned out to be a moderate who voted in favor of gay rights and abortion rights. James Dobson had branded him "one of the most dangerous men in America." The Catholic activist's warning irked Ken Hutcherson, an influential black megachurch pastor from Washington State. Hutcherson argued that "it's not the same thing" when inferring the ideology of a serious evangelical, who was certain to be a true-blue conservative.

As the rift between the two sides widened, one of the evangelical activists on the call began praying out loud for guidance. "I was very surprised" by the prayer, Miranda said. "It's not something I'm used to seeing. My contact with evangelicals is limited."

But the biggest bombshell on the call came from a representative of the Arlington Group. She said that James Dobson would be coming out strongly in support of Miers. That changed everything. Even some of the nonevangelical activists, who just moments ago had expressed outrage over Miers's nomination, said they would now need to learn more about what Dobson knew before they could decide how to proceed.

The White House had placed phone calls to evangelical leaders on the night of the Roberts nomination the previous July, but its evangelical outreach on the Miers nomination went much further. The administration organized a conference call with thirteen members of the Arlington Group's executive committee, including James Dobson, Tony Perkins, Gary Bauer, and Paul Weyrich, that took place just an hour or two after Bush announced Miers's nomination. The call featured Miers's old friend Nathan Hecht, of the Texas Supreme Court, and a federal judge from Dallas, Texas, named Ed Kinkeade, who was also close to Miers. According to *The Wall Street Journal*, one of the Arlington Group members asked the two judges if they believed that Miers, if given the chance, would vote to overturn *Roe v. Wade*. "Absolutely," Kinkeade replied. Hecht spoke up, too: "I agree with that. I concur."[6]

In an interview afterward, Hecht said that he could not recall if he discussed *Roe* on the Arlington Group conference call, but said that many Christian Right activists were reading too much into Harriet Miers's evangelical faith. "People want to know the character of a person, and faith plays into that," Hecht said. "But they're trying to extrapolate judicial views from that, and you simply can't do it."

But with a growing rebellion against the Miers nomination among Washington's conservative elite—the same crowd that had done so much to promote John Roberts—extrapolations from Miers's evangelical faith and church involvement were all that was keeping her nomination alive. Former Bush speechwriter David Frum, *Weekly Standard* editor William Kristol, and conservative columnists George Will and Charles Krauthammer all publicly lambasted Miers's nomination. Aides to Republican senators on the Judiciary Committee were leaking their doubts to the press. Prominent evangelical political activists were among Miers's few big-name defenders. "The preponderance of those who have been the most critical are not only inside the Beltway, they're also nonevangelicals," said the Southern Baptist Convention's Richard Land, a Miers supporter, in an interview at the time. "An extraordinarily close bond has been formed between [the president] and evangelicals."

While some prominent Arlington Group members—like Paul Weyrich and Gary Bauer—came out against Miers, other coalition members were standing firmly behind her. "Harriet is going to make a great justice," said Russell Johnson, the pastor and Arlington Group member who'd founded the Ohio Restoration Project. "I base it on this: You don't become a long-standing member and a Sunday school teacher in a [nondenominational evangelical] church without having some convictions. . . . The Sherlock Holmes school of deduction says that she has a worldview very much like George W. Bush's. This is somebody who believes in the literal interpretation of the Bible when it says tithe."

To Johnson and some other evangelical Arlington Group members, conservative activists who were ganging up on Miers just didn't get it. Miers was an active member of a conservative nondenominational evangelical church, the kind of church that Johnson led outside of Columbus, Ohio. As such, she was theologically barred from ruling in favor of abortion rights or same-sex marriage or against the incorporation of religion into public life. "You can be a member of some denominations and what the Bible says doesn't mean one whit," Johnson said. "But not with Ms. Miers. You can be a churchgoing member of many congregations and have a disconnect between private and public life. It's much more difficult to do that in Valley View Christian Church."

If much of the support for Miers inside the Arlington Group was a product of her evangelical background, a great deal of it was also in deference to James Dobson, who'd come out strongly for Miers on the very day she was nominated, as the Arlington Group rep said he would be doing on Manuel Miranda's conference call that day. Across the country, evangelical pastors too busy to keep abreast of political developments had long taken their cues from Dobson. "If Dobson hadn't come out with a strong statement that the lady was fine from a judicial worldview, it would have been a signal that we did not have enough information to support her," said Maryland pastor and Arlington Group member Harry Jackson after the Miers nomination. "There's a lot of faith being placed on Dr. Dobson's recommendation because we basically have no information. Without that, I'm not so sure we'd been able to pull this [evangelical support for Miers] off. . . . I don't think even [*Purpose-Driven Life* author] Rick Warren can rival the personal credibility of James Dobson when he says, 'I think this is good for the nation.'"

*   *   *

If Dobson's endorsement of Harriet Miers was propping up evangelical support for her, his vaguely worded pronouncements about his confidential conversations with Karl Rove were causing a stir in Washington. From the beginning, Dobson made it clear that his support for Miers was at least partly based on secret information from the White House. "Some of what I know I am not at liberty to talk about," he told *The New York Times* on the day of the Miers announcement. He also said, "I have reason to believe she is pro-life." He made similarly cryptic statements later that evening on the Fox News Channel.[7]

Two days later, Dobson devoted his entire *Focus on the Family* broadcast to the Miers nomination, playing up her reputation as a "deeply committed Christian" and announcing that he knew the "person who led her to the Lord." He also made more references to having secret information from the White House. "When you know some of the things I know," Dobson told his listeners, "that I probably shouldn't know, that take me in this direction, you'll know why I've said with fear and trepidation [that] I believe Harriet Miers will be a good justice."[8] Saying that he could not discuss his conversations with Rove, Dobson told listeners, "You will have to trust me on this one." Then he prayed on the air that he was not making a mistake in supporting Miers and asked the Lord to chastise him if he was. "If I have made a mistake here," Dobson said, "I will never forget the blood of those babies that will die that will be on my hands to some degree. That's why I don't take this lightly."

On the broadcast that day, Dobson insisted that he was not acting as "a shill" for the Bush administration. Then, the following afternoon, he joined a White House–led conference call that had been convened to stop the drain of conservative support for Miers. The call was led by Republican National Committee chairman Ken Mehlman and Tim Goeglein, the White House envoy to the evangelical community. A slate of high-profile, mostly evangelical religious conservatives, including Chuck Colson and Richard Land, took turns defending Miers as hundreds of activists across the country listened in. "This is one scary moment," Dobson said, according to a leaked recording of the call. "Every-thing I care about is on the line."

But Dobson reasoned that Bush was trustworthy on Miers because the president had thus far fulfilled his promise to appoint conservative judges to the federal bench, and because Bush had advanced the pro-life cause by signing the partial-birth abortion ban. "His commitment on the pro-life position," Dobson said of the president, "this is his per-sonal belief and philosophy, and I think probably theology. . . . [A]ll the conservatives out there who are beating him up . . . I think they ought to take a deep breath. . . . I have drawn the conclusion that Harriet Miers will be an excellent justice."

Within a week of Miers's nomination, Dobson's public remarks about the confidential information he'd gleaned from Karl Rove had prompted some senators, including Judiciary chairman Arlen Specter, to threaten him with a subpoena. As calls mounted even among evan-gelical conservatives for him to explain his support, Dobson announced that he would devote an installment of his daily radio broadcast to dis-closing what Rove had told him.

Dobson opened the program by noting, "I have been a topic of con-versation from the nation's capital to the tiniest burg and farming com-munity." Then he said that Karl Rove had given him clearance to reveal what he couldn't earlier: First, that some conservative candidates on President Bush's short list of Supreme Court nominees had requested they be taken off because the confirmation process had grown so ra-dioactive. And second, that Miers was an evangelical "from a very con-servative church, which is almost universally pro-life"; that she had challenged the American Bar Association's pro–abortion rights posi-tion; and that she'd been a member of the organization Texas Right to Life. (As president of the Texas Bar Association, Miers had challenged the American Bar Association on how it *formulated* its position on abor-tion rights and other controversial issues, but her personal stance re-mained unclear. Whether Miers was ever a member of Texas Right to Life also remained unclear, and the White House quickly distanced it-self from the claim.)

Dobson concluded the program by saying, "I want to speak directly to members of the Judiciary Committee about the possibility of my coming to testify. If they want to do that, then I just suggest that they quit talking about it and just go do it."

Dobson's willingness to go to bat for Miers mystified many of his Christian Right allies, who wondered when the political strongman who'd threatened to leave the GOP in the 1990s had begun carrying the White House's water. "Dr. Dobson is putting a whole lot of moral capital on the line," said Mike Schwartz, the longtime Christian activist turned chief of staff to Oklahoma senator Tom Coburn, "to put himself at the service of the White House in a political cause such as this."

Even if they didn't oppose Miers's nomination outright, many Christian Right organizations outside the Arlington Group, like Concerned Women for America and Phyllis Schlafly's Eagle Forum, were vocal in their skepticism about her for the same reasons other conservatives were. Even Family Research Council president Tony Perkins shelved plans for a Justice Sunday III broadcast upon getting word of the Miers nomination. "It's a gross miscalculation," Perkins said of the White House at the time. "To support Roberts was a step of faith. Miers is more a leap of faith." Some FRC sources said the organization was hamstrung from coming out forcefully against Miers because of Dobson's support for her.

Why was Dobson so supportive of Miers? Off the record, some activists said Dobson's full-throated endorsement was a testament to the success of the White House in winning trust from a leader who had long been wary of politicians. "The president is an evangelical Christian and that plays well with the evangelical leadership," said one Family Research Council source. "When they get calls from the White House and are reassured that this person is going to be what we want them to be, they feel like they have every reason to believe him. Dobson didn't call here asking for any advice. He just relied on the word of Karl Rove. The only comment I have is complete puzzlement."

Karl Rove worked hard to cultivate Dobson's support for Miers in the days leading up to her nomination, calling him several times before President Bush made the announcement public. Rove also called Chuck Colson, who would compare notes with Dobson afterward. Asked in an interview if he had as much confidence in Miers as Dobson did, given Rove's assurances, Colson said, "I'd rather not answer that."

Of course, Dobson himself had said that his support for Miers was born of her evangelical faith and his trust in Bush. Former Focus on the Family president Don Hodel spoke with Dobson during Miers's nomination ordeal, and said Dobson was wise to show steadfast support for the nominee, at least until confirmation hearings began. Otherwise, Hodel said, the White House might come to view him as an undependable ally and lock him out in the future. "The White House, and particularly Karl Rove, has earned his trust," said Hodel. "And the White House has increasingly come to trust Dobson."

But a cozy relationship with the White House could burn up the independence and credibility that have won Dobson his enormous influence. "Certain groups care more about Karl Rove taking their phone call than they do about virtually anything else," said a strategist familiar with Republican thinking during the Miers nomination. "So they're very willing to be deputized, willing to shill. I've been around this movement long enough to know you can't swing a dead cat without hitting an ulterior motive."

Dobson claimed that his support for Miers also stemmed from discussions with sources in Texas who were close to Miers. But Ron Key, Miers's pastor for twenty-five years—who'd spoken to World editor Marvin Olasky on the eve of Miers's nomination—said he never spoke to Dobson. Dobson's radio cohost John Fuller called Key to tape an interview, but not until a few days after Dobson had already pledged his support. "They wanted to talk to me to help people understand why Dr. Dobson had supported her," Key said. But the interview never aired.

Dobson also said he talked to Texas judges Nathan Hecht and Ed Kinkeade about Miers. But Hecht said he talked to Dobson only as part of the Arlington Group conference call, and that his presentation lasted all of five minutes. Kinkeade declined interview requests, but another top evangelical source spoke to Kinkeade at Dobson's behest, and said Kinkeade assured him that Miers "shared your [evangelical Christian] worldview."

If Miers's religious worldview was winning her evangelical supporters in the American heartland, however, some evangelical activists and Republican aides in Washington were distressed both by the White House strategy of using Miers's evangelical faith to promote her and by Dobson's cooperation. Such activists and aides began citing Christian historian Mark Noll's book *The Scandal of the Evangelical Mind*, which argues that American evangelicalism has jettisoned the robust intellectualism of earlier generations, and too often embraces identity politics.

"We'd argued when it came to [President Bush's other] nominations that making any sort of big deal about their faith was absolutely not acceptable," said one strategist familiar with Republican thinking. "Why are [Dobson and other evangelical leaders] being chosen as advocates for her? Is it because they are evangelicals? Is their argument that because Miers is an evangelical Christian she will make a better judge, suggesting that her religious faith will influence her judging? If I believed that, I would vote against her. The Founding Fathers would say, 'Why do you think we put no religious test of public office in the Constitution?'"

Three weeks after Miers's nomination, Manuel Miranda announced the formation of a new coalition of conservative organizations calling for Miers to withdraw her nomination. The group included former Family Research Council president Ken Connor and such Religious Right mainstays as Eagle Forum. Its Web site was, simply, WithdrawMiers.org.

Two days after Miranda unveiled the new group, *The Washington Post* reported that Miers had provided the Senate Judiciary Committee with a copy of a speech she made in the early 1990s in which she endorsed a principle of "self-determination" in thinking about abortion rights. In the same speech, Miers, who was then serving as president of the State Bar of Texas, said, "We gave up [long ago on] legislating religion or morality." The speech defended jurists who had invited charges of judicial activism because they ordered state legislatures to address thorny social issues. And it referred admiringly to feminist icon Gloria Steinem.[9]

The following morning, the conservative evangelical group Concerned Women for America called for Miers to withdraw.

One day later, she did. Her official reason for the withdrawal, that the Senate Judiciary Committee was seeking documents related to her White House work that the Bush administration considered privileged, was widely dismissed as a smoke screen.

James Dobson quickly issued a statement applauding the move. "In recent days I have grown increasingly concerned about her conservative credentials," Dobson said, "and I was dismayed to learn this week about her speech in 1993, in which she sounded pro-abortion themes and expressed so much praise for left-wing feminist leaders." Claiming that he had expressed only "tentative support" for Miers's nomination, Dobson said, "Based on what we now know about Miss Miers, it appears that we would not have been able to support her candidacy. Thankfully, that difficult evaluation is no longer necessary."

After Miers's withdrawal, the White House lost little time in nominating Samuel Alito to the Supreme Court. Like John Roberts, Alito was an apparently serious Catholic. Unlike Roberts, he had accumulated a fifteen-year judicial record by serving on the Third Circuit Court of Appeals in Philadelphia. Most reassuring to the Christian Right was Alito's dissenting opinion in the 1991 case *Planned Parenthood v. Casey*, in which he argued to uphold a Pennsylvania law that required a woman's spouse to be notified of her intent to have an abortion. There were other signs that Alito would be amenable to ruling against abortion rights, perhaps even to voting to overturn *Roe*. In 1985, while working as a lawyer in the office of the U.S. Solicitor General, he had written in a memo that he was "particularly proud" of his work trying to show that "the Constitution does not protect a right to an abortion."

The Arlington Group and the Third Branch Conference, which had splintered over Miers largely on evangelical/nonevangelical lines, were unified again. A new round of conference calls in support of the nominee quickly got underway. After Alito's 52 to 48 Senate confirmation in January 2006, which marked the second highest number of "no" votes for a successful nominee in the last one hundred years, conservatives finally felt that Robert Bork's legacy had been reversed. With the possibility of more high court vacancies in Bush's second term, Alito had proved that a proudly conservative nominee with a long paper trail could survive confirmation. "Call it what you want," said Kelly Shackelford, president of Focus on the Family's Texas Family Policy Council, after Alito's confirmation. "I think it's divine intervention. I saw decades of history change in five weeks. Harriet Miers was martyred for an incredible change in history."

9

Looking for God in the Democratic Party

"Democrats are big proponents of Social Security. We see it as a faith-based program, about taking care of widows and orphans, and that is what the Old Testament teaches."

—m—

Like many liberal twenty-somethings, Mara Vanderslice caught Howard Dean fever in the summer of 2003.

Working at the time for a nonprofit group in Washington, D.C., she was drawn to Dean's outspoken opposition to the war in Iraq and to his willingness to challenge the Bush administration in his insurgent campaign to win the Democratic nomination for the presidency. Many of the other Democratic presidential candidates appeared to be more pre-occupied with burnishing their national security credentials for what would be the first post–September 11 presidential election. Vander-slice, a born-again Christian, considered Dean to be a "prophetic voice." But she was also worried for the former Vermont governor. She was worried for her Democratic Party, too. With the 2004 election on the horizon, Vanderslice feared that the Dean campaign was ignoring religious Americans and, worse, alienating them with its secular image. After reading a cover story in *The Washington Monthly* warning the Democratic Party that it risked losing the election by writing off tens of millions of religious voters, Vanderslice quit her job, drove to Des Moines, and talked her way onto the Dean campaign staff as director of religious outreach.

As autumn came and went and the January 2004 Iowa caucuses closed in, however, Vanderslice's fears about the Dean campaign only deepened. In September Dean told *ABC News* that he had left his Episcopal Church because it blocked construction of a bike path on its property. The maneuver prompted Dean to become a Congrega-tionalist. "People felt like anyone who has a relationship with God or Christ is not going to leave their faith over a bike path," Vanderslice said. Shortly after New Year's, Dean answered a reporter's question about his favorite New Testament book by citing the Old Testament Book of Job. When he was asked how he planned to appeal to religious voters, Dean suggested he'd wait until the campaign took him to the Deep South. "I remember sitting in Des Moines and printing these things out on the printer and running them up to the communications director and saying, 'Do you know how horrible this is?' " said Vander-slice, who has a long oval face. "And they said, 'This is a primary, and that's why people like us, because we're secular. We always get the biggest applause at rallies when we bash the Religious Right.' So I didn't get very far."

With Dean leading the Democratic presidential pack in the polls, Vanderslice's concerns were viewed with skepticism by the campaign staff, which dubbed her the "church lady." Just before the Iowa caucuses, the top Dean campaign officials, including campaign manager Joe Trippi, stopped by Des Moines headquarters, where the Iowa staff took turns introducing themselves and explaining their roles in the campaign. "When it got to be my turn, I said, 'I'm doing religious outreach.' And a top adviser, whose name I won't say, literally looked at me and said, 'How the hell did you get hired?'" The person who'd hired Vanderslice came to her defense, manufacturing other campaign duties for her on the spot.

After Massachusetts senator John Kerry's surprise victory in Iowa, Vanderslice returned to Washington. But her fears about the Democratic Party's religion problem persisted, and she told every Democrat she knew that it could cost them the election. Word of her admonitions got back to Kerry, who emerged as the clear Democratic front runner in early 2004. By the end of April, the Kerry campaign had hired Vanderslice to be its director of religious outreach.

At that point in the election cycle, Ralph Reed had been at work for six months assembling his vast evangelical outreach machine for President Bush's reelection effort. He had appointed chairpersons for religious conservative outreach in battleground states and had armed them with databases containing information on thousands of churches. He had signed up tens of thousands of evangelical volunteers. The Bush campaign and the Republican National Committee had begun collecting church directories and using them to sign up millions of new conservative voters.

Vanderslice's operation inside the Kerry campaign was more modest. It consisted of herself, then twenty-nine years old, and an unpaid intern. She had no field staff or volunteer lists at her disposal. With the exception of Kerry's appearances before African American congregations, the campaign had resolved to stay out of churches. "They didn't have any vision at all," Vanderslice said of the Kerry campaign's religious outreach strategy, before breaking into an incredulous giggle. "I didn't have marching orders. I just kind of had to make it up."

There were six months left till Election Day.

* * *

One of Vanderslice's first actions on the Kerry campaign was to assemble a kitchen cabinet of religious outreach advisers, including Florida senator Bill Nelson and his wife, Grace, both evangelicals; Mike McCurry, a press secretary under President Clinton who was active in the Methodist Church; a number of Protestant and Catholic clergy; and a few major Democratic Party donors. Apart from the long tradition of Democratic candidates visiting black churches, it was the first time in memory that a Democratic presidential campaign included a concerted religious outreach effort. "I was trying to change the culture of the entire party," Vanderslice said. "We didn't have time to build a ground game in a way the RNC had been doing for a decade. So our hope was to influence the big-ticket items. Some of what we were trying to do was triage."

Even before Kerry emerged as the Democratic front-runner, he had drawn fire from a handful of Catholic bishops over his support for abortion rights. Just after the Iowa caucuses, Saint Louis archbishop Raymond Burke said publicly that he would refuse to give Holy Communion to Kerry, a former altar boy and lifelong Catholic, because he was pro-choice. The previous year, Archbishop Sean O'Malley, serving in Kerry's hometown of Boston, had declared that pro-choice Catholic politicians should not take communion. And in May 2004, Colorado Springs bishop Michael Sheridan went so far as to instruct Catholic voters who backed candidates supportive of abortion rights, gay marriage, or embryonic stem cell research to forgo communion.

Kerry was surprised and hurt by the cascade of attacks, according to campaign aides. "I've met with many bishops, many cardinals on this very subject before and after the campaign," Kerry said in an interview in his Senate office after the election. "And key prelates in the church have indicated to me that nowhere in canon law is there any refusal of the Eucharist to a parishioner." He also pointed out that only a small handful of the more than 250 active U.S. Catholic bishops had made public remarks that could be construed as critical of his candidacy.

Kerry responded swiftly at the time in the news media, taking pains to express his respect for the bishops' stance while affirming his own Catholic commitment and his opposition to "legislating articles of faith."

Beyond Kerry's personal reactions in the press, however, his campaign declined to dispatch credible Catholic figures in his defense or to reach out to Catholics with Kerry's response to the influential bishops. The way the story was playing out in the media, it was easy to infer that a rift had opened between Kerry and the Roman Catholic Church he claimed to belong to. "There were many conversations about it, but there was a lot of fear and indecision about how to respond," Vanderslice said. "The [campaign] didn't understand the Catholic world, and not having some backup within the broader Catholic community made it even more timid." Nervous that it would only make matters worse, the Kerry campaign decided to simply ignore the bishops who were criticizing its candidate.

Still, one of Vanderslice's primary goals remained getting Kerry himself to open up about his faith, particularly about how his Catholicism influenced his life and politics. She noticed that Kerry's appearance at Ronald Reagan's funeral in June 2004, where he crossed himself over Reagan's coffin, went a surprisingly long way in making religious people comfortable with him. "People were longing to understand who was the person of John Kerry," Vanderslice said, "what was guiding him, what his motivations were, and how he was making decisions." But Kerry was reluctant to speak publicly about his faith, a fact noted often in the press, frequently in contrast to President Bush, whose tale of conversion from drunk to born-again Christian was well known. In summer 2004, a *Washington Post* story remarked that Kerry "rarely talks about his religious faith unless he is speaking at an African American church."[1]

Kerry, for his part, rejected that characterization. "In every speech I gave I talked about values, our values versus theirs," he said in the interview after the election. "The values of choosing children versus the wealthiest people in America; the values of having another tax cut for people earning more than a million dollars a year rather than having children get cut from Medicaid." But Kerry said he was battling historical forces that had long branded the Democratic Party as secular. "The problem is we're trying to make up for twenty-five years of an impression being built," he said. "It isn't done overnight."

It was true that Kerry didn't shy away from religious themes altogether. In his nominating speech at July's Democratic National Convention, he acknowledged both his faith and his reluctance to speak publicly about it. "I don't wear my religion on my sleeve," he said before invoking Abraham Lincoln's line about wanting to be on God's side rather than claiming that God was on his. Vanderslice's religious outreach cabinet considered the speech a major victory. But it wasn't until the last week of October, nine days before Election Day, that Kerry delivered what his campaign called his "faith and values speech." Appearing at a campaign stop in Florida, Kerry spoke of his faith in a way he hadn't before, quoting from all four Gospels, the Ten Commandments, and "Amazing Grace." He spoke of how his Catholicism played into his upbringing and his service in the Vietnam War, the centerpiece of his campaign. "Faith was as much a part of our daily lives as the battle was," he said. "I prayed, as we all did. And I even questioned how all the terrible things that I saw could fit into God's plan. But I got through it. And I came home with a sense of hope and a belief in a higher purpose." In the same Florida speech, Kerry discussed the Catholic notion of the "common good" and connected it to his pledge to put lower- and middle-class Americans above the wealthy. *The Washington Post* called it "perhaps the most overtly religious speech of the campaign by either candidate."[2]

Vanderslice welcomed the speech, but thought it came much too late in the campaign. She had tried for months to insert religious themes into message development and speechwriting but was stymied by more senior campaign officials. She also felt that Kerry's "faith and values" speech was delivered in the wrong venue: to a largely Jewish audience in Fort Lauderdale. Vanderslice had long pressed for Kerry to appear in an overtly Christian setting, like an evangelical or Catholic college, but she met with strong resistance from the campaign. "Some people [in the campaign] didn't think it was a priority and that we were never going to win those people anyhow," she said. "Then there were some people who had an actual aversion, who would purposefully take requests out of the pile."

The Kerry campaign's fears about its religious outreach effort backfiring—which had provoked the decision to remain mum in the face of criticism from the Catholic bishops—seemed to be vindicated in June 2004, when the conservative Catholic League for Religious and Civil Rights issued a press release attacking Kerry for hiring Vanderslice. The group charged that she was "raised without any faith and didn't become an evangelical Christian until she attended Earlham College, a Quaker school known for its adherence to pacifism." Vanderslice was in fact raised in a Unitarian home. She said she was deeply affected by the missionary work she witnessed on a trip to Colombia while in college, and that upon returning to Earlham, in rural Indiana, she began attending the evangelical Intervarsity Christian Fellowship. By the time she graduated, Vanderslice had become a born-again. "I fell in love with Jesus of Nazareth," she said. "It's the most important thing that ever happens to you."

The Catholic League assailed Vanderslice for her involvement with the Earlham Socialist Alliance, and for speaking at rallies sponsored by the AIDS activist group ACT UP, which the Catholic League called "anti-Catholic." It noted her role as an organizer for World Trade Organization protests in Seattle and IMF and World Bank protests in Washington. "Her résumé is that of a person looking for a job working for Fidel Castro, not John Kerry," the press release said. "Just wait until Catholics and Protestants learn who this lady really is."

After the Catholic League attack, Vanderslice was barred by the Kerry campaign from speaking to the press. She had been hired barely a month earlier. When the Catholic League later criticized the religious outreach director for the Democratic National Committee, she was silenced as well. The result was that the Democrats' ties to the religious press, including widely read publications like the *Baptist Press* and *Christianity Today*, were completely severed. "Reporters from the religious press would call and they didn't get their phone calls returned for two or three months," Vanderslice said. "The campaign made a decision not to work with *Christianity Today*, which is in the mainstream part of the evangelical community. It's not like *Focus on the Family* magazine. They didn't return *CT*'s calls."

That helps explain why *Christianity Today*'s October 2004 profile of John Kerry read like a hatchet job. The magazine noted that the Democratic nominee invoked God's name just once in the three days that its reporter rode aboard his campaign press plane, and then in a secular context. "I was flying down the Hood River and the gorges," Kerry had told a crowd in Oregon. "I was thinking, God! I need to get back here! I was planning on doing a little windsurfing." Denied an interview with Kerry, *Christianity Today* resorted to citing his 1998 interview with *American Windsurfer* magazine as a source for "some of his most detailed public comments about his theological ideals." The story skewered Kerry's stances on a range of issues, including his support for abortion rights and gay rights: "This windsurfer's open-mindedness translates into some jarring stances on public policy."[3]

Christianity Today's profile of President Bush was no valentine, but it didn't question the authenticity or consistency of Bush's faith commitment, as it had Kerry's. The Bush profile included a Christian talk show host remarking, "The church community is more strongly supportive of this President than any other I can remember in my lifetime."[4]

With a readership in the hundreds of thousands, *Christianity Today* wasn't the only evangelical concern that felt shunned by the Kerry campaign. "I was shocked when my office told me that the Kerry campaign will not return our phone calls," said National Association of Evangelicals then-president Ted Haggard. Whenever Haggard was asked in the evangelical media about his views on John Kerry during the presidential campaign, he would respond by saying simply that his phone calls were going unreturned. "I said it on TBN [Trinity Broadcasting Network] probably ten times," Haggard recalled. "I said it on *Focus on the Family*. I said it on [Christian broadcasting giant] Bott Radio. I was not trying to angle the campaign. I was trying to get Kerry to call me. It was because he didn't have anybody on his team that listens to those things. All he needed was somebody that was an evangelical on his team. That would have swung Ohio."

Of course, Kerry did have an evangelical on his team. But because Mara Vanderslice was marginalized within the campaign and barred from speaking to the press, she focused on quietly organizing religious volunteers at the grass roots. The Bush campaign had signed up three hundred thousand conservative religious volunteers by Election Day. Vanderslice worked with a national volunteer list of seven hundred. Rather than actively courting religious volunteers, she simply tried to keep up with the phone calls and e-mails coming in from religious Kerry supporters. They were requesting everything from bumper stickers and buttons to talking points on how Catholics could enthusiastically support Kerry despite the criticisms he'd received from some Catholic bishops.

The 2004 election returns confirmed the fears that provoked Mara Vanderslice to join the Kerry campaign in the first place. Evangelical turnout surged by 9 percentage points over 2000 and broke for Bush over Kerry by 78 to 21 percent, a more lopsided result than any on record. Kerry lost the Catholic vote, despite his own Catholicism. He did receive more support from mainline Protestants than any recent Democratic presidential candidate, but almost all the increase came from the least observant "modernist" mainliners, while traditionalist and centrist mainliners backed Bush.[5]

The religious commitment gap between Bush and Kerry voters was, in fact, the most significant dividing line in the electorate in 2004. Church attendance actually tied with race as the single best predictor of voting behavior, having much greater impact than factors like union membership, income level, or urban versus rural residency.[6] Voters who attend religious services more than once a week supported Bush over Kerry by 64 to 35 percent, while those attending services weekly backed Bush by 58 to 41 percent. Those two constituencies together made up roughly a third of the electorate.

Secular voters cast their ballots in almost exactly the opposite way. Americans who never attend religious services supported Kerry over Bush by 62 to 36 percent, while those who attend just a few times a year broke for Kerry by 54 to 45 percent. Those two constituencies together also made up about a third of the electorate. In its postelection analysis, the Pew Forum on Religion & Public Life called this religious-partisan divide "by far the most powerful new reality at the intersection of religion and politics." "This is becoming such a familiar dividing line in modern politics," the analysis noted, "that it is easy to overlook how unusual it is from a historical perspective."[7]

Insisting that his religious outreach effort was "very effective," Kerry, who began positioning himself for a 2008 presidential run soon after the 2004 election was over, said the campaign had nonetheless taught him some important lessons about faith and the American electorate. "I've been doing much more Bible reading than ever before," he said during the interview in his office. "I have a Bible that sits on my night table, and [my wife] Teresa has the same Bible, which I gave to her as a Christmas present. . . . I find it absolutely beautiful reading."

Since the election, Kerry has befriended *Purpose-Driven Life* author Rick Warren, who he said helped him develop a deeper appreciation for the staunch anti–abortion rights position of religious conservatives. "*Believe* is a powerful word," Kerry said. "If you really believe that life begins at conception and that that's a living person with full ensoulment, and that is the image of God, then for that person, whatever number of abortions are a Holocaust, and I have to be prepared to say, 'I respect that.' Now, if you do respect that, then the language of 'It's my body, I can do whatever I want with it' is frankly not correct. It doesn't mean you don't have the right to make a choice. . . . But it still means there is a morality that we have to acknowledge in that choice.

"I think the word *choice* is a bad word, personally," Kerry continued. "I'm firmly where I have been with respect for the notion that the government doesn't make that decision; it's between a woman and God and her doctor. It's an individual's job to acknowledge the morality, though, and for a long time I'm not sure we [pro-choice Democrats] did a good enough job with that. I consider myself more thoughtful and understanding of that now."

Kerry has also become more open about his personal faith. "It's not a question of a new thing," he said. "It's a question of making sure people know who you are and making sure people aren't suffering distortions and outright lies." As an example, he pointed to a 2004 Republican National Committee mailing that accused "liberals" of trying to ban the Bible. "How dare somebody suggest that I'm going to ban the Bible," he said. "That's tomfoolery. And I think [Democrats] are reacting by saying, 'Look, if that's the way they're going to play, then we need to make sure they know who we are. We have to counter stereotypes. But you don't counter them with a tactic. You counter them with the truth and honesty. If it isn't, people see through it in ten seconds."

—◊◊◊—

Not long after the 2004 election, newly elected Colorado senator Ken Salazar was trying to counter stereotypes of his party with truth and honesty when he called Focus on the Family "the antichrist of the world." One of the few Democratic success stories of the 2004 election, Salazar was responding to newspaper and radio ads targeting him for threatening to filibuster some of President Bush's judicial nominees.

The ads were part of Focus on the Family's joint campaign with the Family Research Council to "stop the filibuster against people of faith." *I am a person of faith*, thought Salazar, an observant Roman Catholic and former seminarian, when he learned of the ads. To strike back, he told a Colorado Springs television station in April 2005 that "From my point of view, [Focus on the Family] are the antichrist of the world."

The jab caused a stir in the press. The following day, Salazar claimed that he had misspoken. He said he'd meant to say that some of Focus's tactics were "unchristian." But James Dobson responded to Salazar's "antichrist" remark in a rare interview with the Associated Press, calling it "so off the wall it's hard to imagine."

As the news media latched onto the contretemps, Salazar did something Democrats rarely do. He made an appointment to see James Dobson at Focus's Colorado Springs headquarters. "I expressed my concern that I'm a Christian, a man of faith, and I don't believe that the agenda of Focus on the Family is a comprehensive Christian agenda," Salazar said in an interview, recalling the fall 2005 meeting. "It seemed to me that what they allowed to happen is that they'd become an appendage of the Republican Party."

The meeting between Salazar and Dobson was not all adversarial. They discussed mutual political goals, like cutting down on minors' access to pornography and stopping a casino from moving into Pueblo, south of Colorado Springs. But the meeting hardly marked the onset of a productive relationship. Rather than reaching a cease-fire, Salazar and Dobson agreed merely to alert one another before either launched his next public attack on the other.

And yet Salazar had no regrets about sitting down with Dobson. He saw the meeting as part of a necessary change in posture for his party. From now on, Salazar thought, Democrats would refuse to be branded as faithless or as antagonistic toward religion. And when the Christian Right wielded that brand, Democrats would strike back forcefully. "I look at my Democratic Catholic colleagues in the U.S. Senate—I think the number is thirteen—and for most of us, part of the reason we're in public service is because of the faith tradition we come from," he said. "The Beatitudes and the Sermon on the Mount gave me a lot of guidance, and I try to live in accordance with those teachings. Catholic [Democrats] and Democrats of faith should not be branded as being faithless, because we're not. And when the evangelical right puts that brand on people of faith, we need to stand up and refute it."

Salazar's thinking mirrored that of John Kerry after his 2004 defeat. Indeed, having lost seats in the Senate and House, on top of losing the White House, and with exit polls showing religious voters to be more pro-Republican than ever, the Democrats' top leaders realized that their party had a major religion problem soon after the polls closed on November 2, 2004. "Certainly, Democrats are faith-filled," House Minority Leader Nancy Pelosi said the next day. ". . . But somehow or other, that did not come across, when 61 percent of those who are regular churchgoers voted for President Bush."

So when the 109th Congress convened in January 2005, one of Nancy Pelosi's first acts was to organize a task force of House Democrats to help the party shed its secular image. "Democrats have been of the notion that it's a bit unseemly to wear your religion on your shirtsleeve," said South Carolina congressman James Clyburn, whom Pelosi tapped to chair the new Faith Working Group. "But it seems as if the voting public has been responding to those people who wear their religion on their shirtsleeve, who preach and don't necessarily practice what they preach. So those of us who have been walking the walk for years have decided maybe it's time we talk the talk."

Some conservative evangelical leaders were quick to dismiss the effort as window dressing. "It can't be a case where Democrats try to append the word God to . . . all their policy discussions," said Richard Cizik, chief lobbyist for the National Association of Evangelicals. "I don't think it will work until they change some policies."

But the Faith Working Group argued that the Democrats' religion problem had little to do with their policy positions. Instead, it promoted the idea that the Democrats needed to do a better job of framing their

positions, articulating their moral—and, where appropriate, biblical—
underpinnings. "Democrats are big proponents of Social Security," said
Clyburn, who is the son of a fundamentalist minister and active in the
African Methodist Episcopal Church. "We see it as a faith-based program, about taking care of widows and orphans, and that is what the
Old Testament teaches. The book of James says faith without works is
dead. And yet we believe in food stamps, and Republicans seem not to.
We believe in funding the school lunch program, and Republicans
seem not to. Republicans believe you fend for yourself, and all of this is
contrary to what the Bible teaches us."

It was, on the surface, a direct challenge to the Christian Right, an
attempt to redefine "moral values" in terms of progressive government.
In another way, though, the Democrats' post-2004 faith offensive represented a major victory for the movement. It was a recognition by one of
the nation's two major political parties, decades after the other party
had done so, that the Judeo-Christian faith should play a central role in
America's public life, including the policy-making process. Two hundred years after the U.S. Constitution had explicitly outlawed religious
tests for public office, the Democrats began studying up on how to pass
them.

Just as Democrats were wrestling with how to close the God gap, a book
called *God's Politics: Why the Right Gets It Wrong and the Left Doesn't
Get It* was shooting up the national bestseller lists. It alleged that the
Christian Right distorted the Bible by fixating on issues like abortion
and homosexuality while largely disregarding causes that the book said
were more important to Jesus, like promoting peace and helping the
poor. But *God's Politics* chided Democrats, too, for allowing the secular
left to gain a stranglehold on their party, and for ceding the entire dia-
logue about religion's role in public life to the Christian Right. Author
Jim Wallis embarked on a fifty-city book tour less than two months after
Election Day. His readings wound up drawing tens of thousands of disillusioned religious liberals.

Around the same time, Wallis's phone began ringing off the hook with calls from concerned Democratic officials. He was invited to address the full Democratic caucuses in the Senate and the House. As the year went on, Wallis sat for one-on-one meetings with new Democratic National Committee chairman Howard Dean, Senators Hillary Clinton and Ted Kennedy, and others. From the beginning, Wallis warned the Democrats that he was about more than message management. When Senate Minority Leader Harry Reid called after the election, Wallis told him, "If you're looking for a few Bible verses and instructions for how to clap at the right time during church, I'm not the person you need."

But Wallis's presentations to the Democrats actually echoed what the Faith Working Group was already advising: that the party should articulate a moral foundation for progressive public policy. It was what Wallis, in his late fifties, had been doing all his life. Raised in an evangelical home in the Midwest, his rejection of his racially segregated congregation led him to Detroit's black churches. While attending divinity school, he joined the anti–Vietnam War movement and co-founded a commune for Christian liberals called Sojourners, which now exists as a monthly magazine devoted to social justice issues. To Wallis, the Democrats simply had to rediscover liberalism's rich religious legacy. "Throughout American history, if you look at what religion has fought for, it's mostly a progressive history," he said in an interview in his Sojourners office, housed in the old Nicaraguan embassy in Washington. "The abolition of slavery, women's suffrage, child labor law reform, civil rights. The Religious Right claims to be in that earlier tradition. They are in the tradition of applying faith to politics, but they can't say they were the first ones to think of it."

Wallis, whose round face and close-cropped white hair give him a monkish appearance, went out of his way to warn the Democrats that appearing to invoke religion in a phony or cynical way would be fatal. "Howard Dean doesn't strike me as knowing the issue of faith very well," he said in his usual deadpan monotone. "He should be careful about saying much of anything about it."

And to emphasize his point that winning over religious voters would require more than dressing up their positions in "values-speak," Wallis called on Democrats to show leadership on a big moral issue. He recommended poverty relief. The head of a coalition of poverty relief groups named Call to Renewal, Wallis had long been an advocate for debt relief and increased aid for third-world nations and, domestically, for a higher minimum wage. He is fond of noting that *evangel*, the root of *evangelical*, comes from Jesus's first sermon in Nazareth, in which he announces that the Lord has anointed him to bring good news to the poor. "Whatever else our gospel does," Wallis said, "if it doesn't bring good news to poor people, it isn't the gospel of Jesus Christ. I say that flat out."

While Wallis coached the Democrats, the Democratic National Committee commissioned polling about Americans' views of religion and morality. The polls seemed to confirm much of what Wallis was saying. A 2005 DNC survey found that most Americans ranked alleviating poverty and funding education as greater moral concerns than hot-button issues like same-sex marriage and abortion rights. A DNC polling memo to congressional Democrats noted that 79 percent of Americans felt it was morally wrong for increasing numbers of children to be growing up in poverty. Only 47 percent of Americans, by comparison, felt it was morally wrong to allow gay marriage.

But the DNC's polling also illustrated the depth of the Democrats' religion problem. One poll found that roughly half the American voters were influenced as much or more by their religious faith as by any other issue when casting their ballots, and that those voters were voting Republican by as much as two to one. And yet these so-called values voters were also among the most economically vulnerable in the country, making them natural allies of the Democratic Party. The finding supported the thesis of the 2004 bestseller *What's the Matter with Kansas?*, which argued that lower- and middle-class Americans supported Republican candidates because of their conservative positions on cultural issues, and that they did so against their own economic interest.

During the two years after the 2004 election, Democrats harnessed the DNC's polls and Wallis's advice into new ways of framing their message. After the Democrats helped derail President Bush's plan to introduce private investment accounts into the Social Security system, House Minority Leader Pelosi called the plan "a charge right at our core values." In November 2005, when a split Senate passed a budget plan that cut billions from federal benefits programs, Senate Minority Leader Harry Reid denounced it as an "immoral document."[8] As the 2006 midterm elections approached, the Democrats pushed for Congress to raise the federal minimum wage for the first time since 1997, while liberal groups across the country promoted ballot initiatives to raise the minimum wage in a handful of states. When Senate Republicans blocked a federal minimum wage increase in June 2006, Senator Ted Kennedy called it a "moral outrage."

The Democrats also stepped up their outreach to religious Americans, with Senate Minority Leader Reid launching a Web site called "A Word to the Faithful," though the site was never updated after its summer 2005 launch. In mid-2005, the Democratic National Committee hired its first full-time religious outreach director. "The most important thing in any twelve-step program is to admit that you have a problem," said a top DNC source. "This is not a fly-by-night, we-want-your-vote effort. This is about the future direction of our party. But we're starting from zero."

—m—

Even as they powwowed with Jim Wallis and worked to recast their positions in a morals and values framework, some Democrats worried that the party was still avoiding the difficult changes that reversing its secular image would require. They thought that much of the Democratic offensive to regain religious voters was cosmetic. The Democratic National Committee's new religious outreach director made no secret that she was focusing almost exclusively on the party's traditional base:

women, Latinos, and African Americans. All the DNC staffers assigned to do religious outreach were African American, a testament to the party's historic alliance with black churches. And rather than urging it to moderate its stances on social issues, the party's new spiritual adviser, Jim Wallis, was to the left even of many Democrats. He supported gay rights, opposed the war in Iraq, and was highly critical of the war in Afghanistan. "Does anybody care that we killed more Afghan civilians who had nothing to do with Al Qaeda than people who died on September eleventh?" Wallis asked. "Is that even a moral issue?"

It was difficult, in other words, to see how the Democrats' faith offensive would appeal to the white evangelical Christians who did so much to deliver President Bush the election in 2004. "The problem with Jim Wallis is that the individuals he appeals to—progressive Christians—are already voting with the Democrats," said Randy Brinson, founder of the group Redeem the Vote, which works to register young evangelicals to vote. "They're not gaining any new votes."

A Montgomery, Alabama-based gastroenterologist by day, Brinson was introduced to the national Democratic Party by a House aide who met him at a post-2004 election forum in Washington, where Brinson was discussing the work of Redeem the Vote. Launched during the 2004 election cycle, the nonpartisan organization worked with Christian Rock acts and Christian radio stations to register tens of thousands of evangelicals. "He said, 'You seem like a very reasonable evangelical,'" Brinson said, recalling how the Democratic aide introduced himself. "I told him that the problem is that if you get back these two issues you all are so adamant about"—promoting abortion rights and opposing efforts to ban same-sex marriage—"there are a lot of other issues that resonate with evangelicals: jobs, trade, all these other things."

Soon, Brinson was fielding calls from the office of Democratic Minority Leader Nancy Pelosi, the Democratic National Committee, and the Democratic Congressional Campaign Committee. A longtime Republican and George W. Bush loyalist, Brinson was nonetheless willing to offer the Democrats some advice. "We get six calls from the Dems for every one we get from the Republicans," he said. "Republicans think they have evangelicals totally engaged and that they don't need anybody else's help. The Democrats realize they need evangelicals."

So when Brinson was invited to DNC headquarters in early 2005 to brief top party officials, he accepted.

In a forty-five-minute presentation, Brinson, who is tall, rail-thin, and speaks at a breakneck speed in a thick southern drawl, laid out his dim prognosis for the Democratic Party. The Democrats' first big problem, in Brinson's view, was that they had no channels through which to reach the white evangelical masses. That was largely because many of the evangelical world's biggest media outlets, including Focus on the Family and Pat Robertson's Christian Broadcasting Network, made little secret of their hostility toward the Democrats. "Democrats have no portal to reach evangelicals, and everything they say is edited," Brinson said, recalling his presentation to the DNC. "Even if they're doing something positive, certain groups have political alliances and are going to question everything they do." Making matters worse, Brinson said, was that Democrats had done virtually nothing to seek out portals to the evangelical world. He said the DNC could change that by booking party spokespeople and airing political ads on Christian radio, a format carried on roughly two thousand U.S. stations.

The Democrats' second big problem, Brinson said, would be more difficult to remedy; it was their policy positions. Unlike Jim Wallis, Brinson wasn't shy about saying that liberal stances on social issues were a major turnoff for white evangelical voters. "Every time they say something about same-sex marriage or protecting the right to choose, those are volatile issues in terms of evangelicals," Brinson said. "There's no reason for going out there talking without changing the message."

Leading on poverty relief, Brinson warned, wouldn't cut it. It was a pressing moral issue, to be sure, but it wasn't what Brinson called "nine-to-five politics," the kitchen table issues that resonated with most middle-class evangelicals, and with most middle-class Americans, period: ensuring adequate funding for public schools, defraying the high

cost of health care, providing stability for pension programs. The problem for Democrats, as Brinson saw it, was that they could realize their
political advantage on such economic issues among evangelical voters
only by neutralizing—at least partially—the GOP advantage on abortion rights and same-sex marriage.

To help prove his point, Brinson told the Democrats about the
Evangelical Sensitivity Index, or ESI, which he devised during the
2004 election cycle. By aggregating the responses voters gave to a host
of questions about their political positions, ranging from the economy
to national security to abortion rights, Brinson found that he could pre-
dict which party or candidate they were likely to support. But when he
aggregated the responses of white evangelical voters, Brinson discovered
that many respondents who answered in a way that suggested a Democratic vote—placing high priority on public education and affordable
health care, for example—were actually more likely to back a Republican. The reason was that opposition to abortion rights and/or gay marriage trumped all of their other concerns. "You see a lot of checks in the
Democratic column, yet who wins the game?" Brinson asked. "The Republicans."

Brinson was not recommending that Democrats co-opt the Republican Party platform. But he advised the Democrats to build a big-tent
party that welcomed socially conservative candidates and elected officials, especially in so-called red states, just as the GOP had embraced
social liberals like Rudolph Giuliani and Arnold Schwarzenegger in
blue ones. On the presidential ticket, meanwhile, Brinson said a candidate like John Kerry, a northeastern liberal who opposed the Partial
Birth Abortion Ban Act of 2003 and was one of fourteen senators to oppose the 1996 Defense of Marriage Act, was more or less your average
evangelical's worst nightmare. It was one point on which he agreed with
Jim Wallis.

Drastic as it was, the Democrats began applying Brinson's advice
soon after the 2004 election. In January 2005, Senator Hillary Clinton
of New York told an audience of family planning providers that "we can

all recognize that abortion in many ways represents a sad, even a tragic choice to many, many women" and that the "primary reason teenage girls abstain [from sex] is because of religious and moral values." Facing an audience of abortion providers, Clinton, weighing a presidential run in 2008, invited pro-lifers to join the Democratic Party: "I, for one, respect those who believe with all their heart and conscience that there are no circumstances under which abortion should ever be available."

Just around that time, Democrat Tim Kaine officially launched his bid to be governor of Virginia, one of the few major races of 2005. Kaine placed the first ads of his campaign on Christian radio, as Brinson had advised. And when his Republican opponent aired television commercials attacking Kaine's anti–death penalty stance, a potentially fatal blow in the strenuously pro–death penalty state, Kaine ripped a page from the Christian Right's own playbook by suggesting that his Catholic faith was under attack. "My faith teaches life is sacred," Kaine said in his response ad. "That's why I personally oppose the death penalty. But I take my oath of office seriously, and I'll enforce the death penalty." Openly discussing his Catholicism all through the campaign, Kaine won by nearly 6 percentage points in November 2005. In early 2006, he was tapped to give the Democratic response to President Bush's State of the Union address. "I worked as a missionary in Honduras when I was a young man," Kaine said at the outset of his response. "And I learned to measure my life by the difference I can make in someone else's life." The Democratic National Committee was active in Kaine's race and saw it as a blueprint for a new generation of Democratic "values" campaigns.

So in looking to field a strong challenger to Pennsylvania's Rick Santorum, one of the Christian Right's staunchest allies in the U.S. Senate, in 2006, the Democratic Party apparatus swung into action behind the pro-life candidate Bob Casey, Jr. Casey's father, former Pennsylvania governor Bob Casey, was famously denied a speaking role at the 1992 Democratic National Convention because of his anti—abortion rights position. In 2006, by contrast, key Democrats like Pennsylvania governor Ed Rendell and Democratic Senatorial Campaign Committee chairman Charles Schumer cleared the primary field for Casey Jr. Rendell and Schumer dissuaded a popular pro-choice Democrat, the former state treasurer, from opposing Casey Jr., invoking the wrath of abortion rights groups like the National Organization for Women. Casey won in a rout, picking up nearly 30 percent of the white evangelical vote.

In Washington, D.C., meanwhile, with a little help from Randy Brinson, a small group called Democrats for Life of America, incorporated in 1999, was finally getting its calls returned by the Democratic National Committee. Previously, the DNC had refused to meet with Democrats for Life, and when asked to provide a link to Democrats for Life on its Web site, the DNC instead removed from its site all links to outside groups. "They thought we were just Republicans trying to infiltrate the party," said Democrats for Life executive director Kristen Day. "Then the 2004 elections happened. Tom Daschle, who was not a rabid pro-abortion supporter, who voted for the partial-birth abortion ban, was painted as pro-abortion. It wasn't true, but it led to his defeat."

After the 2004 election, the DNC established official ties to Democrats for Life. It also hosted a spring 2005 press conference to announce the group's most ambitious project to date, a package of more than a dozen legislative proposals designed to reduce the number of abortions in the United States by 95 percent in ten years. The "95-10 Initiative" included calls for federally funded pregnancy counselors on college campuses, a stricter federal parental notification law for minors seeking an abortion, the establishment of a toll-free number to notify pregnant women of the support services available to them, and a national study into how to decrease demand for abortion. Democrats for Life had seen little success in passing parts of the plan through Congress by late 2006, but its very existence marked a new, distinctly Democratic approach to reducing abortion. "The fight until now has been keep abortion legal versus make it illegal," said Day. "Nobody has been talking about the woman facing an unplanned pregnancy who doesn't have any support or health care. It's four hundred dollars for an abortion versus twenty thousand dollars to have the baby. We're trying to change the debate."

Of course, Republicans will be loath to grant Democrats victories on one of their signature issues, working for the elimination of abortion. But the Democratic pro-life movement and the party's broader effort to shed its secular image may face stiffer resistance from elements in its own base, like Hollywood donors and pro-choice activists. "With all due respect to Jim Wallis," National Organization for Women president Kim Gandy told an audience after the 2004 election, ". . . I don't want an evangelical progressive movement any more than I want the conservative one we have right now." Indeed, the secular Americans who are among the most dependably Democratic voters now represent the fastest growing "religious" tradition in the nation. In 1996, 44 percent of Americans reported going to church infrequently or never, up from 29 percent in 1965.[9] The Democrats' secular bloc could thwart the party's religious offensive before it has a chance to succeed.

But not if Mara Vanderslice has her way. Vanderslice's stints as religious outreach director for Howard Dean's and John Kerry's presidential campaigns may have confirmed her fears about Democrats botching religious outreach, but they also gave her something more useful: the credentials to finally be taken seriously by her own party. In summer 2005, Vanderslice partnered with a former Democratic Capitol Hill staffer to launch Common Good Strategies, a political consulting firm whose mission is helping Democrats—candidates, elected officials, and party operatives—connect with evangelicals and other committed Christians. From the start, Vanderslice adopted Republican National Committee chairman Ken Mehlman's mantra for his campaign to woo black voters: "Give us a chance, we'll give you a choice."

Rather than encouraging Democrats to reframe their message or change their positions, Common Good Strategies aimed simply to help Democrats build relationships with Christian communities, most importantly, the evangelical subculture. "It kind of sounds silly when talking about Democrats," said Eric Sapp, Vanderslice's business partner, "but our party has some serious prejudices and misconceptions about evangelical Christians." When he was an aide in the Senate, Sapp said, his Democratic colleagues viewed him with suspicion. He said he was taken off an assignment on genetic counseling legislation because his superiors thought his religious beliefs presented a conflict. "A lot of what we're doing [at Common Good]," Sapp said, "is what I heard happened with my grandparents in the South when they started integration: to get people to sit down with one another."

Shortly after opening its doors, Common Good was hired by the Democratic Senatorial Campaign Committee to work on races across the country, including the Casey campaign in Pennsylvania, the Democratic Senate and gubernatorial campaigns in Ohio, and by the Democratic Party in a handful of states. In Michigan, the firm arranged meetings between state party officials, who were plotting to reclaim the state legislature from the Republicans in 2006, and evangelical, mainline Protestant, and Catholic clergy. They also set up meetings between the clergy and representatives from the campaigns of Governor Jennifer Granholm and U.S. senator Debbie Stabenow, both facing difficult reelection battles in 2006. Michigan includes some conservative evangelical strongholds—the family of Granholm challenger Dick DeVos has been one of the Family Research Council's biggest benefactors—but some of the state's most powerful evangelical pastors accepted Common Good's invitation. Because they had grown accustomed to being courted by the GOP, evangelical pastors were actually more responsive than their mainline Protestant counterparts. "Everywhere we go, we're getting the same reaction: Evangelicals want to talk to Democrats," said Sapp. "The Democrats often come in a little scared, a little wary, thinking Do they have horns? And they start talking and realize these people are not going to yell at them."

That was true even when the conversation turned to hot-button issues like abortion, inevitably one of the first topics to surface in the meetings Common Good set up between Democrats and evangelical

pastors. Rather than succumbing to arguments over the legitimacy of
Roe v. Wade, however, Vanderslice and Sapp and their Democratic
clients promoted Democrats for Life's 95-10 Initiative and other ways to
reduce unwanted pregnancy without criminalizing abortion. "These
evangelical pastors never thought about it that way," Sapp said. "And
they said, 'Where we disagree theologically, we can agree on the best
public policy.'"

In fact, Sapp and Vanderslice were surprised at the number of evangelical pastors they met with who had reservations about supporting the
outright criminalization of abortion. "When you talk about sending
women to jail, they don't want to do it," Vanderslice said. "They'd much
rather take a step back and say, 'Let's acknowledge this is a problem and
we're going to work together to solve it.' And that's what they don't hear.
They only hear Democrats say, 'It's a choice between a woman and her
doctor,' like it's morally neutral. That's what's offensive. They have to
have a sense that we understand there is moral significance to it."

As basic as that sounds, it captures Common Good's mission: convincing religious Americans that Democrats recognize a moral dimension. "We're the party of the Second Great Commandment: Love your
neighbor as yourself," said Sapp. "What we don't get is the First Great
Commandment: Love your God with all your heart, mind, and soul.
And for Dems to get legitimacy within the religious community, we
have to pass the sniff test on the first."

With Democrats reclaiming the House and Senate in 2006 by picking up seats in culturally conservative red states, the party had begun
making progress toward that goal. White evangelical support for Democratic House candidates ticked up from 25 to 28 percent since 2004.
The party's gains among the broader weekly churchgoer demographic
were more dramatic, particularly in states where Common Good
Strategies was active, like Pennsylvania, Ohio, and Michigan, where
Granholm and Stabenow survived their challenges and Democrats reclaimed the state House of Representatives. Internal Democratic National Committee polls showed that 2006's national Democratic wave

came largely because the party narrowed the Republican lead among "values first voters"—those who say that their faith is as much as or more of an influence in how they cast their ballot than any other factor. In some states, such voters constitute nearly 60 percent of the electorate. Democrats cut the GOP's lead among those voters from 22 points in summer 2005 to 10 points by Election Day 2006.

But the DNC's polls also showed that gains among values voters had been born mostly of disillusionment over Republican scandals, from Jack Abramoff to Congressman Mark Foley's lewd electronic messages to male congressional pages, rather than because of anything the Democrats had done. Religious voters "haven't fallen in love with us," said DNC pollster Cornell Belcher after the election. "They're just really ticked off at Republicans. The idea that greed and corruption were being rewarded really sticks with them." Which means the real test of whether the Democratic evangelical and broader religious outreach is working will come in 2008, when—with control of the White House hanging in the balance—the stakes will be as high as in 2004.

Epilogue:
The Post-Dobson Christian Right

". . . the Sierra Club is not going to change

the minds of conservative Republicans. But

is it conceivable that the National Associa-

tion of Evangelicals could? It's conceiv-

able."

—w—

A staunch social conservative and fervent supporter of Presidents
Ronald Reagan and George W. Bush, the Reverend Richard Cizik had
looked skeptically on the environmental movement for decades. "Environmentalists were adherents to New Age faiths," Cizik said in an interview. "It was a kind of mother earth mentality that said, 'Evangelicals

need not apply.'" As the chief Washington lobbyist for the National Association of Evangelicals, Cizik knew he was not alone. A 1996 Brookings Institution study found that committed white evangelicals were by
far the most antienvironment religious group in the nation.[1] The study
theorized that such attitudes were explained largely by dispensationalist
theology, the belief among many evangelicals that the world will de-
scend into chaos just before Jesus's return. Such a view tends to render
attempts at environmental preservation useless.[2]

That's what made Cizik's signature-gathering campaign for the
Evangelical Climate Initiative remarkable. Drawn up by Cizik and
other evangelical leaders in 2005, the Evangelical Climate Initiative
was a petition that declared global warming was happening and that the
Bible demanded a response from evangelical Christians. It called on
the Bush administration and the Republican-controlled Congress to begin taking steps to combat the problem. With enough signatures, its
drafters thought they would send a bold message to the Republican
Party: that a huge chunk of its base was demanding action on an issue
the Democratic Party had more or less owned since the emergence of
the environmental movement in the late 1960s. If successful, the Evangelical Climate Initiative could turn the traditional politics of the environment on their head and open doors to bold new environmental laws.

Cizik's own environmental awakening had begun in 2002, when a
fellow evangelical pastor who had launched an anti-SUV "What Would
Jesus Drive?" campaign pressured Cizik into attending a conference on
climate change in England.[3] The conference featured a handful of
evangelical scientists, most notably Sir John Houghton, a retired Ox-
ford professor and member of the Intergovernmental Panel on Climate
Change, the main international scientific body studying global warming. Houghton and others convinced Cizik that global warming was
real and that it had disastrous consequences for life on earth. "Houghton
said, 'Richard, if you come to conclusions about this, you have an obligation to speak out,'" recalled Cizik, whose lanky build and high-toned
voice give him the air of a bluegrass singer. "'That's the role God has

given you.'" Cizik told *The New York Times* that he experienced a "conversion" in England around the climate change issue that was so intense as to be comparable to an "altar call," the part of a Protestant church service when nonbelievers are called forward to accept Jesus as their savior.[4]

After returning to the United States, Cizik helped organize meetings of evangelical leaders aimed at formulating an evangelical response to global warming. He began studying evidence that linked mercury pollution to birth defects. He bought hybrid Toyota Priuses for himself and his wife. Asked about the biblical basis for his newfound environmentalism, Cizik would cite Genesis 2:15: "The Lord God took the man and put him in the Garden of Eden to work it and take care of it."[5] In granting man dominion over the earth, Cizik reasoned, God had also entrusted man with the care of his creation. "I don't think God is going to ask us how he created the earth," Cizik would say. "But he will ask us what we did with what he created."[6] Indeed, Cizik refused to refer to his global warming activism as environmentalism; he insisted it be called "Creation Care."

He wasn't just being cute. Cizik, whose organization includes upward of thirty million American evangelicals and whose 1983 convention was the staging ground for Reagan's famous "Evil Empire" speech, knew that born-again Christians had long frowned on the environmental movement's embrace of government regulation and on its calls for population control.[7] Of course, many evangelicals also saw environmental activists as keeping what Cizik called "kooky religious company."[8] But polls suggest that evangelical attitudes toward the environment are complex. A 2004 Pew Research Center poll found that while many more evangelicals oppose environmental regulations than do adherents of other religious traditions, a slight majority of evangelicals actually favor stronger environmental regulations, even when they cost jobs or lead to higher prices.[9] Cizik thought that the secret to convincing more evangelicals to adopt some tenets of environmentalism was to dispense with the traditional environmentalist plea to protect nature for its own sake. "I think the environmentalists have framed the issue all wrong," Cizik said. "It has to be framed as a people issue. Evangelicals will understand it more clearly that way."

That's what the Evangelical Climate Initiative was for. "For most of us, until recently this has not been treated as a pressing issue or major priority," the document acknowledged. "Indeed, many of us have required considerable convincing before becoming persuaded that climate change is a real problem and that it ought to matter to us as Christians." The document briefly laid out the scientific evidence for global warming. It framed global warming as a "people issue," arguing that the expected environmental fallout, including a rise in sea level, droughts, floods, and the accelerated spread of tropical diseases, would wreak havoc on the world's poor. It cited more than a half-dozen biblical passages on mankind's stewardship duties toward nature. And it called for federal legislation to curb carbon dioxide emissions, possibly through a "cap and trade" program. Such a program would impose a cap on CO_2 emission levels, then allow manufacturers to buy and sell emissions credits, providing flexibility and financial incentives for compliance.

Collecting signatures for the Evangelical Climate Initiative was not easy. Leaders of some evangelical denominations told Cizik that signing on to such a traditionally liberal platform would be too risky unless he could give them political cover. They wanted him to first sign up an evangelical star with solid conservative credentials, someone like Rick Warren. So Cizik and other Evangelical Climate Initiative boosters lobbied Warren over to their side, then used his support to prod the fence-sitters. As the unveiling of the document approached in early 2006, Cizik was visibly excited, especially over the prospect of lobbying traditional Republican allies in Congress—who were with him on issues like opposing gay marriage—on a cause so far outside their comfort zones. "The Natural Resources Defense Council or the Sierra Club is not going to change the minds of conservative Republicans," Cizik said.

"But is it conceivable that the National Association of Evangelicals could? It's conceivable."

The Evangelical Climate Initiative was unveiled in February 2006, bearing the signatures of eighty-six evangelical luminaries. In addition to Warren, they included Salvation Army chief Todd Bassett, *Christianity Today* editor David Neff, and the presidents of thirty-nine evangelical colleges, including such highly regarded institutions as Wheaton College and Calvin College.

But two signatures were conspicuously absent: those of National Association of Evangelicals then-president Ted Haggard and NAE Washington lobbyist Richard Cizik.

Cizik's name had originally been on the Evangelical Climate Initiative—he was, after all, one of the document's chief architects and advocates. But at the last minute before its Washington unveiling, he'd requested that it be withdrawn. In January, as Cizik was coaxing other evangelical leaders to sign his document, the NAE received a one-page letter from a coalition of Christian Right leaders requesting that the NAE forgo adopting an official position on climate change. "Global warming is not a consensus issue, and our love of the Creator and respect for His creation does not require us to take a position," the letter read, charging squarely at the central pillars of the Evangelical Climate Initiative. Written under the auspices of a group called the Interfaith Stewardship Alliance, its signatories included Chuck Colson, the Southern Baptist Convention's Richard Land, the American Family Association's Don Wildmon, and James Dobson.

In retrospect, Cizik should have seen it coming. When the National Association of Evangelicals had convened in Washington the previous year to discuss a handbook it was drafting on Christian political engagement, Focus on the Family had sent its political chief just to voice objections to the document's section on Creation Care. "For Rich Cizik, the [global warming] issue is paramount," the Focus rep, Tom Minnery, said in an interview later. "My concern is that the issue is not paramount among American evangelicals."

In fact, Cizik had consistently stressed that Creation Care was not the paramount political concern for himself or for the evangelical community, but that it was an urgent matter nonetheless. In the eyes of Dobson and other Christian Right leaders, however, the Evangelical Climate Initiative was not only a concession to its liberal enemies, but a threat to the movement's core agenda: fighting same-sex marriage, abortion, and the removal of religion from the public square. America's cultural crisis was too dire for the evangelical movement to be distracted by a bunch of Christian tree huggers.

Cizik believed that taking a stand on global warming would actually lend more credibility to the Christian Right's traditional agenda, which he wholly endorsed. If the evangelical movement succeeded in swaying key Republicans to pass global warming legislation, his thinking went, it would be much harder for the movement's opponents to characterize it as out of the mainstream on causes like the Marriage Protection Amendment and curbing abortion rights. Plus, successfully lobbying for a climate change bill could give the Christian Right something it rarely got: a legislative victory, which would remind Washington policy makers of the movement's influence. "If the evangelical movement is described as having passed only the partial-birth abortion ban, then what kind of strength do we have?" Cizik reasoned. "We are a toothless tiger."

The January 2006 letter from Dobson and other Christian Right leaders did have teeth, however. Cizik removed his name from the Evangelical Climate Initiative before its public launch at the National Press Club in Washington the following month. NAE president Ted Haggard, a Creation Care advocate who was expected to sign the document, announced that he would withhold his name, too.

With no congressional votes scheduled on major global warming legislation in the period between the launch of the Evangelical Climate Initiative and this writing, it is difficult to assess the impact of the document on lawmakers, particularly on those Republicans who have until now opposed sweeping environmental laws. But without Cizik promoting the Evangelical Climate Initiative in the halls of Congress, its power has most likely been considerably reduced.

Cizik has by no means given up on Creation Care, however. One of his top tasks continues to be convincing Bible-believing Christians, including, most importantly, Christian Right leaders, that environmentalism is nothing short of a biblical mandate. "Fundamentally, we are rescuing evangelicalism from bad theology," he said. "If we, who claim to be the 'people of the book,' are shown to be hypocrites about what the Bible itself teaches, then we bring disrepute to the Gospel itself. That's how important this is. On every score, it's historic."

Cizik's ongoing Creation Care activism riled Christian Right leaders, including Dobson. In May 2006, Cizik even showed up in a provocative photograph in *Vanity Fair*'s "green issue," where he appeared to be walking on water, barefoot. The NAE lobbyist, it seemed, still hadn't gotten the message. So in spring or early summer of 2006, Dobson wrote to NAE's Colorado Springs headquarters calling for Cizik's firing, according to a source knowledgeable about the action. The NAE expressed its surprise at Dobson's request, the source said— Dobson is a member neither of the organization's board of directors nor of its executive committee—and vowed to stand by Cizik, who'd been at the organization for more than twenty-five years.

As intent as Dobson and his organizational empire are on focusing the evangelical constituency on a narrow social agenda—and despite such successes as keeping signatures off the Evangelical Climate Initiative— the movement is clearly branching out politically, bending the very definition of the term *Christian Right*. Beyond the burgeoning Creation Care movement, evangelicals in the last decade have played a leading role in the passage of major legislation to promote international human rights, to crack down on instances of rape in U.S. prisons, and to increase U.S. funds for HIV/AIDS in Africa. None of those issues had been historically championed by the Christian Right, but it is unlikely that any of those laws would have passed without evangelical advocacy.

"For the first time in twenty-five years, since the rise of the New Right, there is really a *new* New Right," said a top Washington strategist familiar with White House thinking. "This is not to say that Dobson is not at the helm of things, but [the new New Right] has a broader agenda. . . . There is a genuine interest in humanitarianism, and in Sudan and sub-Saharan Africa. When you talk about the social issues now, it's not just abortion and same-sex marriage. You also have to have something to say on Sudan and HIV/AIDS. In those [evangelical] subcultures, people want to know: What's your plan?"

The most high-profile example of this "new" New Right leader is Rick Warren, probably the most influential church pastor in the country. After his book *The Purpose-Driven Life* became the bestselling hardback in American history following its 2002 release, Warren devised an ambitious plan for his twenty-thousand-plus-person megachurch in Southern California to adopt villages in the war-ravaged African nation of Rwanda. His goal is slowing the spread of HIV/AIDS, alleviating hunger, and teaching literacy. Launching the effort in 2005, Warren has closely coordinated it with Rwandan president Paul Kagame, hoping it will inspire similar projects by other evangelical churches. "Dobson is how old now?" asked Mark Rodgers, the evangelical staff director for the Senate Republican Conference in late 2005, when Dobson was sixty-nine. "We're probably entering a transition phase, and it will be interesting to see who fills that gap. Rick Warren has that potential. He could be the next generation's Dobson. Although absolutely orthodox in things like abortion or marriage between a man and a woman, his agenda has expanded to include international justice. His set of concerns will possibly redefine evangelicalism in the public's eye."

Rick Warren's embrace of HIV/AIDS and poverty relief is a recent development. But the expansion of the evangelical political agenda beyond hot-button domestic issues could be traced to the mid-1990s, largely to the work of a Washington insider named Michael Horowitz, who happens to be Jewish. A White House lawyer under Ronald Reagan, Horowitz continued to be an influential Beltway legal thinker into the 1990s. From his perch at the conservative Hudson Institute, a think tank, Horowitz's work revolved mainly around promoting tort reform.[10] It wasn't until 1995, when he and his wife hired a live-in housekeeper who was an Ethiopian-born Christian evangelist, that he began to pay attention to the issue of international religious persecution. The housekeeper shocked Horowitz with stories of the torture he endured under Ethiopia's communist regime—and, after the regime fell, at the hands of Muslim radicals—because of his role as a leader in the underground church. "He described to me how he was hung upside down, how they poured hot oil over him and beat him with steel rods," Horowitz recalled in an interview. When Horowitz attempted to get the U.S. Immigration and Naturalization Service to grant his housekeeper asylum, he discovered that the agency was leery of Christian asylum seekers who claimed they'd been persecuted because of their religion. With roughly two billion adherents, Christians are the most populous religious group on the planet.[11] To the INS, Christians' claims of religious persecution seemed suspect on their face.

The experience prompted Horowitz to look into cases of persecuted Christians elsewhere in the world, through reports from the conservative Washington-based human rights group Freedom House and from a loose coalition of other organizations and activists that had been quietly working on the issue. They had documented the abuse of religious liberties under undemocratic regimes in North Korea, China, and Turkmenistan and in majority Islamic countries like Iraq, Iran, Sudan, and Nigeria. Religious minorities suffering in such places included Baha'is, Buddhists, Jews, Sufi Muslims, Shia Muslims living in Sunni-ruled nations, such as Iraq, and Sunni Muslims living in Shia-ruled nations. But partly due to the sheer size of the international Christian community and its explosive growth rate, particularly in the third world, it was estimated that tens of million of Christians were facing persecution in their home countries.[12] Africa and Asia, home to many of the nations with the most egregious records for religious persecution, had seen their evangelical Christian populations shoot up by 207 percent and 326 percent, respectively, since the 1970s.[13] It was these believers whom Horowitz most identified with. "Evangelicals really are the scapegoats of choice for the thug regimes around the world, just as the Jews had been," he said. "Not because of activism, but because they were seen as symbolizing the West. And because they live beyond the reach of bribes and threats that many of these dictatorial regimes thrive on."

Horowitz, bespectacled and white-haired, with a voice that frequently crescendos into a full-blown shout, tried talking to others in Washington about the plight of persecuted evangelicals abroad. He got little traction on the issue. "I began to see," Horowitz said, "that the rhetorical treatment of evangelical Christians was verbatim what had happened in the same kind of dinner parties seventy years ago to the Jews: 'I wouldn't want one as a neighbor; they bring it on themselves; they're clannish.' Every damn line that justified silence and indifference as Hitler was coming to power was happening here."

Horowitz, however, was having just as much trouble getting a hearing in evangelical circles, even after publishing an op-ed piece on international Christian persecution in *The Wall Street Journal*. Many evangelical leaders were simply fixated on the culture wars. Others felt that shining a light on persecuted Christian communities abroad could be counterproductive, antagonizing already unfriendly regimes into taking an even more hostile line toward believers. Sensing that he was getting nowhere, Horowitz began phoning Christian Right leaders. He'd tell the story of a group of American Jews who tried to dissuade Franklin Roosevelt from appointing Felix Frankfurter to the Supreme Court for fear it would inflame Hitler. "I said, 'Look, I'm a Jew,'" Horowitz said, recalling his pitch. "'Silence is not the answer. It's silence that makes it worse. I will work with you, but if need be I will shame you. You are not going to be silent.'"

Horowitz organized a conference in Washington on Christian persecution and invited his Christian Right contacts to attend. Held in early 1996, the event was officially sponsored by the National Association of Evangelicals, largely due to the influence of Richard Cizik.

Cizik's early receptivity to Horowitz's cause anticipated his later attempts to push the Christian Right beyond its traditional agenda on Creation Care. At the conference, Horowitz was able to convince Christian Right leaders to take up his cause. "Mike was coaching us, in some cases beating us onward with a strong whip," Cizik remembered. The conference culminated with the release of an NAE-endorsed "Statement of Conscience" on international religious persecution. Drafted by Horowitz, it included specific recommendations for the U.S. government, including the appointment of a special adviser to the president for religious liberty; a plan for U.S. diplomats to advocate religious liberties and to seek out religious dissidents abroad; and a program to train officials at the Immigration and Naturalization Service on handling religious persecution cases.[14]

Following the conference, Horowitz, Cizik, and others began assembling a coalition of religious groups to push for federal legislation to codify the Statement of Conscience. The coalition included such Christian Right stalwarts as Chuck Colson, Richard Land, and Family Research Council president Gary Bauer.[15] What was coming to be known as the "religious freedom coalition" didn't include just conservative religious organizations. Rabbi David Saperstein, the Washington lobbyist for the liberal Reform Judaism movement, was an early ally of Horowitz. His interest in helping persecuted Christians abroad stemmed partly from the active support he had witnessed from Christians in the 1970s, when the United States was helping persecuted Jews emigrate from Communist Russia.

Saperstein acted as a liaison between the conservative core of the religious freedom coalition and the liberal groups it was trying recruit into its ranks. Soon, the Anti-Defamation League, the International Campaign for Tibet, and the Washington office of the Episcopal Church were all attending the coalition's meetings. "Before that, there had hardly ever been any interaction between the fundamentalist evangelical communities and the Jewish community," said Saperstein, who has battled the Christian Right on issues like gay rights and school prayer. "We're at odds over two radically different visions of the proper role of religion in American politics and public life."

Nevertheless, the unlikely marriage of conservative evangelical groups and liberal Jewish organizations held up through the two-year process of drafting, negotiating, and redrafting the International Religious Freedom Act of 1998. The bill won unanimous support from both houses of Congress and was signed into law by President Clinton, who had originally fought the legislation on the basis that it would elevate religious freedom above other rights and would complicate the State Department's already tense relations with many nations.[16] Indeed, religion and politics scholar Allen Hertzke called the new law "one of the most sweeping human rights statutes on the books and the only one of its kind in the world."[17] It created a new ambassador-at-large for international religious freedom at the State Department; required the State Department to release annual, country-specific reports on religious freedom; and set up the independent U.S. Commission on International Religious Freedom to monitor the situation internationally and make policy recommendations independent of the State Department.[18]

In championing the International Religious Freedom Act, the Christian Right was moving onto terrain long occupied by secular liberals: the promotion of international human rights. Many liberal human rights groups had actually expressed skepticism or opposition toward the International Religious Freedom Act, for the same reasons the Clinton administration did. Such organizations included Human Rights Watch, and even the mainline Protestant National Council of Churches. There were accusations that, rather than making a good-faith effort to promote international human rights, evangelicals were advancing the cause of fellow believers abroad out of self-interest.[19]

If the American evangelical community had abandoned its human rights work after passage of the International Religious Freedom Act, those charges might have stuck. But the religious freedom coalition that emerged around the law has reconstituted itself to lobby successfully for

a flurry of other human rights laws, often in areas that have received
scant attention from secular human rights organizations. These include
2000's Trafficking Victims Protection Act, which imposed sanctions on
countries that failed to crack down on human trafficking for forced
prostitution and labor;[20] 2002's Sudan Peace Act, which established a
framework for negotiating the end of the twenty-year civil war between
the Sudanese government and southern rebels that had claimed an estimated two million lives;[21] and 2003's Prison Rape Elimination Act,
which authorized the creation of a national plan to reduce prison rape.
More recently, the religious freedom coalition helped pass 2004's North
Korea Human Rights Act, which aimed to make human rights concerns
a key part of U.S. negotiations with North Korea and pledged more support to North Korean refugees. "Clearly, the driving political force that
got these bills through Republican-dominated Congresses and the administration," said Saperstein, "was the strong, assertive voice of the fundamentalist Christian community."

Such human rights laws, and the role of conservative evangelicals
in passing them, have received little attention from the news media,
even as Christian Right advocacy around fighting gay marriage and
abortion rights regularly makes headlines. "Underneath the radar
screen of a press that's either blind or bigoted, the evangelical community has become the principal force for international human rights in
the country today," said Horowitz. "But it's like a man bites dog story.
The media scratch their heads, or they deprecate it by saying it's a sop
to the Christian Right." David Saperstein attributes the scarcity of news
coverage to the media's lack of interest in human rights issues generally,
rather than to a bias against portraying evangelicals as human rights advocates.

If James Dobson hasn't worked to stymie the evangelical movement's activism on human rights, as he did with the 2006 Evangelical Climate Initiative, he has been largely absent from such campaigns. Dobson devoted
a *Focus on the Family* radio program to promoting 1998's International

Religious Freedom Act, an effort in which the Family Research Council was active. But Dobson was conspicuously quiet in the campaigns to push for the Trafficking Victims Protection Act, the Sudan Peace Act, the Prison Rape Elimination Act, and the North Korea Freedom Act, even as Christian Right figures like Chuck Colson and Richard Land took on high-profile roles. On the rare occasions when Dobson has featured Michael Horowitz on his radio show, he has focused narrowly on the persecution of Christian communities abroad, avoiding broader human rights issues. "I would say, 'Wait a minute—what about discussing Christian involvement in stopping the trafficking of women or ending prison rape or taking on the North Korean regime—why only focus on ending religious and anti-Christian persecution?'" Horowitz recalled of a recent appearance on Dobson's show. "The default option for him is to come back to the standard old issues too quickly, too easily. He tends to be into a much more parochial set of issues."

Horowitz stressed his respect for Dobson, who he credits with saving his career in the Reagan administration. As general counsel for the White House Office of Management and Budget, Horowitz had unleashed an uproar in Washington by proposing a rules change in how contractors and nonprofit groups applied for federal contracts and grants. With some outside groups calling for his resignation, Dobson devoted part of his *Focus on the Family* radio broadcast to Horowitz's cause, triggering a windfall of mail into the White House that Horowitz said saved his job. Horowitz also shares many of Dobson's conservative views, but believes those views would be more effectively advanced, and that he would be harder to caricature and demonize, if Dobson better communicated his commitment to human rights issues that he shares with liberals. But Horowitz's characterization of Dobson's issue set as "parochial" is one that Dobson probably would not quarrel with. "Those issues like the poor and the needy are all important to us," he said in a 2004 interview. "But when you compare those issues . . . with killing forty-three million babies, it's not in the same league. We're talking the unborn holocaust here. . . . When it comes to preserving the in-

tegrity of the family, it's very hard to put anything else in that arena. . . .
Everything that has been predictable and stable for the last five thousand years has been based on the family.

"You can't shoot at everything—you won't hit anything," Dobson
continued. "You have to decide the things that matter most and then
talk about those. If that makes us sound extreme, I'll take it, brother."

But Horowitz suspects that Dobson has declined to participate for
another reason: He can't abide working with traditional enemies on the
left. Starting with 1998's International Religious Freedom Act, every
major human rights law pushed by evangelical groups has seen them
enter into alliances with liberal groups. Such arrangements maximize
bipartisan support and boost the odds of success. In promoting the Trafficking Victims Protection Act, for instance, Christian Right activists
joined feminist leaders like Gloria Steinem to confront the problem of
sex trafficking. That kind of partnership is anathema to Dobson. "I wish
so much that he understood that people on the other side are more
reachable than he imagines them to be," Horowitz said, "so that he
would not be out there perpetuating an 'us against them' approach."

That approach has led the Christian Right to try to elect as many
conservative Republicans as possible, in hopes of enacting a hard-core
legislative agenda. But with the evangelical movement showing greater
willingness to work with traditional adversaries in the pursuit of non-
hot-button policy objectives, and achieving major victories in doing so,
it has arrived at a crossroads. Will the movement continue to break with
its history to make headway on humanitarian causes, or will Christian
Right leaders swing attention back to the culture war? With Dobson's
age expected to force him off the political stage in the not-too-distant
future, the answer depends partly on who replaces him as evangelicalism's top political power broker. But the unique nature of Dobson's influence through the rise of Focus on the Family makes it hard to
imagine a figure that could single-handedly exert as much control over
the movement as he has. The Christian Right's humanitarian awakening may only accelerate in his absence.

Notes

1 The Crossroads

1. William Martin, *With God on Our Side: The Rise of the Religious Right in America*, rev. ed. (1996; repr., New York: Broadway Books, 2005), 68.
2. Dale Buss, *Family Man: The Biography of Dr. James Dobson* (Wheaton, Ill.: Tyndale House Publishers, 2005), 380.
3. Ibid., 151.
4. Ibid., 336.
5. Brad Carson, "Vote Righteously!" *New Republic*, November 22, 2004.
6. Buss, *Family Man*, 381–382.
7. Allen was given probation before judgment, meaning his record will be cleared after his probation is complete. Stephen Manning, "Former Bush Advisor Accused of Theft Gets Two Years Probation," Associated Press, August 4, 2006.

2 Billy Graham's Heir

1. Dale Buss, *Family Man: The Biography of Dr. James Dobson* (Wheaton, Ill.: Tyndale House Publishers, 2005), 21.
2. Ibid.
3. Ibid., 21–22.
4. Ibid., 11–14.
5. Ibid., 15–16.
6. Tim Stafford, "His Father's Son: The Drive Behind James Dobson, Jr.," *Christianity Today*, April 22, 1988, 16.
7. Ibid.; J. Gordon Melton, *Encyclopedia of American Religions*, 6th ed. (Detroit: Gale, 1999), 439.

8. Church of the Nazarene, "Nazarene Church Statistics/Statistical Comparison—2004," Official Site of the International Church of the Nazarene, www.nazarene.org/gensec/statistics_04.html (accessed August 5, 2006).

9. Buss, *Family Man*, 13.

10. Peter W. Williams, *America's Religions: From Their Origins to the Twenty-First Century*, 2nd ed. (Urbana: University of Illinois Press, 2002), 273.

11. Buss, *Family Man*, 13.

12. Ibid., 24.

13. Ibid., 27, 31–32.

14. Stafford, "His Father's Son," 20.

15. John C. Green, "Seeking a Place: Evangelical Protestants and Public Engagement in the Twentieth Century," in *Toward an Evangelical Public Policy*, ed. Ronald J. Sider and Diane Knippers, 16–18 (Grand Rapids, Mich.: BakerBooks, 2005).

16. Rolf Zettersten, *Dr. Dobson: Turning Hearts Toward Home* (Dallas: Word Publishing, 1989), 86–87.

17. Buss, *Family Man*, 46.

18. Ibid., 47; Zettersten, *Dr. Dobson*, 90.

19. Stafford, "His Father's Son," 20.

20. Buss, *Family Man*, 59.

21. Ibid., 67–68.

22. Ibid., 79.

23. John Dart, "A Force in Conservative Protestant America; Dobson's Influence Based on Family Issues," *Los Angeles Times*, April 2, 1988.

24. Ann Cooper, "Families and Texas," *National Journal*, August 3, 1985.

25. Gustav Niebuhr, "Advice for Parents, and for Politicians," *New York Times*, May 30, 1995.

26. Stafford, "His Father's Son," 22.

27. Peter Perl, "Tom DeLay Is Certain That Christian Family Values Will Solve America's Problems. But He's Uncertain How to Face His Own Family," *Washington Post*, May 13, 2001.

28. Matthew Scully, "Right Wing and a Prayer—Still Alive and Kicking," *Washington Times*, November 8, 1989.

29. William Martin, *With God on Our Side: The Rise of the Religious Right in America*, rev. ed. (1996; repr., New York: Broadway Books, 2005), 174.

30. Ibid., 164.

31. A former Arkansas congressman, Tucker was convicted of charges related to his role in the Clinton Whitewater scandal in 1996. Then serving as governor of Arkansas, he was forced to step down.

32. Stafford, "His Father's Son," 22.

33. Sara Diamond, *Not by Politics Alone: The Enduring Influence of the Christian Right* (New York: Guilford Press, 1998), 34.

34. Dart, "A Force."

35. Buss, *Family Man*, 87, 92.

36. John Dart, "Porno Foe Has Unusual Ally in Killer Bundy; Religious Broadcaster Tapes Interview Before Execution," *Los Angeles Times*, January 25, 1989.

37. Robert Zwier, "The Christian Right and the Cultural Divide in Colorado," in *The Christian Right in American Politics: Marching to the Millennium*, ed. John C. Green, Mark J. Rozell, and Clyde Wilcox, 187 (Washington, D.C.: Georgetown University Press, 2003).

38. Diamond, *Not by Politics Alone*, 35.

39. Zwier, "The Christian Right," 187–188.

40. Diamond, *Not by Politics Alone*, 173.

41. Ibid., 175.

42. Ibid., 173.

43. Grover G. Norquist, "Home Rule," *American Spectator*, June 1994.

44. Anna Greenberg and Jennifer Berktold, "Re: Evangelicals in America," *Religion & Ethics Newsweekly*, www.pbs.org/wnet/religionandethics/week733/results.doc (accessed August 5, 2006).

45. Martin, *With God on Our Side*, 275–276.

46. Ibid., 289.

47. Buss, *Family Man*, 256.

48. Ibid., 257.

49. Ibid., 194; Mike Ward, "Christian Radio Suit Dismissed by Judge," *Los Angeles Times*, June 25, 1991.

3   Vatican West

1. Focus asks journalists not to use the names of callers to Focus's correspondence department or the names of persons mentioned by callers.

2. Evangelical Christians point to Ephesians 5:22 as the basis of the call for wives to submit to their husbands.

3. Dale Buss, *Family Man: The Biography of Dr. James Dobson* (Wheaton, Ill.: Tyndale House Publishers, 2005), 121–122.

4. Ibid., 325–326.

4   The Long War

1. John C. Green, "Seeking a Place: Evangelical Protestants and Public Engagement in the Twentieth Century," in *Toward an Evangelical Public*

Policy, ed. Ronald J. Sider and Diane Knippers, 16 (Grand Rapids, Mich. BakerBooks, 2005).

2. Ibid., 18.
3. Cal Thomas and Ed Dobson, *Blinded by Might: Can the Religious Right Save America?* (Grand Rapids, Mich.: Zondervan Publishing House, 1999), 31–32.
4. Green, "Seeking a Place," 18–19.
5. Ibid., 19.
6. Ibid., 20.
7. Ibid., 21–23.
8. Ibid., 22.
9. William Martin, *With God on Our Side: The Rise of the Religious Right in America*, rev. ed. (1996; repr., New York: Broadway Books, 2005), 149.
10. Ibid., 154.
11. Ibid., 156.
12. Ibid., 169.
13. Ralph Reed, *Active Faith: How Christians Are Changing the Soul of American Politics* (New York: Free Press, 2005), 105.
14. Martin, *With God on Our Side*, 172.
15. Ibid., 198.
16. Sara Diamond, *Not by Politics Alone: The Enduring Influence of the Christian Right* (New York: Guilford Press, 1998), 67.
17. Reed, *Active Faith*, 108; Martin, *With God on Our Side*, 203.
18. Martin, *With God on Our Side*, 205.
19. Ibid., 208.
20. Ibid., 213.
21. Ibid., 209.
22. Ibid., 215; Diamond, *Not by Politics Alone*, 68.
23. Diamond, *Not by Politics Alone*, 67.
24. Ibid., 62.
25. Ibid., 69.
26. Martin, *With God on Our Side*, 221–222.
27. Ibid., 227.
28. Ibid., 228.
29. Linda Greenhouse, "Consistently, A Pivotal Role," *New York Times*, July 2, 2005.
30. Martin, *With God on Our Side*, 226–227.
31. Ibid., 233.
32. Ibid., 238–239.
33. Ibid., 240–241.
34. Ibid., 241.

35. Ibid., 242–245.
36. Ibid., 249–252.
37. Ibid., 256.
38. Diamond, *Not by Politics Alone*, 72.
39. Martin, *With God on Our Side*, 258.
40. Diamond, *Not by Politics Alone*, 25.
41. Ibid., 26; Martin, *With God on Our Side*, 258.
42. Diamond, *Not by Politics Alone*, 25.
43. Ibid.
44. Ibid.
45. Martin, *With God on Our Side*, 259–262.
46. Ibid., 265–267.
47. Ibid., 285.
48. Ibid., 262–267.
49. Ibid., 299–300.
50. Ibid., 300.
51. Ibid., 299–300.
52. Thomas B. Edsall, "In Ga., Abramoff Scandal Threatens a Political Ascendancy," *Washington Post*, January 16, 2006.
53. Nina Easton, *Gang of Five Leaders at the Center of the Conservative Crusade* (New York: Simon & Schuster, 2000), 210.
54. Martin, *With God on Our Side*, 304.
55. Easton, *Gang of Five*, 210.
56. Ibid., 212.
57. Reed, *Active Faith*, 131–132; Easton, *Gang of Five*, 214–215; Martin, *With God on Our Side*, 305.
58. Easton, *Gang of Five*, 216.
59. Ibid., 217.
60. Reed, *Active Faith*, 122.
61. Ibid.
62. Ibid., 121–122.
63. Martin, *With God on Our Side*, 317.
64. Reed, *Active Faith*, 132–133.
65. Ibid., 136; Easton, *Gang of Five*, 247.
66. Martin, *With God on Our Side*, 310.
67. Ibid., 316.
68. Ibid., 314–316.
69. Reed, *Active Faith*, 136.
70. Martin, *With God on Our Side*, 325.
71. Easton, *Gang of Five*, 253.
72. Reed, *Active Faith*, 156.

73. Ibid., 121.
74. Ibid., 120.
75. Easton, *Gang of Five*, 257.
76. Ibid.
77. Ibid.
78. Ralph Reed, *Active Faith*, 158.
79. Ibid., 161–163.
80. Easton, *Gang of Five*, 271.
81. Reed, *Active Faith*, 185.
82. Easton, *Gang of Five*, 256.
83. Reed, *Active Faith*, 154.
84. Martin, *With God on Our Side*, 340.
85. Ibid.; Easton, *Gang of Five*, 288–289.
86. Reed, *Active Faith*, 200–201.
87. Ibid., 204.
88. Easton, *Gang of Five*, 344.
89. Ibid., 345.
90. Ibid., 346–347.
91. Ibid., 347.
92. Ibid., 350–351.
93. Ibid., 351.
94. Ibid., 389.

5 The Beltway's Bible Belt

1. Michael J. Gerson, "A Righteous Indignation," *U.S. News & World Report*, May 4, 1998.
2. Dale Buss, *Family Man: The Biography of Dr. James Dobson* (Wheaton, Ill.: Tyndale House Publishers, 2005), 168–169; J. Gerson, "A Righteous Indignation."
3. Ralph Reed, *Active Faith: How Christians Are Changing the Soul of American Politics* (New York: Free Press, 1996), 252.
4. William Martin, *With God on Our Side: The Rise of the Religious Right in America*, rev. ed. (1996; repr., New York: Broadway Books, 2005), 344.
5. Reed, *Active Faith*, 252.
6. Ibid., 240.
7. David D. Kirkpatrick, "Club of the Most Powerful Gathers in Strictest Privacy," *New York Times*, August 28, 2004.
8. Buss, *Family Man*, 166.
9. Ibid.
10. *National Journal's CongressDaily*, "Dems, Conservative GOP Join Forces Against Bankruptcy Bill," November 15, 2002.

11. Buss, *Family Man*, 177.
12. Ibid., 312.
13. Ibid.
14. Ibid., 312–313.
15. Ken Connor, "Ominous Implications for the Handicapped," *Washington Times*, February 6, 2005.
16. David D. Kirkpatrick and Sheryl Gay Stolberg, "How Family's Cause Reached the Halls of Congress," *New York Times*, March 22, 2005.
17. Keith Epstein, "Congressmen Rush Schiavo Bill," *Tampa Tribune*, March 9, 2005.
18. Senator Martinez's legal counsel admitted to writing the memo and resigned the following month.
19. Recording provided by the Americans United for Separation of Church and State.
20. Elisabeth Bumiller, "Bush Says $2 Billion Went to Religious Charities in '04," *New York Times*, March 2, 2005.
21. Thomas Edsall, "Grants Flow to Bush Allies on Social Issues; Federal Programs Direct at Least $157 Million," *Washington Post*, March 22, 2006.

6 Dobson's D-Day

1. Cate Terwilliger, "Finances Get Blurry for Focus on the Family," *Denver Post*, February 23, 2003.
2. David D. Kirkpatrick, "Conservatives Using Issue of Gay Unions as a Rallying Tool," *New York Times*, February 8, 2004.
3. Franklin Foer, "Marriage Counselor: Matt Daniels believes he's found a solution to the political problem of gay marriage. So why do his fellow conservatives want to divorce him?" *Atlantic Monthly*, March 2004.
4. Ibid.
5. Mark O'Keefe, "Religious Right Frustrated Despite Friends in High Office," Newhouse News Service, July 10, 2003.
6. Cal Thomas and Ed Dobson, *Blinded by Might: Can the Religious Right Save America?* (Grand Rapids, Mich.: Zondervan Publishing House, 1999), 36.
7. Kirkpatrick, "Conservatives Using Issue."
8. Ibid.
9. Ibid.
10. Ibid.
11. Kevin Freking, "White House to Enforce Abortion-Fetus Law," Associated Press, April 22, 2005; Robert Pear, "New Attention for 2002 Law on Survivors of Abortions," *New York Times*, April 23, 2005.

12. Ceci Connolly, "Doctors Are Warned on Fetus Care; Guidelines Are Issued on Born-Alive Infants Protection Act," *Washington Post*, April 23, 2005.

13. John C. Green, Mark J. Rozell, and Clyde Wilcox, *The Christian Right in American Politics: Marching to the Millennium* (Washington, D.C.: Georgetown University Press, 2003), 13.

7 The Values Vote

1. Clem Boyd, "Hometown Heroes: Marriage Man," *Citizen* magazine, March 2005.

2. Alan Johnson, "Even Foes Like Leader of Group Opposing Gay Marriage," *Columbus Dispatch*, August 22, 2004.

3. Tom Minnery, *Why You Can't Stay Silent: A Biblical Mandate to Shape Our Culture* (Wheaton, Ill.: Tyndale House Publishers, 2001), 176.

4. Ibid., 174.

5. Ibid., 175.

6. John C. Green, "The Bible and the Buckeye State," in *The Values Campaign?*, ed. John C. Green, Mark J. Rozell, and Clyde Wilcox, 79–97 (Washington, D.C.: Georgetown University, 2006).

7. Ibid., 15–16.

8. Todd Donovan, Caroline Tolbert, and Daniel Smith, "Do State-Level Ballot Measures Affect Presidential Elections? Gay Marriage and the 2004 Election" paper presented at the annual meeting of the American Political Science Association, Washington, D.C., September 1–4, 2005.

9. Ibid., 19.

10. Andrew Welsh-Huggins, "Ohio GOP Fighting Scandal, Each Other on Convention Eve," Associated Press, August 28, 2004.

11. Polls suggest that more than half of Americans attend worship services at least once monthly.

12. Richard L. Berke, "Aide Says Bush Will Do More to Marshal Religious Base," *New York Times*, December 12, 2001.

13. Rachel Zoll, "Republican Request for Church Directories Angers Some Religious Leaders," Associated Press, July 23, 2004.

14. John C. Green, Corwin E. Smidt, James L. Guth, and Lyman A. Kellstedt, *The American Religious Landscape and the 2004 Presidential Vote: Increased Polarization* (Washington, D.C.: Pew Forum on Religion & Public Life, 2005), 8.

15. Pew Forum on Religion & Public Life, "Religion and Public Life: A Faith-Based Partisan Divide," in *Trends 2005* (Washington, D.C.: Pew Research Center, 2005).

16. Green et al., *American Religious Landscape*, 7.

17. Pew Center for People & the Press, *Voters Liked Campaign 2004, But Too Much "Mud-Slinging"/Moral Values: How Important?* (Washington, D.C.: Pew Research Center, November 2004).

18. Green et al., *American Religious Landscape*, 11.

19. Ibid., 7, 11.

20. Ibid., 5.

21. Pew Forum, "Religion and Public Life," 12–13.

22. "Conservative Leaders Shining a Light," *Fairfield Citizen*, August 2005.

23. Susan Page, "Shaping Politics from the Pulpits," *USA Today*, August 3, 2005.

24. Matt Curry, "Perry Mobilizes Evangelicals as Texas Governor's Race Heats Up," Associated Press, June 12, 2005.

25. Kelley Shannon, "As Texans Gear Up to Decide on Gay Marriage Ban, a Novel Opposition Strategy Looms," Associated Press, November 3, 2005.

8   The Bench Press

1. After resigning under pressure from several Republican senators, Miranda filed a lawsuit in federal court in 2004 seeking a declaratory judgment on the MemoGate allegations. At press time, the court hadn't yet ruled on the case. (Alexander Bolton, "Political Comeback: Fall and Rise of Miranda," *The Hill*, November 9, 2005.)

2. Jeanne Cummings, "Crowd Control; In Judge Battle, Mr. Sekulow Plays a Delicate Role," *Wall Street Journal*, May 17, 2005.

3. Michelle Roberts, "Religious Public Interest Law Firm Grows from One to 100 Workers," Associated Press, November 24, 2005.

4. Sheryl Gay Stolberg, "G.O.P. Colleagues Backing Specter in Judiciary Post," *New York Times*, November 19, 2004.

5. David D. Kirkpatrick, "Frist Set to Use Religious Stage on Judges Issue," *New York Times*, April 15, 2005.

6. John Fund, "Judgment Call: Did Christian Conservatives Receive Assurances That Miers Would Oppose *Roe v. Wade*?" *Wall Street Journal*, October 17, 2005.

7. David D. Kirkpatrick, "Conservatives Are Wary Over President's Selection," *New York Times*, October 4, 2005.

8. "Focus on the Family Founder Questions Own Support for Miers," Associated Press, October 6, 2005.

9. Jo Becker, "In Speeches from 1990s, Clues About Miers Views; Nominee Defended Social Activism," *Washington Post*, October 26, 2005.

9   Looking for God in the Democratic Party

1. Jim VandeHei, "Values Become Key Campaign Issue; Kerry, Bush Show Their Differences," *Washington Post,* July 9, 2004.
2. Jim VandeHei and Mike Allen, "Kerry Speaks of Faith's Role; Bush Touts 'Record of Results,'" *Washington Post,* October 24, 2004.
3. Mark Stricherz, "John Kerry's Open Mind," *Christianity Today,* October 2004.
4. Tony Carnes, "Wooing the Faithful," *Christianity Today,* October 2004.
5. John C. Green, Corwin E. Smidt, James L. Guth, and Lyman A. Kellstedt, *The American Religious Landscape and the 2004 Presidential Vote: Increased Polarization* (Washington, D.C.: Pew Forum on Religion & Public Life, 2005), 8.
6. Pew Forum on Religion & Public Life, "Religion and Public Life: A Faith-Based Partisan Divide," in *Trends 2005* (Washington, D.C.: Pew Research Center, 2005), 5.
7. Ibid., 2.
8. Robert Pear, "Senate Passes Budget with Benefit Cuts and Oil Drilling," *New York Times,* November 2, 2005.
9. Andrew Kohut, John C. Green, Scott Keeter, and Robert C. Toth, *The Diminishing Divide: Religion's Changing Role in American Politics* (Washington, D.C.: Brookings Institution, 2000), 24.

Epilogue: The Post-Dobson Christian Right

1. Andrew Kohut, John C. Green, Scott Keeter, and Robert C. Toth, *The Diminishing Divide: Religion's Changing Role in American Politics* (Washington, D.C.: Brookings Institution, 2000), 47–48.
2. Ibid., 48–49.
3. Laurie Goodstein, "Evangelical Leaders Swing Influence Behind Effort to Combat Global Warming," *New York Times,* March 10, 2005.
4. Ibid.
5. Michael Janofsky, "When Cleaner Air Is a Biblical Obligation," *New York Times,* November 7, 2005.
6. Goodstein, "Evangelical Leaders."
7. Ibid.; Melissa Jones, "Evangelicals and 'Creation Care,'" *National Catholic Reporter,* June 17, 2005.
8. Deborah Solomon, "Earthy Evangelist," *New York Times,* April 3, 2005.
9. Pew Forum on Religion & Public Life, *Religion and the Environment: Polls Show Strong Backing for Environmental Protection Across Religious Groups* (Washington, D.C.: Pew Research Center, October 2004).

10. Allen D. Hertzke, *Freeing God's Children: The Unlikely Alliance for Global Human Rights* (Lanham, Md.: Rowman & Littlefield, 2004), 155.
11. Ibid., 17.
12. Ibid., 19.
13. Ibid., 59.
14. Ibid., 186–187.
15. Ibid., 193.
16. Ibid., 203–204.
17. Ibid., 183.
18. Ibid., 183–184.
19. Ibid., 203.
20. Ibid., 316.
21. Ibid., 239, 291.

Interviews

Unless otherwise noted, all quotations are drawn from interviews with the author. Most interviews were conducted in person, but some were done via telephone, or, in a very few instances, by e-mail. The following individuals granted on-the-record interviews; those granting background or off-the-record interviews are not listed. Most interviews were conducted expressly for this book, though a few were done in the course of reporting for *U.S. News & World Report*. Titles given are from the time of the interview. Where sources were interviewed for previous positions, former titles are given and noted.

Wayne Allard
U.S. Senator (R-Colo.)

Amanda L. Banks
Federal Issues Analyst
Focus on the Family
Colorado Springs, CO

David Barton
Founder and President
WallBuilders
Aledo, TX

Gary L. Bauer
President
American Values
Arlington, VA

J. Kenneth Blackwell
Ohio Secretary of State
Columbus, OH

Peter L. Brandt
Senior Director, Public Policy
  Division
Focus on the Family
Colorado Springs, CO

Rob Brendle
Associate Pastor
New Life Church
Colorado Springs, CO

R. Randolph "Randy" Brinson
Founder
Redeem the Vote
Montgomery, AL

Sam Brownback
U.S. Senator (R-Kans.)

Phil Burress
President
Citizens for Community Values
Cincinnati, OH

Frank Carl
Senior Pastor
Genoa Baptist Church
Westerville, OH

David Cauthen
Senior Pastor
Genesis Church
Spring Hill, TN

Joseph J. Cella
President
Fidelis
Chelsea, MI

Warren Chisum
Representative
Texas House of Representatives
Austin, TX

Richard Cizik
Vice President for Governmental
   Affairs
National Association of Evangelicals
Washington, DC

James Clyburn
U.S. Congressman
   (D-S.C.)

Tom Coburn
U.S. Senator (R-Okla.)

Chuck Colson
Founder
Prison Fellowship
Lansdowne, VA

Joann Condie
Licensed Professional Counselor
Focus on the Family
Colorado Springs, CO

Ken Connor
Chairman
Center for a Just Society
Washington, DC

Alan Crippen II
Rector, The Witherspoon Fellowship
Family Research Council
Washington, DC

Michael Cromartie
Vice President
Ethics and Public Policy Center
Washington, DC

Jim Daly
President and CEO
Focus on the Family
Colorado Springs, CO

Matt Daniels
President
Alliance for Marriage
Merrifield, VA

Kristen Day
Executive Director
Democrats for Life of America
Washington, DC

Sheryl DeWitt
Director of Faculty
Focus on the Family Institute
Colorado Springs, CO

James C. Dobson
Founder and Chairman
Focus on the Family
Colorado Springs, CO

Carrie Gordon Earll
Director, Issue Analysis
Focus on the Family
Colorado Springs, CO

Ted Engstrom
Board member
Focus on the Family
Colorado Springs, CO

Jerry Falwell
Founder and Chancellor
Liberty University
Lynchburg, VA

Michael Farris
Cofounder
Home School Legal Defense
    Association
Purcellville, VA

Robert Flanegin
Chief Internet Officer
Focus on the Family
Colorado Springs, CO

Trent Franks
U.S. Congressman (R-Ariz.)

Melissa Fryrear
Gender Issues Analyst
Focus on the Family
Colorado Springs, CO

John Fuller
Vice President, Broadcasting
Focus on the Family
Colorado Springs, CO

Robert George
McCormick Professor of
    Jurisprudence
Princeton University
Princeton, NJ

C. Boyden Gray
Chairman
Committee for Justice
Washington, DC

John C. Green
Director, Ray C. Bliss Institute of
    Applied Politics
University of Akron
Akron, OH

Jim Guth
Professor of Political Science
Furman University
Greenville, SC

Ted Haggard
President
National Association of Evangelicals
Colorado Springs, CO

Mike Haley
Director, Gender Issues Department
Focus on the Family
Colorado Springs, CO

John Hart
Communications Director
U.S. Senator Tom Coburn
Washington, DC

Bruce Hausknecht
Judicial Analyst
Focus on the Family
Colorado Springs, CO

Nathan L. Hecht
Justice
The Supreme Court of Texas
Austin, TX

Phil Heimlich
President
Hamilton County Board of
    Commissioners
Cincinnati, OH

Paul L. Hetrick
Vice President
Focus on the Family
Colorado Springs, CO

Don Hodel
Board member, former President
    and CEO
Focus on the Family
Colorado Springs, CO

Michael Horowitz
Senior Fellow
Hudson Institute
Washington, DC

Harry Jackson
Founder and Chairman
High Impact Leadership Coalition
College Park, MD

Peb Jackson
Former Vice President of Public
    Affairs
Focus on the Family
Colorado Springs, CO

Stan John
Vice President of Constituent
    Response
Focus on the Family
Colorado Springs, CO

Russell Johnson
Founder, Chairman, CEO
Ohio Restoration Project
Lancaster, OH

D. James Kennedy
President
Coral Ridge Ministries
Fort Lauderdale, FL

John Kerry
U.S. Senator (D-Mass.)

Ron Key
Pastor
Cornerstone Christian Church
Dallas, TX

Richard Land
President
The Ethics & Religious Liberty
    Commission of the Southern
    Baptist Convention
Nashville, TN

H.B. London, Jr.
Vice President of Ministry
    Outreach/Pastoral Ministries
Focus on the Family
Colorado Springs, CO

Christopher Long
Executive Director
Christian Coalition of Ohio
Columbus, OH

Connie Mackey
Vice President of Government Affairs
Family Research Council
Washington, DC

Steve Maegdlin
Vice President, Constituent
    Acquisition
Focus on the Family
Colorado Springs, CO

Bill Maier
Vice President, Psychologist in
    Residence
Focus on the Family
Colorado Springs, CO

Gary Marx
Executive Director
Judicial Confirmation Network
Alexandria, VA

Thomas E. McClusky
Director of Government Affairs
Family Research Council
Washington, DC

Edwin Meese III
Ronald Reagan Distinguished Fellow
    in Public Policy
Heritage Foundation
Washington, DC

Brad Miller
National Representative, Family
    Policy Councils
Focus on the Family
Colorado Springs, CO

Tom Minnery
Vice President of Public Policy
Focus on the Family
Colorado Springs, CO

Manuel Miranda
Founder and Chairman
Third Branch Coalition
Washington, DC

Lindy Morgan
Phone Correspondent
Focus on the Family
Colorado Springs, CO

Duane P. Murray
Executive Pastor
Thompson Station Church
Thompson Station, TN

Paul Nelson
Former Executive Vice President and
    CEO
Focus on the Family
Colorado Springs, CO

Marvin Olasky
Editor-in-Chief
World Magazine
Austin, TX

Pam Olsen
Florida Chairwoman for Social
    Conservative Outreach
Bush-Cheney 2004
Tallahassee, FL

Gary Palmer
President
Alabama Policy Institute
Birmingham, AL

Diane Passno
Executive Vice President
Focus on the Family
Colorado Springs, CO

Tony Perkins
President
Family Research Council
Washington, DC

Joe Pitts
U.S. Congressman (R-Pa.)

David Price
U.S. Congressman (D-N.C.)

Bruce Purdy
Assistant Director of Columbus
    Operations
Citizens for Community Values
Cincinnati, OH

Ralph E. Reed, Jr.
President
Century Strategies
Atlanta, GA

Mark Rodgers
Staff Director
Senate Republican Conference
Washington, DC

Sean Rushton
Executive Director
Committee for Justice
Washington, DC

Ken Salazar
U.S. Senator (D-Colo.)

David Saperstein
Director and Counsel
Religious Action Center of Reform
    Judaism
Washington, DC

Eric Sapp
Senior Partner
Common Good Strategies
Washington, DC

Rick Scarborough
President
Vision America
Lufkin, TX

Michael Schwartz
Chief of Staff
U.S. Senator Tom Coburn
Washington, DC

Jay Sekulow
Chief Counsel
American Center for Law and Justice
Washington, DC

Kelly J. Shackelford
President
Free Market Foundation
Plano, TX

Barry Sheets
Governmental Affairs Director
Citizens for Community Values
Cincinnati, OH

Doug Sommer
Senior Manager, Briargate Media
Focus on the Family
Colorado Springs, CO

Wil Spaite
Associate Discipleship Pastor
Crossroads Nazarene Church
Chandler, AZ

Peter Sprigg
Vice President for Policy
Family Research Council
Washington, DC

Gwen Stein
Manager, Media & Public Relations
Focus on the Family
Colorado Springs, CO

Colin Stewart
President
Center for a Just Society
Washington, DC

Del Tackett
President
Focus on the Family Institute
Colorado Springs, CO

John Thune
U.S. Senator (R-S.D.)

Mike Trout
Former Co-Host
Focus on the Family
Colorado Springs, CO

Bobbie Valentine
Former Executive Producer
Focus on the Family
Colorado Springs, CO

Mara Vanderslice
President
Common Good Strategies
Washington, DC

Richard A. Viguerie
Chairman
American Target Advertising
Manassas, VA

Kathryn Vorce
Vice President, Constituent
    Communications
Focus on the Family
Colorado Springs, CO

Jim Wallis
President and Executive Director
Sojourners/Call to Renewal
Washington, DC

Paul M. Weyrich
Chairman and CEO
Free Congress Foundation
Washington, DC

Laurence L. White
Chairman
Texas Restoration Project
Houston, TX

Don Wildmon
Chairman
American Family Association
Tupelo, MS

Ron Wilson
Vice President of Human
    Resources
Focus on the Family
Colorado Springs, CO

Ken Windebank
Vice President of Public Affairs
Focus on the Family
Colorado Springs, CO

Frank Wolf
U.S. Congressman (R-Va.)

Genevieve Wood
Vice President
Center for a Just Society
Washington, DC

Wilford D. Wooten
Senior Director, Department of
    Counseling
Focus on the Family
Colorado Springs, CO

Charmaine Yoest
Analyst
Family Research Council
Washington, DC

Index

ABC, 80
abortion
    curbs on methods of, 122, 165
    discouraging it (the 95–10 initiative),
        263
    as a moral issue, 251–52, 257, 261
    restrictions on minors, 111, 122, 166
abortion rights, 78, 86
Abramoff, Jack, 92–93, 130, 134, 267
abusive homes, 49
Abzug, Bella, 31
Adams, John, 60, 192
Adventures in Odyssey (radio show),
    62
Afghanistan War, 119
African Americans, 2, 103, 180–81,
    210, 244, 259
    outreach to, by political campaigns,
        179, 244
    social conservatives, 179
AIDS, 63, 87, 121–22
Alabama, 152
Alabama Policy Institute, 152
Alabama Supreme Court, 1–5
Alexander, Lamar, 108
Alito, Samuel, 42, 240–41
Allard, Wayne, 161
Allen, Claude, 16, 283n7
Alliance Defense Fund (ADF), 222

Alliance for Global Human Rights,
    278–80
Alliance for Marriage, 143–44, 149
Amendment 2 (Colorado), 34–35
America
    at a historic crossroads, 4
    social ills of, 60
America Coming Together (ACT), 188
American Bar Association, 236
American Center for Law and Justice
    (ACLJ), 216, 222
American Civil Liberties Union
    (ACLU), 76, 189, 222
American Family Association, 139,
    180, 181
American Psychiatric Association, 56
American Psychological Association,
    56
American Restoration Project, 207
Americans with Disabilities Act, 96
American Windsurfer, 249
Americas United for Separation of
    Church and State, 193
"America the Beautiful" (national
    hymn), 44
Amish, 181
Anti-Defamation League, 278
Anti-Evolution League of America, 76
Arizona, 151

Arkansas, 151
Arlington Group, 11–12, 139–40,
    156–62, 167–72, 174, 178, 207,
    210–11, 213, 217–19, 224–25,
    228, 232–34, 241
Armey, Dick, 112
Ashcroft, John, 15
Aspen, Colorado, 34
Associated Press, 253
Association of Christian Schools
    International, 44
Atwater, Lee, 92
Australia, 63

Baha'is, 276
Baker, James, 30
Bakker, Jim, 41, 88
bankruptcy bill, 119–21
Baptist Press, 249
Barton, David, 191–94, 210
Bassett, Todd, 272
Bates, Katharine Lee, 44
"Battle for Marriage" rallies, 167
Bauer, Gary L., 6–7, 32, 39, 40, 64,
    101, 109, 116, 117–18, 126, 131,
    144, 148, 181, 225, 227, 232, 233,
    278
Beasley, David, 102
Be Intolerant (book), 41
Belcher, Cornell, 267
Belgium, 63
Bennett, Bill, 185
Bible, 153, 191, 192–93, 198, 220, 221,
    251
"Big Tent," 111
Billings, Robert, 79–80
Billy Graham Evangelistic Association,
    61
Blackwell, J. Kenneth, 157, 179, 180,
    183, 202–4
Blunt, Roy, 16, 132
Boehner, John, 133
Bork, Robert, 142, 213, 231
Born-Alive Infants Protection Act, 122,
    165
Boulder, Colorado, 34
Brandt, Peter L., 152
Breakaway (magazine), 62

Brinson, R. Randolph "Randy,"
    259–61, 263
Brio (magazine), 62
Brio & Beyond (magazine), 62
Brokaw, Tom, 45
Brookings Institution, 77
Brown, Janice Rogers, 226, 227
Brownback, Sam, 112, 116, 122, 124,
    133, 148, 225
Bryan, William Jennings, 76
Buchanan, Angela "Bay," 103
Buchanan, Pat, 97, 102–3, 108
Buddhists, 276
Bundy, Ted, 33–34
Burke, archbishop Raymond, 245
Burress, Phil, 173–83, 198–99, 202,
    207–8, 222
Burress, Vickie, 176
Bush, George H. W., 59, 62, 90–92,
    96–97, 229
    evangelicals' suspicion of policies of,
    96–97
Bush, George W., 15, 16, 62, 118–19,
    122, 125, 131, 134–35, 161–66,
    169–72, 173, 181–83, 186–87,
    189–90, 192, 205, 220, 223, 226,
    227–29, 231, 236–38, 246, 249,
    252
    administration, 37, 235, 269
    appeal of, to evangelicals, 190
    endorsed by Dobson, 15
Bush, Jeb, 126
Bush-Cheney 2000 campaign, 186, 188
Bush-Cheney 2004 campaign, 12, 179,
    184, 186–96, 244
Buss, Dale, 11

Call to Renewal, 257
Calvin College, 272
Campaign for Working Families, 181
Campaigns & Elections (magazine), 98
Campus Crusade for Christ, 27
Carl, Frank, 185
Carson, Brad, 12–14
Carter, Jimmy, 15, 31, 78–79, 84, 85
    administration, 78–79
    evangelicals' initial welcoming of and
    later disillusionment with, 78–79

Casey, Bob, 262
Casey, Bob, Jr., 262–63, 265
Catholic League for Religious and
    Civil Rights, 248–49
Catholics
    in Congress, 253–54
    U.S. bishops, 245–46
    voters, 77, 80, 155, 190, 196, 210,
        250
    See also Roman Catholic Church
Caviezel, Jim, 185
Center for a Just Society, 127–29
Centers for Disease Control, 87
Century Strategies, 188
"chapelteria," 53
Chapin, Harry, 8
charismatic movement, 75
Child Custody Protection Act, 122,
    166
Childrens Hospital Los Angeles, 21
child tax credit, 118
China, 276
Chisum, Warren, 208, 210
Christian Broadcasting Network
    (CBN), 89–90, 93–94, 260
Christian Coalition, 7, 10, 27, 36, 39,
    64, 91, 93–103, 107–9, 112, 117,
    132, 135, 149, 151–52, 177, 187,
    200, 209
    rise and fall of, 93–103
Christian Coalition of Ohio, 180
Christianity, importance of, to
    Founding Fathers, 59–61
Christianity Today (magazine), 30, 32,
    45, 104, 249, 272
Christian radio, 260
    Dobson's leadership of, 39
Christian Right, 8–9, 10, 11, 16, 29,
    36, 39, 72–78, 80, 84–105
    backlash toward, after Schiavo
        episode, 125, 131–32
    core agenda of, 273
    history of, 71–75, 80–105
    and Reagan, 84–88
Christians, worldwide, persecution of,
    276–79
Christian School Action, 79
churches, tax exemption of, 193–94

Churchill, Winston, 10
Church of the Nazarene, 20
Cincinnati, Ohio, 175–77, 179
Citizen (magazine), 32, 36–37, 62
Citizens for Community Values
    (CCV), 152, 175–83, 198–200
Citizen USA (newspaper), 202
civil rights movement, 2
Civil Rights Restoration Act, 33
Cizik, Richard, 254, 268–74, 277–78
Clement, Edith, 219
Clinton, Bill, 8–9, 97, 107, 279
    administration, 38–39, 100, 118
    impeachment of, 104
    personal character of, 8–9
Clinton, Hillary, 97, 256, 261–62
cloning, 122
Clubhouse Jr. (magazine), 62
Clyburn, James, 254–55
Coats, Dan, 30
Coburn, Tom, 12–14, 112, 114, 156,
    164, 225
College Republicans, 92, 100
Colorado, 10, 14, 34–35, 54, 218
Colorado Springs, Colorado, 34,
    43–46, 253
Colson, Chuck, 38, 40, 121, 157, 167,
    226, 235, 238, 272, 278, 281
Columbus, Ohio, 176
Commission on Pornography, 32, 33
Committee for the Survival of a Free
    Congress, 77
Common Good Strategies, 264–66
Compassion International, 44
Concerned Women for America, 112,
    118, 139, 156, 159, 160, 237,
    240
Condie, Joann, 50–52
condoms, 111, 121
Congregationalists, 243
Congress
    Democratic control after 2006
        election, 266–67
    Republican control after 2004
        election, 17
    workings of, 88, 118
    See also House of Representatives;
        Senate

Connor, Ken, 126–29, 144–45, 146–49, 154, 239
Conservative Caucus, 81
Constitution, U.S., 11, 60, 221–22, 239, 255
    amending of, 156
Contemporary Christian Music, 66–67
Contract with America, 100–101
Contract with the American Family, 101
Coors, Joseph, 72
Coors, Peter, 14
Costa Rica, 63
Council for National Policy, 109
Court of Appeals for the District of Columbia, 214
covenant marriage, 150
Coverdell, Paul, 99
Creation Care, 270, 272–74
Crippen, Alan, II, 154
Criswell, W. A., 80
Culbertson, Paul, 20–21
culture war, 5, 14, 55, 97, 104, 136, 282

Dallas, 80
Daly, Jim, 54, 64–65, 66–70
Daniels, Matt, 142–47, 149, 156, 160
Dare to Discipline (book), 7, 22–23, 37, 67
Darrow, Clarence, 76
Darwinian evolution, 22, 76
Daschle, Tom, 5–7, 12, 263
Da Vinci Code (book), 9
Day, Kristen, 263–64
Dean, Howard, 242–44, 256
death penalty, 262
Defense of Marriage Act, federal (DOMA), 118, 170, 177–78, 182, 261
Defense of Marriage Acts, state, 142, 221
DeGeneres, Ellen, 56
DeLay, Tom, 30, 112, 113, 114, 120, 125, 128–30, 132, 167, 228
Democratic National Committee, 215, 249, 256, 257–60, 262–63, 266–67

Democratic National Conventions
    1976, 78
    1992, 262
    2004, 247
Democratic Party, 12, 87, 104, 188, 197, 204, 243–45, 247, 253–67, 269
    advised to be a "big tent," 261
    gains in 2006 election, 266–67
    religious position of, 242–67
    secular image of, 258
Democratic Senatorial Campaign Committee, 265
Democrats
    black, 180
    congressional, 17
    House, 133, 254, 256
    Senate, 5–7, 172, 226, 253–54, 256
Democrats for Life of America, 263–64
Denver, Colorado, 34
DeVos, Dick, 265
DeVos, Richard, 118
DeWitt, Sheryl, 58
dispensationalist theology, 269
divorce, 150
Dobson, Danae, 41
Dobson, Ed, 157
Dobson, James C., Jr., 1–5, 7–17, 18–73, 79, 106–13, 117–21, 123, 125, 132, 136–37, 139–40, 147–50, 153–55, 157, 158–61, 163–64, 166, 167, 169, 170, 174, 181, 184, 186, 216–17, 219, 221, 222, 223, 225, 226–28, 232–40, 253, 272–75, 280–82
    ancestry and background, 18–21, 61
    books by, 22–24
    campaigning by, 12–13
    close relations with Bush White House, 235, 237
    interviews with, xi, xiv, xvii, 40, 45
    management style, 28–29
    manner and appearance, 9
    Montgomery, Alabama, visit and speech, 1–5
    political activities, 9–10, 29–30
    political influence, 39–40
    radio advice program, 7, 24–27
    retirement of, 64, 282

scientific and academic career, 21
spotless personal reputation of, 41
support for candidates, 108–9
wife and children of, 41
Dobson, James C., Sr., 18–19, 62
Dobson, Myrtle, 19–20
Dobson, Ryan, 41
Dobson, Shirley Deere, 20, 38, 41, 61
Dole, Bob, 91, 102–3, 108–9, 186, 190
Donaldson, Sam, 108

Eagle Forum, 237, 239
Earlham College, 248
Eastern Orthodox Church, 181
Edwards, Jonathan, 23
Egypt, 63
Eisenhower, Dwight D. administration, 16
elections
    1980 presidential, 84–85
    1984 presidential, 87
    1988 presidential, 90–92
    1992 presidential, 97
    1994 midterm, 100–101
    1996 presidential, 101–3, 108–9, 112, 187
    1998 midterm, 104, 112
    2000 presidential, 15, 186–88
    2002 midterm, 119
    2004 presidential, 15–16, 123, 124–25, 161, 163, 167, 169, 170, 173–74, 180–86, 194–97, 223, 225, 250–51, 259, 263–64
    2005 off-year, 169, 208, 262
    2006 midterm, 123, 124, 132, 164, 169, 204, 211, 258, 262–63, 266–67
    2008 future presidential, 225, 251, 262, 267
    See also Bush-Cheney 2000 campaign; Bush-Cheney 2004 campaign; Kerry, John: campaign
Engstrom, Ted, 37
environmentalism, 268–74
Ephesians, Epistle to the, 5:22, 285n2
Episcopal Church, 243, 278
Equal Rights Amendment, 77, 78, 84, 140

Ethics and Public Policy Center, 141–42, 145
Europe, modern, paganism of, 4
Evangelical Climate Initiative, 269–74
evangelicals
    antienvironmental attitude of, 269
    election turnout of, 161, 170, 186–87, 194, 250
    history of, 75–77
    mailing lists of, 189–91
    members of Congress, 132–33
    shunning of politics, 37, 77, 134, 186
Evangelical Sensitivity Index (ESI), 261
Exodus International, 55

Fabrizio, Tony, 131
faith-based charities, 135
Faith Working Group (House Democrats), 254, 256
Falwell, Jerry, 2, 7, 31, 32, 36, 40, 72–73, 79, 80, 81–83, 85, 86–89, 104, 157, 163, 185, 201
family, disintegration of the, 21–22, 143
Family Man: The Biography of Dr. James Dobson (book), 11
Family Minute (radio short), 63
Family News in Focus (radio feature), 32, 62
family.org, 48
family planning, funding of centers abroad, 135
Family Policy Councils, 32, 63, 129, 142, 151–53, 168, 174, 183–84, 200, 204, 209, 211, 213
    Alabama, 3
    Ohio, 173, 175
    Texas, 169, 209
Family Research Council (FRC), 10, 13, 16, 32, 39, 47, 101, 115, 116–18, 120–21, 123, 125, 126–29, 136, 141, 144–50, 153–55, 159, 163–65, 167, 171–72, 181, 199–200, 204, 207, 213, 217, 218–19, 226, 227–28, 237, 253, 265, 281

Family Research Council (FRC) (*continued*)
founding of, 32
Pastor's Resource Council, 47
Farris, Michael, 35, 108, 113, 137, 157, 159, 160–61
Fauntroy, Walter, 144
Faye, Tammy, 41, 88
Federal Administration for Children, Youth, and Families, 34
Federal Council of Churches, 77
Federal Election Commission (FEC), 103
Federal Marriage Amendment (FMA), 143–50, 154–72, 178, 181–82, 183, 208, 224
Feminists for Life, 214, 217
Ferraro, Geraldine, 87
fetuses, personhood of, 166
filibusters, 124, 224, 225–26
Flanegin, Robert, 69
Florida, 14
Florida Prayer Network, 189–90
Focus on the Family, 2–5, 8–9, 16, 19, 29–39, 41–72, 107, 117, 120, 139, 147–55, 158, 159, 168, 174, 175, 177, 178, 181, 183–84, 186–87, 213, 218, 252–53, 260, 272
advertising by, 68
advice databank, 28–29, 65–66
income and budget, 27, 139
IRS status, 37
mailing list, 39
moral behavior expected of staff, 42
parenting advice from, 36
phone attendants and counselors, 46–52
political involvement, 34, 38
publications and media produced by, 62–64
tour of buildings and operations, 45–54
working with Congress on legislation, 113–16
Focus on the Family (radio program), 7, 9, 19, 24–29, 33, 35–36, 47, 62–64, 66–67, 117–18, 139, 235, 280–81

Focus on the Family Action, 6, 14–15, 54–55, 69, 168, 226
Focus on the Family Institute, 57–61
"Focus on the Family" seminars, 24
Focus on the Family series (film), 24
focusonyourchild.com, 63, 68, 69
Focus on Your Child newsletters, 68
Foley, Mark, 267
Food and Drug Administration, 134
Ford, Gerald, 85
Fortas, Abe, 231
Founding Fathers, 59–61, 191, 221, 239
"four horsemen," 215–16, 231
FOX News Channel, 40, 123, 202
Frankfurter, Felix, 277
Franks, Trent, 84
Free Congress Foundation, 77
Freedom Council, 90
Freedom House, 276
Free Market Foundation, 209
Frist, Bill, 16, 42, 125, 127, 132, 148, 167, 213, 224, 225, 226
Frum, David, 233
Fuller, John, 64, 65, 66, 197, 238
fundamentalists, history of, 75–77
Fundamentals, The: A Testimony to the Truth (booklets), 76

Gandy, Kim, 264
gay marriage
courts' rulings on, 141, 161, 178
legalizing of, 162, 174
legislative bans on, 14, 118, 122, 140, 171, 174, 205, 208–11
as a moral issue, 257, 261
threat of, to the heterosexual family, 11
gay rights laws, 34, 179
opposition to, 168, 177
gays
Focus on the Family's ministry to, 55–57
in the military, 97, 118
Genesis 2:15, 269
Genoa Baptist Church, 185
George, Robert, 142, 145, 149
Georgia, 99, 133–34

Gerson, Mike, 134
Gibson, Mel, 188
Gillespie, Ed, 17
Gingrich, Newt, 53, 100–101, 111–13
Giuliani, Rudolph, 261
global warming, 269–71
God, 29, 73, 266, 270
God's Politics: Why the Right Gets It Wrong and the Left Doesn't Get It, 255
Goeglein, Tim, 216, 235
Goldwater, Barry, 5
Gonzalez, Alberto, 227–28
Gore, Al, 194
Graham, Billy, 6, 15, 77, 176
Graham, Franklin, 121, 187
Gramm, Phil, 108–9
Granholm, Jennifer, 265, 266
Gray, C. Boyden, 215
Green, John C., 75, 76
Gregg, Judd, 164
Griswold v. Connecticut, 155
Guth, Jim, 133

Hadley, Martha, 67
Haggard, Ted, 2, 3, 41, 44–45, 157, 216, 224, 250, 272, 273
Hahn, Jessica, 41
Haley, Mike, 55, 57
Hannity, Sean, 53, 185
Harry Potter and the Goblet of Fire (film), 62
Hart, John, 13
Hastert, Dennis, 132, 134
Hate Crimes bill, 96
Hawaii, 141, 177–78
HBO, 45
Health and Human Services Department, 165
Heche, Anne, 56
Heche, Nancy, 56
Hecht, Nathan L., 230, 232–33, 238–39
Heimlich, Phil, 203–4
Helms, Jesse, 95
Heritage Foundation, 72, 77, 98, 136
Hertzke, Allen, 279
Hispanics, 210
Hitler, Adolf, 277

HIV/AIDS, 275
Hodel, Don, 39, 64–65, 158, 159, 238
Hogan & Hartson, 214, 218
home schooling, 35–36
Home School Legal Defense Association, 35
homosexuality, 48, 55–57, 98, 167
  no longer defined as illness by psychiatric associations, 56
  See also gay rights; gays
Horowitz, Michael, 275–78, 280, 281–82
Hostettler, John, 146
Houghton, Sir John, 269
House of Representatives, U.S., 106–7, 127, 130–31, 132–33, 160, 163
Huckabee, Mike, 189
Hudson Institute, 276
Human Life Amendment, 171
human rights, evangelicals' involvement in fostering, 279–82
Human Rights Watch, 279
Hurricane Gloria, 90
Hurricane Katrina, 47
Hutcherson, Ken, 232
Hutchison, Kay Bailey, 205–6
Hybels, Bill, 38–39

Immigration and Naturalization Service, 276, 278
Incapacitated Persons Legal Protection Act, 127
Indian casinos, 93
Interfaith Stewardship Alliance, 272
Intergovernmental Panel on Climate Change, 269
Internal Revenue Service (IRS), 4, 14, 37, 79, 103, 139, 184–85, 193–94, 203
International Bible Society, 44
International Campaign for Tibet, 278
International Council of Christian Churches, 77
International Religious Freedom Act, 279, 280–81, 282
Iowa, 91, 102, 244
Iran, 276
Iraq, religious persecution in, 276

Iraq invasion and war (2003–), 119, 134, 195, 202, 242
Ireland, 63
I, Rigoberta Menchú, 59
Israel, 40
Issue One, 178–83
"I Vote Values" campaign, 183–84

Jackson, Harry, 234
Jackson, Peb, 25, 26, 28
James Dobson Family Minute (radio short), 66
Japan, 63
Jefferson, Thomas, 60
Jesus
    return of, and the environment, 269
    talking about, 15, 187
Jews
    as interest group, 83
    persecution of, 276, 277
    Russian, 278
    voters, 247–48, 277
Jim Crow laws, 2
Jindal, Bobby, 16
Job, Book of, Howard Dean's citing of, 243
John Birch Society, 77
Johnson, Lyndon, 123
    administration, 2
Johnson, Russell, 197–99, 201–4, 233–34
Johnson, Tim, 6
Judeo-Christian faith, 22, 255
judicial activism, 220–21
"Justice Sunday" rallies, 226, 228, 237

Kagame, Paul, 275
Kaine, Tim, 262
Kansas, 112
Kemp, Jack, 91, 109
Kennedy, Anthony, 4, 232
Kennedy, D. James, 95, 157
Kennedy, Ted, 256, 258
Kerry, John, 12, 15, 81, 173, 182, 194–95, 244, 251–52, 261
    2004 campaign, 244–51
    religious beliefs of, 247, 251
Kerry, Teresa, 251

Key, Ron, 230, 238
Keyes, Alan, 108
Kilgore, Jerry, 193
King, Martin Luther, Jr., 3
King, Martin Luther, Sr., 78
Kinkeade, Ed, 233, 238–39
Koop, C. Everett, 87
Krauthammer, Charles, 233
Kristol, William, 233

LaHaye, Beverly, 118
LaHaye, Tim, 95, 109
Land, Richard, 2, 7, 112, 158, 161–62, 190, 233, 235, 272, 278, 281
Largent, Steve, 107
Last Temptation of Christ, The (film), 33
Latin America, 63
Latinos, 259
Lawrence v. Texas, 4, 148, 155
Leavitt, Mike, 165
Leo, Leonard, 215, 219
Liberty Foundation, 88
Liberty Singers, 83
Liberty University, 40, 82, 150
Lincoln, Abraham, 247
"litmus tests," 111, 224
Log Cabin Republicans, 162
London, H. B., Jr., 184
Lott, Trent, 132
Louisiana, 14, 150–53
Louisiana Family Forum, 152
Love Must Be Tough (book), 51–52
Love Must Be Tough (radio series), 50–51
Love Won Out ministry, 55–57, 63
Lowry, Rich, 136
Lutheran Church - Missouri Synod, 75
Lynchburg Baptist College, 82
Lynn, Barry, 193

Mackey, Connie, 120–21, 218–19
Madison, James, 60
Maegdlin, Steve, 68–69
Maier, Bill, 56, 65
Mapplethorpe, Robert, 107, 177
marriage
    definition of, 144
    threat to institution of, 143, 147

Marriage Protection Amendment, 164
Martin, William, 89
Martinez, Mel, 127
Marx, Gary, 12, 188, 191, 195
Massachusetts, 11, 122, 161, 174,
    178–80, 182, 221
Massachusetts Family Institute, 142–43
McCain, John, 40
McCarrick, Cardinal Theodore, 121
McCarthy, Joseph, 77
McClusky, Thomas E., 123, 163–64
McConnell, Mitch, 132
McCurry, Mike, 245
McGovern, George, 85
Meese, Edwin, III, 53, 215
Mehlman, Ken, 235, 264
Melkite Greek Catholic Church, 73
"MemoGate," 215, 291n1
Menchú, Rigoberta, 59
Mercy Corps International, 91
Michigan, 90–91, 265, 266
middle class, issues important to, 260
Miers, Harriet, 42, 70, 229–41
Miller, Brad, 184, 201
Miller, Zell, 185
minimum wage, 258
Minnery, Tom, 177, 187, 272
Miranda, Manuel, 212–18, 229–32,
    239, 291n1
Moegerle, Gil, 42
Mondale, Walter, 87
Montgomery, Alabama, 1–5
Moore, Ray, 2–5
Moral Majority, 7, 12, 31, 32, 36, 41,
    73, 80–84, 87–88, 93–96, 104,
    132, 157, 201
  history of, 80–83
Moral Majority Report, 82
Morgan, Lindy, 47–50
MoveOn.org, 188
Musgrave, Marilyn, 160, 161
Muslims, 276

NARAL Pro-Choice America, 166, 215
National Association of Evangelicals, 2,
    3, 41, 44, 77, 249–50, 254,
    269–70, 272–74, 277–78
National Council of Churches, 279

National Council on Bible
    Curriculum in Public Schools,
    191
National Day of Prayer, 38, 121
  Task Force, 38, 62
National Endowment for the Arts, 107,
    113–14
National Organization for Women, 31,
    263, 264
National Religious Broadcasters, 87
National Retail Federation, 120
National Women's Conference, 31
Natural Resources Defense Council,
    271
Nazis, 42, 132
NBC, 45
Neff, David, 272
Nelson, Bill, 127, 245
Nelson, Grace, 245
Nelson, Paul, 25, 28–29
New Age faiths, 268
New Hampshire, 91, 102
New Life Church, 44–45
New Mexico, 162
New Right, 31, 72, 77, 275
  Dobson's leadership of, 31
Newsom, Gavin, 162, 222
Newsweek (magazine), 78
New Testament, 53
New York City, 68
New York Times, 102–3, 104, 107,
    111
Nigeria, 276
1960s, 21–23
95–10 Initiative, 263, 266
Nixon, Richard, administration, 38
Noll, Mark, 239
No Nonsense, 209–11
Norquist, Grover, 92
North, Oliver, 53, 103
North Carolina, 14, 95
North Korea, 276, 280
North Korea Human Rights Act, 280
"nuclear option," 224, 225–26

obscenity laws, 175–76
O'Connor, Sandra Day, 86, 213, 227,
    229

Ohio, 152, 169, 173–83, 203–4, 207–8, 222, 265, 266
Ohio Campaign to Protect Marriage, 180
Ohio Restoration Project, 197–204, 206–7
Oklahoma, 12–14, 112
Oklahoma City, 20
Olasky, Marvin, 229–30
Old Time Gospel Hour (TV show), 81, 89
Olsen, Pam, 189–90, 196
O'Malley, archbishop Sean, 245
Operation Rescue, 10
Oregon, 168
originalism, 221
Origin of the Species (book), 76
Owen, Priscilla, 226, 227

Parks, Rosa, 1–2
Partial Birth Abortion Ban Act, 166, 221, 261
Pasadena College, 20–21
"Passion Crowd," 188
Passion of the Christ, The (film), 185, 188
Passno, Diane, 29, 34, 65–66
pastors, involvement in politics, 184–85, 197–206
Patrick Henry College, 57, 137, 159
Patriot Pastors, 201–4, 206
Paulk, John, 56–57
Pelosi, Alexandra, 45
Pelosi, Nancy, 254, 258
Pennsylvania, 200, 262–63, 265, 266
Pentecostal movement, 75
People for the American Way, 215
Perkins, Tony, 150–55, 167, 172, 199–200, 207, 217, 225, 226, 227–28, 232, 237
Perot, Ross, 97
Perry, Bob, 81
Perry, Rick, 205–7
Peterson, Laci, 166
Petro, Jim, 203–4
Pew Forum on Religion & Public Life, 251
Pew Research Center, 195, 270

Phillips, Howard, 81, 109, 186
Pitts, Joe, 115, 119–21, 160
Planned Parenthood, 107, 110, 121
Planned Parenthood v. Casey, 240
Plugged In (magazine), 62
Plugged In (radio short), 66
Policy Review (magazine), 98
Pomona, Calif., 34
pornography, 33, 48, 175
poverty, alleviating, 257, 260
Powell, Colin, 108
prayer, public, banned, 86, 220
Preparing for Adolescence (book), 7, 24
Prison Rape Elimination Act, 135, 280
Proposition 2 (Texas), 205–11
Protestants
   fundamentalists' split, 75
   mainline, 22, 75, 96, 196, 250

Quayle, Dan, 85, 91, 96

radio, 66–67
   AM vs. FM audience penetration, 66
Reagan, Ronald, 34, 53, 61–62, 74, 78, 84–87, 96, 104, 163, 229, 246, 270
   administration, 10, 30, 32, 85–88, 232, 281
   evangelists' attitudes toward, 84
Redeem the Vote, 184–85, 259
Reed, Ralph, 7, 39, 64, 79, 91–103, 107–9, 133–35, 149, 168, 187, 188–90, 244
Rehnquist, William, 214, 228, 229
Reid, Harry, 256, 258
religion
   courts' war against public presence of, 3, 86, 220
   as a progressive force in history, 256
Religion & Ethics Newsweekly (TV show), 40
Religious Right, 78
Religious Roundtable, 81
Rendell, Ed, 263
Republican National Committee, 73, 190, 191–94, 210, 244, 264

Republican National Conventions
  1980, 84
  1984, 87
  1992, 97
  2004, 126
Republican Party, 15–16, 36, 72,
    73–75, 78, 81–82, 84–87, 90–92,
    96–97, 99–104, 107–21, 124,
    132–36, 146–47, 162–67, 169–71,
    197, 253, 255, 261, 269
  business wing of, 124
  Dobson's attack on, 109–10
  evangelists' suspicion of motives of,
    146–47, 163
  Ohio, 180, 183, 203–4, 207–8
  Texas, 205, 210
Republican Revolution, 104, 110
Republicans
  candidates, 10–14
  congressional, 30, 130–33
  House, 106–7, 114
  Senate, 206, 220, 223
Right to Life Amendment, 140–41, 160
Rios, Sandy, 139, 160
Road to Victory conferences, 96, 102
Roberts, John, 213–19
Robertson, Pat, 7, 36, 39, 40, 73, 78,
    79, 85, 88–97, 135, 216, 222, 260
Robison, James, 80, 84, 85, 87
robocalls, 209
Rodgers, Mark, 113, 124, 275
Roe v. Wade, 3, 16, 77, 126, 155, 216,
    217, 220, 223, 231, 233, 240, 266
Rogers, Adrian, 80
Roman Catholic Church, 73, 181,
    262. See also Catholics
Romer v. Evans, 218
Roosevelt, Franklin, 277
Rove, Karl, 42, 70, 123, 161–62,
    170–71, 186, 194, 216, 235–36,
    237–38
Rush, Benjamin, 60
Rwanda, 275

Salazar, Ken, 252–54
Salvation Army, 27, 47, 272
same-sex marriage. See gay marriage
San Francisco, California, 162, 222

Santorum, Rick, 148, 223, 262
Saperstein, David, 278–79, 280
Sapp, Eric, 265–66
Scaife, Richard, 72
Scalia, Antonin, 4, 148, 217
Scarborough, Rick, 201
Schaeffer, Francis, 82, 83, 87
Schiavo, Michael, 126, 131
Schiavo, Terri, 124–32, 138, 222
Schlafly, Phyllis, 77, 237
schools, Christian, 78–79
Schumer, Charles, 119, 263
Schwartz, Michael, 13, 114–15, 156,
    160, 163–64, 166, 237
Schwarzenegger, Arnold, 261
Scopes Trial, 75–76
Scorsese, Martin, 33
Sekulow, Jay, 215–16, 222
Senate, U.S., 5–7, 9, 12–14, 15–16, 85,
    124, 127, 132, 163–64, 206
Senate Judiciary Committee, 223, 233,
    236–37, 239
Senate Republican Conference, 113,
    275
September 11, 2001, terrorist attacks,
    119
serial killers, 33
Serrano, Andres, 107
700 Club, The (cable program), 89–90
sex behaviors, advice from Dobson
    about, 25
sex education, 87, 111
Shackelford, Kelly J., 207–11, 241
Sharing Life Together (radio show), 67
Sharon, Ariel, 40
Sheridan, bishop Michael, 245
Shia Muslims, 276
Shows, Ronnie, 160
Sierra Club, 271
"Sinners in the Hands of an Angry
    God" (sermon), 23
Snow, Tony, 123
social problems, evangelicals' role in
    alleviating, 274–82
Social Security, 258
Solomon and David, 19
Souter, David, 216–17, 229
South Africa, 63

South Carolina, 14, 102, 200
South Dakota, 5–7, 12, 182
Southern Baptist Convention, 2, 75, 78, 80, 112, 183, 190
Spaite, Polly, 21
Spaite, Wil, 21
Specter, Arlen, 223–25, 236
Spock, Benjamin, 21, 23
SpongeBob SquarePants, 42, 70
Stabenow, Debbie, 265, 266
"Stand for Family" rallies, 6, 14
State Department, 279
"Statement of Applicant's Christian Faith," 52–53
"Statement of Conscience" (on international religious persecution), 278
Steinem, Gloria, 240, 282
stem cell research, 135
Stewart, Colin, 127, 129, 154
Strickland, Ted, 204
Strong-Willed Child, The (book), 37
Students for America, 92, 94
sub-Saharan Africa, 275
Sudan, 135, 275, 276
Sudan Peace Act, 280
Sufi Muslims, 276
Sunni Muslims, 276
Supernanny (TV show), 67–68
Supreme Court, 3–5, 15–16, 35, 70, 72, 73–74, 86, 122, 131, 134, 148, 155, 166, 172, 212–20, 227–41
    nominees favored by the Right, 212–19, 227–41
    rulings unpopular with the Right, 220–21
Swaggart, Jimmy, 41, 88
Swift Boat Veterans for Truth, 81

Tackett, Del, 59–61
Taft, Bob, 183
Talent, Jim, 107
Tarrance, Lance, 80–81
Tate, Randy, 112
tax code, 37
Taylor, Ken, 175
Temple in Jerusalem, 19
Ten Commandments, 4, 220

Ten Commandments monument ("Roy's Rock"), 1–5
"Terri's Law," 126
Terry, Randall, 10, 99
Texans For Marriage, 209
Texas, 169, 192, 205–11
Texas Bar Association, 236
Texas Family Policy Council, 205, 207
Texas Restoration Project, 205–9
Texas Right to Life, 236
thetruthproject.org, 63
Third Branch Conference, 213–18, 229–32, 241
This Week with David Brinkley, 108
Thomas, Cal, 157
Thomas, Clarence, 217
Thomas Road Baptist Church, 81
Thompson, Tommy, 165
Thune, John, 6–7, 12, 111, 134
Trafficking Victims Protection Act, 280, 282
Trippi, Joe, 244
troubledwith.com, 48, 68
Trout, Mike, 26–27, 40, 42
Tucker, Jim Guy, 31–32, 284n31
Turkmenistan, 276

Unborn Child Pain Awareness Act, 122, 166
Unborn Victims of Violence Act, 122, 166
United Nations, 135
U.S. Appeals Courts, 5
U.S. Commission on International Religious Freedom, 279
U.S. Council of Catholic Bishops, 155
USC School of Medicine, 21
U.S. News & World Report, 40
U.S. Taxpayers Party, 109, 186

Valentine, Bobbie, 33
Values Action Teams (VAT), 119–22
    House, 115–17, 132, 147, 160
    Senate, 116–17, 124
values voters, 132, 173, 183, 195, 257
Vanderslice, Mara, 242–50, 264–66
Vanity Fair (magazine), 274
Vatican, 155

"Vatican West" (Colorado Springs), 44
Vermont, 145, 154
Viguerie, Richard A., 36, 82
Virginia, 103, 262
voter registration, 191, 197, 259

Wallis, Jim, 255–59
Warren, Rick, 184, 251, 271, 275
Washington, D.C., 30–32, 57, 136–37
Washington, George, 59
Washington (state), 200
Washington Post, 107, 111, 239, 247
Wead, Doug, 91, 96
Web sites, Focus, 69
Weekend Magazine (radio show), 62, 65
Weldon, Dave, 127
Weyrich, Paul M., 12, 30, 72–75, 77–82, 85–86, 88, 95, 101, 104–5, 109, 111, 114, 131, 136, 158, 169–70, 217–18, 224–25, 232, 233
WFAA, 80
Whatever Happened to the Human Race? (book and film), 87
What's the Matter with Kansas? (book), 257
What Wives Wish Their Husbands Knew about Women (book), 7, 23–24

Wheaton College, 272
Where's Dad? (film), 8, 24, 30
White, Laurence L., 206–7
White House, 29, 38, 44
White House Conference on the American Family, 31
White House Office of Public Liaison, 96, 216
Whitman, Christine Todd, 15
Why You Can't Stay Silent (book), 177
Wildmon, Don, 139–40, 157, 168, 181, 272
Will, George, 233
Willow Creek Community Church, 38
Wisconsin, 74
WithdrawMiers.org, 239
Witherspoon Fellowship, 136
Wolf, Frank, 7–8, 30
Wood, Genevieve, 154, 167
Wooten, Wilford D., 52
Working Mother (magazine), 68
World (newsweekly), 229–31
World's Christian Fundamentals Association, 76
World Vision International, 37
Wright, Jim, 30

Zettersten, Rolf, 36, 38